Magnificently Insignificant

Published by Brolga Publishing Pty Ltd
ABN 46 063 962 443
PO Box 12544, A'Beckett St, Melbourne, VIC, 8006, Australia
email: admin@brolgapublishing.com.au

National Library of Australia Cataloguing-in-Publication entry:

Odou, Noël
Magnificently insignificant: travel stories and life lessons.
9781921221866 (pbk.)
Odou, Noël.
Personal coaching
Travel – Anecdotes.
Life.
Conduct of life – Anecdotes.
Counselors – Biography.
920.710994

Printed in Indonesia
Cover design by David Khan
Typeset and design by Imogen Stubbs

Magnificently Insignificant

Travel stories and life lessons

Noël Odou

Dedicated to Johann and Natasha
with thanks for helping me to be a dad.

'In order to explore and explain our own mystery, we write.'

Carmel Bird, *Dear Writer*

Contents

Part Two: The Inward Journey

Part Three: The Domestic Journey

Acknowledgements

First and foremost I want to thank Joy for suggesting many years ago that I write my story for the sake of the children. Many people who read early drafts have given me valuable feedback and have encouraged me to continue working at it. I especially want to thank, in no particular order and with apologies to those I missed: Jonathan Billington, Josh Ciechanowski, Ann and Tony Yacono, Lois Edwards (who is now also writing her story), Very Sheaffer, Graham Joy (who even took me to see a movie producer), Graham Moore (my personal Hypnotherapist), Stephan Knorles, Steven and Cathy Hogan, Callandra Gilligan, Robbie Wesley, and for her especially perceptive insights, Trudi Reeves.

I am grateful to Maria Saldaña for allowing me to reproduce 'Life at Liffey' by my wonderful friend Rafael, who inspired me in so many ways.

I owe a great deal of gratitude to Sandra Giles and Diann Payne not only for their enduring friendship and contributions to my life lessons but to the manuscript itself.

Special thanks to the people at Brolga, in particular Mark Zocchi and Imogen Stubbs for their creative contributions and flexibility.

Finally and most importantly thanks Natasha and Johann for adding enormous satisfaction to my life and providing me with the most significant fulfilment of my purpose.

Preface

THIS story tells of my travels but is not a travel book. I am simply sharing it as one might over dinner or a drink because humans are wont to communicate.

This story is based on my own life and experiences but some names and some parts have been changed to protect the privacy of the people who were also there. I have even protected myself whenever I thought I needed protecting. As for you, the reader, there is no protection at all. If you read this there is no guarantee what it may do to you. I certainly do not intend to offend, but if for some reason anything in my story has this effect on you, I am confident you will get over it, eventually.

Writing has been recognised as a tool of reflection in the service of self-exploration and a way to grow through understanding more about oneself so one can live a better life. If it does that then it is also worth sharing with others on the off-chance they may also benefit.

Noël Odou
Melbourne, Australia.
2009

A chronology of travel and events

My story is written in a non-chronological order, including flash-backs and incidental reminiscing. To facilitate a sense of flow, if needed, refer to the charts below.

Year	Travelled...	Leading to...
1942	Through the birth canal	Being born
1947	To kindergarten	Meeting the nuns
1949	To primary school	Problems with learning
1950	To Yper	Feeling abandoned
1951	To boarding school	Learning about survival
1958	To work	Becoming a ladies hairdresser
1961	To Germany	Learning about the Military Postal Service
1963	To Australia	Becoming me and meeting Annie
1964	To Papua & New Guinea	Owning a salon and meeting Sylvia
1966	To Japan and USSR	Trans-Siberian railway and meeting Emma
1966	To London	Learning about sexuality
1967	To Syria & Afghanistan	Meeting Gunther and a 1926 Rolls Royce
1967	To Libya	Searching Benghazi for my car
1968	Back to Australia	Becoming a Theosophist
1971	To India	Meeting Nataraja Guru
1974	To Armidale, NSW	First Class Honours in Philosophy of Education
1980	To Phillip Island	Meeting Joy and marriage
1994	Around the globe	Revisiting Belgium
2000	To Blackburn	Travelling 'solo'

Maps of travels

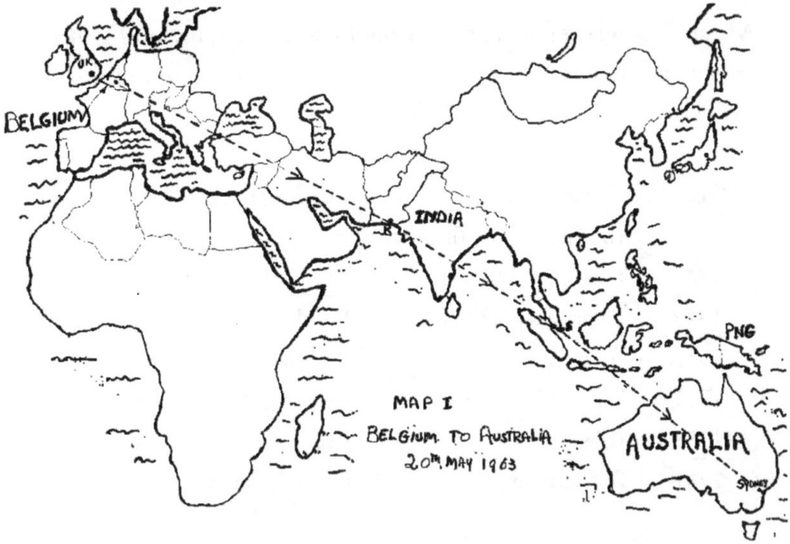

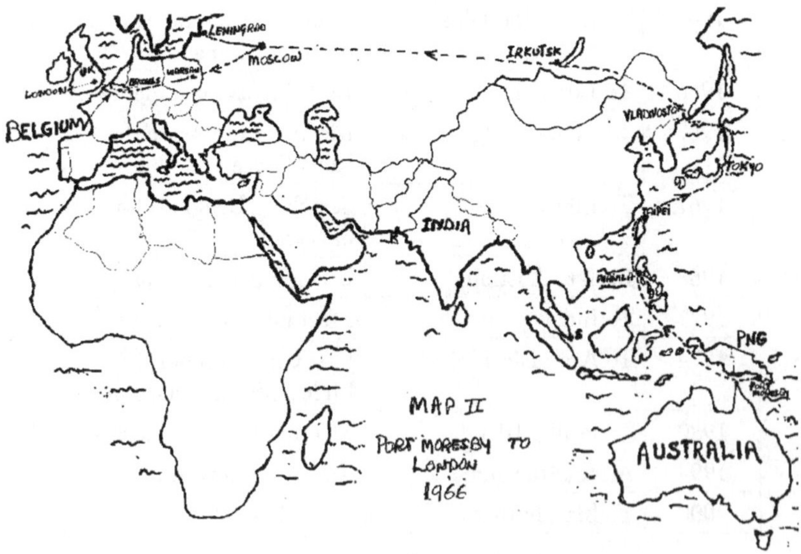

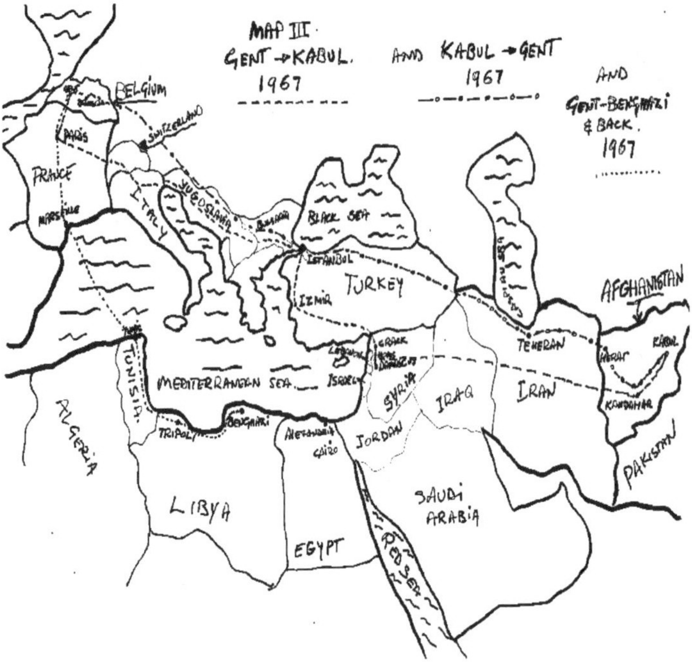

MAP III
GENT → KABUL
1967
AND KABUL → GENT
1967
AND
GENT-BENGHAZI
& BACK
1967
BELGIUM
PARIS
SWITZERLAND
FRANCE
MARSEILLE
ITALY
YUGOSLAVIA
BULGARIA
BLACK SEA
ISTANBUL
TURKEY
IZMIR
AFGHANISTAN
TEHERAN
KABUL
HERAT
KANDAHAR
SYRIA
IRAQ
IRAN
PAKISTAN
MEDITERRANEAN SEA
TUNISIA
ALGERIA
TRIPOLI
BENGHAZI
LIBYA
ALEXANDRIA
CAIRO
EGYPT
JORDAN
SAUDI
ARABIA
RED SEA

INDIA
K
KERALA
MADRAS
PENANG
MALAYSIA
S
SINGAPORE
PNG
DARWIN
CAIRNS
TOWNSVILLE
AUSTRALIA
ARMIDALE
SYDNEY
MAP IV
SYDNEY - KERALA
& BACK
1971

PART ONE

THE OUTWARD JOURNEY

It is good to have an end to journey towards,
but it is the journey that matters in the end.

Ursula Le Guin

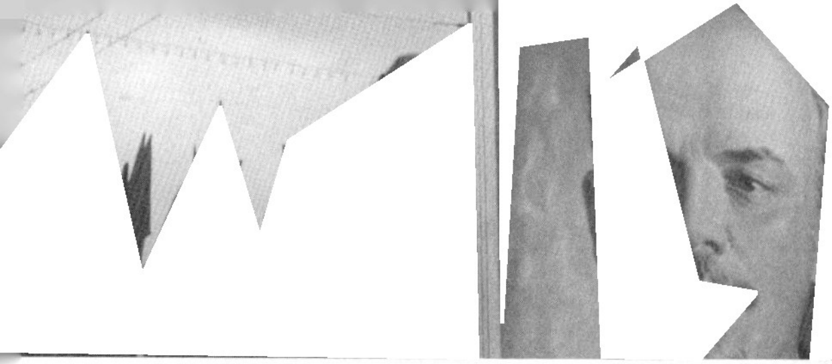

1.

Emma and the Trans-Siberian Railway

Part of the Port Moresby to London trip 1966

AFTER passing through customs and looking around the chaotic Victoria Station hall, I was relieved when I spotted Emma's big squinting smile. I was about to embrace her passionately when I noticed a man about her own age following her towards me. His murky blond curls made a halo around his head but his smile revealed some embarrassment. She half turned around to see if he was still there and then, with a slight awkwardness, introduced him to me as *'Peter, my husband.'* 'What!? You never told me you were married!' I felt like screaming at her, but of course I didn't. Instead I shook his rather limp hand, said *'Hello'* and took an instant, if grossly unfair, dislike to him.

I had never been to London before and while travelling on the creaky old ferry from Oostende, I had been thinking what I would do if she hadn't been there. I also had time to recall the ten exciting days we had spent together, openly enjoying each other's company.

Four weeks earlier I had met Emma Wilson and Bill

Kriatcheck, her travel companion not her husband she told me early on the ship in the bar of the *Khabarovsk* taking us from Yokohama to Nhakodka, even before the anchor had lifted. When you meet other English-speaking people in a foreign land it is easy to be drawn into their company. She was English and had just spent a year with the British Council in Kabul as a kindergarten teacher for the English expatriate community there. While in Kabul she had met Dr Kriatcheck, a medical doctor of Ukrainian parentage working with the Peace Corps. They had shared an apartment, amongst other things, and when I met them they were sharing the trip back home via Japan.

There were two things that immediately attracted me to Emma. One was her absolutely infectious and sensuous-looking smile, which revealed a row of beautifully regular teeth. The other was her striking resemblance to a younger version of Glenda Jackson, one of my favourite actresses. After several vodkas (what else would you drink on a Russian boat?) the dinner gong interrupted our animated conversation and Emma and I parted company. About half an hour later, to our amused surprise, we found ourselves sitting next to each other at the captain's table. We discovered we were part of a group of tourists lumped together by virtue of the regulation prohibiting unaccompanied travel through the then USSR. The Cold War still raged; it was 1966.

I politely inquired if Bill was indisposed with seasickness already. She explained that they were not registered as a couple and hence were not invited together. My focus was firmly on Emma now and, by the time we got to liqueur, we had hardly spoken to any of the other guests at the table and they must have thought us either very rude or madly in love or both. As the journey progressed, Bill and Emma behaved less and less like a couple, or even travelling companions, which made it easier for me to move closer to her. It just happened very naturally. I liked her, she liked me.

When I awoke the next day suffering a decent-sized hangover, the ship rolling considerably added to my discomfort. Between nursing my head and my stomach, I managed to meet most of the other people in our group. Apart from Emma and Bill, who were both, like me, in their mid-twenties, there were two wives of American diplomats stationed in Japan going on a 'little tour to Paris'. Pamela Brenner and Jane Fleischer were in their late thirties. They were loud, brash Americans, excessively friendly, and stereotypically they smoked like chimneys and drank like fish. I made the mistake of telling them I was a ladies hairdresser so they had me in their cabin the following morning doing their hair. They offered to pay but I said they could buy me a drink instead, which they continued to do for practically the entire trip. It did not occur to me then, naïve as I was, that they had ulterior motives.

There was a softly spoken Spaniard, about forty, who didn't participate much, but when I eventually got to speak with him, he confided to me that he was a Catholic priest travelling in civilian clothes. He was on his way to Spain for biannual leave from his mission in Japan. When I told him I had been brought up a Catholic, but before I got around to telling him that I had lapsed, he shared with me his frustration with the Japanese resistance to adopting Catholicism. When later I learned about Shinto and Zen Buddhism I could see why they would have preferred what they already had rather than this Western priest's brand of religion.

Then there was the German businessman who lived in Hong Kong and who was making big money with an insurance company. He had escaped from the Nazis in 1939 and was going back to his birthplace for the first time since the war. Another member of the group was a Danish sailor, sporting a generous, rusty-red beard. He told me he had lost his yacht somewhere on one of the Caroline Islands. I never worked out whether he was shipwrecked, had gambled it away or simply had mislaid it! I also never found out where the Caroline Islands were. Apart from the middle-aged Swedish nurse and the very quiet gay-looking Frenchman, neither of whom I got to know, the others were mostly Japanese.

They showed a documentary film about Russia one evening in the ship's library which was clearly propaganda, but given the very strong presence of *Intourist* personnel (the Russian national tourist bureau), half of whom we suspected to be KGB, nobody walked out. Four days later when we arrived at Nhakodka, about a hundred kilometres East of Vladivostok, the full impact of the *Intourist* machine hit us.

Mass tourism in Russia was still in its early stages then and the function of *Intourist* was clearly much more to control the tourists rather than provide a service to their clients. It became a standard joke that *'you can't complain about the service – there isn't any.'* On boarding the ship they had confiscated our passports, for *'safe keeping'*, but now that we were on land some people wanted theirs back and *Intourist* categorically refused. *'When you leave the country,'* they told us. The amount of confusion, misunderstanding and plain inefficiency was incredible. Everything had to be triple checked with their superiors, who were the ones making decisions as to who could do what, but by what rules it was impossible to say. After a considerable delay we were taken by bus from the ship to the local railway station, presumably to make sure we were all off the ship, where an even longer delay prevented us from getting on the train. Apparently it had been discovered that a middle-aged American gentleman, who was part of another group, was a professor of Archaeology. He, so the rumour went, had insisted a little too much on getting his passport back and was now under suspicion, of what we didn't know. We speculated that they must have thought he could have left the group if he had his passport and spied on something. The professor had demanded he be allowed to contact the American Embassy in Moscow, which stopped us from boarding the train, severely testing our patience.

It was dark, cold and miserable by the time we boarded the train, which took us the thousand kilometres north to Khabarovsk, the city this time, not the ship. The following morning at Khabarovsk station we were met by a bus to take us to the Imperial Hotel. To our surprise the two American ladies, Pamela and Jane, were invited to travel in a private car escorted by two military officials. By the time the interminable check-in procedure was completed and we had settled in our rooms, we were invited to lunch even though it was only about eleven.

No sooner had we taken our places around the various tables, more military officials came in and locked the doors around the room. We now realised that it wasn't an early lunch after all, but rather that an investigation was under way. Pamela and Jane had been seen talking to the professor during the delay at Nhakodka and when it was discovered they were connected to American Embassy staff in Japan, the Russians put two and two together and came up with six. This is why it is called *'Political Science'*.

Later, when we were reunited with them after our 'lock-up', during which none of us were interrogated, they shared their story. Being fellow Americans, they had naturally chatted to the professor if for no other reason than to offer moral support. It is easy to read conspiracy into whispered conversations. They each had been questioned separately, but not unpleasantly. On the contrary, when the inquisitors were satisfied there was no connection between her and the professor, Jane was taken by one of the KGB officers to lunch, just the two of them, and he had offered to escort her on a tour of the city, which she courageously refused under the pretext of a headache. A 'cold war' tone marked the trip from then on, more to our amusement than anything else. It is hard to take any sort of politics seriously when so much of what they do amounts to a joke, except that most of the time it isn't funny.

That day, 22 April, was Lenin's birthday and there was a special celebration dinner that night. There was much boisterous singing, dancing and, of course, drinking. Russians like their beer, which they call *'piva'*, but which we thought should have been 'pee' for short, it being so weak. By eleven that night it was announced that the dining room was closing because they had run out of beer. The Russians running out of beer? This was highly unlikely. We thought that it was probably because there were too many military uniforms staggering around amongst the tourists, courting both personal and national risks.

I had by now experienced Russian sea and rail transport, both of which were rather average considering I was supposed to be travelling first class. My travel agent in Port Moresby had strongly suggested the extra expense since otherwise *'you end up with the peasants'*. It was now time to fly Russia's Aeroflot from Khabarovsk to Irkutsk near Lake Baikal in central Siberia.

My original plan had been to go across the entire Russian continent from East to West on the Trans-Siberian Railway. However, security regulations prohibited travel in the Eastern part of Siberia at that time because, we speculated, they could have been building nuclear installations which we might have been able to see from the train. So we flew Aeroflot. Besides an Afghan Ariana flight which I would fly later, the Aeroflot flight was the most unpleasant, uncomfortable and unsafe-feeling flight

I have ever undertaken. There was a constant shaking, a musty metallic smell and again practically no service. All we were given during the three-hour flight was a cup of terrible coffee, most of which spilt onto the saucer because of the shaking of the aircraft. Absolutely no sign of first class. Then it struck me that this was communism – no class distinction on public transport.

The rather darkly luxurious hotel in Irkutsk was the first sign of my first-class status and immediately put me with a smaller group of people, which fortunately included Emma, but unfortunately also included Bill and Pamela and Jane. I remember Irkutsk well for two reasons. The first is that we went to visit Lake Baikal. At 5,715 feet, it is the deepest lake in the world. It is very large as well, stretching 12,162 square miles, most of it frozen over in the winter. At the small but well-organised maritime museum we learned how they take the eggs from the sturgeon, a fish plentiful in the lake, and produce *'caviar'*. This did not put us off eating plenty of it whenever it was on the menu, which was almost every day. It was fresh and very cheap.

The second memory about Irkutsk, a more sentimental one, is that I cut Emma's hair there. Emma did not think she could trust a Russian hairdresser so she asked if I would do it for her. I was delighted. I had continued to enjoy her company and was looking forward to getting a little closer still. The hotel where we stayed had a salon attached to it. When we asked if we could borrow a chair and a pair of scissors, they had to clear it with the hotel manager first. The manager (a KGB agent, we jokingly speculated), all the hairdressers and apprentices, and our tour guide came to watch my performance. Presumably they didn't want us to steal any hairpins or trade secrets. It was the first time I touched Emma in more than a deliberately engineered 'accidental' manner. It is part of the profession of a ladies hairdresser to touch a woman and it is part of the subtle art of making clients feel good about themselves. I chiselled Emma's thick black hair precisely the way she liked it and I wallowed in pleasing her every wish. She was delighted and so grateful that she gave me a kiss on the cheek in front of all those people. I am sure I blushed. I did not know then that much more was to come later.

The following morning we left Irkutsk, back on a train for the second half of the Trans-Siberian journey to Moscow. It took four long days and by the end of it I was glad they hadn't allowed us to go all the way by train.

I remember the journey as very pleasant most of the time and generously sweetened by Emma's presence. What do you do on a Russian train for four days? You drink terrible Russian beer. You drink excellent Russian vodka. You play chess and cards with the Russians and anyone else who wants to play. You move around compartments a lot, visiting other members of your group and talking to people who want to talk to you. Many Russians wanted to talk to us, albeit in very bad English, mostly about politics and culture, and though they may be poor, they are a very cultured people and love their motherland dearly. The train was crammed with soldiers on their way to Moscow for the May Day parade, where they were to represent their part of the country. Pamela and Jane were openly flirting with some of them. I supposed it was some sort of political perversity on their part or maybe sheer opportunism.

After a day or two, crowdedness turned to chaos and sanitary conditions deteriorated rapidly. The smell of tobacco smoke was a welcome disguise for some of the more pungent food, alcohol and body odours hanging around people.

Most of my time was spent with Emma in the dining car. She had a very warm engaging manner, was very intelligent and, in contrast to the Americans, was not in the least overbearing. We talked about art, music, French cinema, Existential literature and philosophy. We played cards, chess and, increasingly it seemed, with each other's mind and emotions. I knew that

Emma and Bill were not married and since she clearly liked me it was perfectly acceptable for me to enjoy her company as much as it was available. Bill did not have the same view, as I discovered later, but he was too much of a gentleman to make a scene, at least in public. He spoke good Russian and seemed to be enjoying chatting with the soldiers on the train.

In Moscow Emma and I went on a couple of half-day tours together without Bill. On one occasion we managed to have our group guide take just the two of us inside the Kremlin. This was highly irregular, the guide told us, and we were under strict instructions to make it short and quick. Walking around inside the inner sanctum of the world's biggest communist party was an eerie experience. We felt like spies since we were foreigners inside the Russian government stronghold. Of course it was hard to take all this seriously and we probably looked more like school children who had jumped the fence to skip classes. What gave this walk a further sense of unreality was to find several churches inside the grounds of the Kremlin. On a rectangular courtyard, appropriately called Cathedral Square, there are three small Byzantine cathedrals, all with bulbous golden domes and surrounded by immaculately kept gardens. At times we expected the ghost of Rasputin to emerge from behind the closed doors of any one of the cathedrals, decrying the excesses of both the system and the Orthodox Church. Unfortunately he didn't.

The most spectacular item inside the Kremlin grounds is the King of Bells, an eleven-tonne bell which took two years to build. It was brought into the Kremlin in 1737 and promptly cracked, due to a nearby fire, before it was ever installed. It never tolled and it just sits there looking sad, forlorn and mute, utterly unfulfilled in its purpose. In some ways the whole setting looked more like a convent or monastery than the seat of a communist superpower. Against the express instructions of our guide, and to her annoyance but our impish delight, we took photos of each other inside the compound, risking, our guide told us, having our cameras confiscated.

It was during another one of those outings that Emma gave me the impression that the quality of her relationship with Bill was slipping in a downward spiral.

My accommodation in Moscow was the Leningradsky Hotel, one of the best I was told. It's a huge Stalin-era style building with lots of marble and brass in the foyer and hallways. The bed was a four-poster set in an alcove, but the sheets had repair patches. The water coming out of the bath taps in the bathroom was a murky pale brown so I settled for a sponge wash.

If some of the services were not up to scratch, the culture certainly was. The first night we saw Swan Lake at the Stanislavski Theatre. The following night we heard the Moscow Philharmonic Orchestra playing Berlioz, Mozart and Stravinsky at the Tchaikovsky Conservatorium. And to top it all off, on 1 May, the big day, we went to the Bolshoi. There was a special celebratory performance of the ballet Don Quixote one of my favourite stories. The audience response was deafening and I thought the encores would never stop. I was close to cultural indigestion. The Russians love their ballet and their music and so they should as it's amongst the most stirring in the world.

Equally stirring was the May Day Parade. The May Day Parade in Moscow was an event of national importance and seemed to me to be celebrated with more intensity, fervour, and food and drink than any Christmas I had ever seen. Apart from the spectacular if somewhat over-the-top military display of the parade itself, against the backdrop of Red Square, everybody was openly of good cheer. Many see it as an opportunity to abandon themselves to excesses and I have never seen so many people in military uniform so drunk as to have completely lost control. Their general boisterousness was often directed towards tourists as they assumed that if you are there at that time, you are obviously a communist sympathiser and therefore a comrade and thus a guest of honour. More than a few medal-covered military officers came to our table to propose a toast to us. That trip through Russia was a big contribution to my political awareness, something severely lacking in my life thus far.

On our last day together in Moscow, during a walk in Gorky Park, she suggested that I should visit her in London and she gave me the address and phone number of her parents. London had not been on my agenda till now, but since there was nothing planned after 'getting home' to Belgium, why not accept the invitation? The day after the May Day parade, we said a very warm goodbye at Moscow Central station, and Emma and Bill went off to London.

One night after Emma and Bill had gone, I had dinner with the Americans where they were staying in the Metropole Hotel. After a good deal of excellent Russian champagne before, during and after dinner, one of the Americans blurted out that she felt 'horny like hell'. While not out of character given the circumstances, what was funny about it was that I didn't know what that word meant then as my English was still developing, so they had to explain it to me. I am not sure what happened after that, but she must have thought that I needed a practical demonstration of the consequences of such feelings. The next thing I became aware of, after considerably more champagne and French cognac, was being in a bed with her beside me. The episode can only be described as an ugly, drunken shemozzle. There is no doubt that we were drunk, but not drunk enough for me not to notice that in the middle of a chaotic struggle, her hairpiece supporting her bee-hive, fashionable in those days, came off in my hand. I am sure hilarity must have killed any hint of eroticism and, in fact, I doubt that anything more than a groping attempt at sex actually happened. Given my profession I was able to reinstall her hairpiece the following morning. What was even funnier, at least to me, was that this rather insignificant event caused a good deal of friction between the two American women, rather ungraciously displayed over breakfast the following morning. Fortunately they left for Paris the next day.

Before starting this journey, I had planned to visit Leningrad and its main attraction, the Hermitage Museum. Leningrad, or St Petersburg, as it was originally called, (and has been again now since 1992) has always been more of a cultural centre than Moscow which, apart from the Kremlin, is rather dull, especially when there is no parade.

Peter I, Tsar of Russia, later dubbed Peter the Great, started building that city himself in 1703 at the mouth of the river Neva. Italian architects were engaged and the city looks like an attempt to copy both Rome and Venice. Fifteen years later it was the new capital of Russia and by 1725, St Petersburg had a population of over forty thousand people, many of whom were aristocrats, artists and intellectuals.

If St Petersburg was the Crown of Peter's achievements, the Hermitage is certainly its jewel. Established by his successor Catherine II in 1764 with an initial 200 paintings, it now boasts three and a half million artefacts. The building itself, originally the Winter Palace for the Russian Emperors, is a magnificent example of classic Italian Baroque and many of the living quarters are on display. The 1812 War Gallery celebrates the Russian victory over Napoleon with opulence and great pride.

My main interest in going there, however, was the vast collection of paintings, one of the best in the world. The Flemish School is extremely well represented by no less than forty-two works by Peter Rubens and other such Flemish masters as van Dyck, Jordaens, Snyders, and Teniers, to name but a few. The Dutch collection is even larger, starting with twenty-four Rembrandts, including the famous and voluptuous Danae beckoning any would-be lover to her bed, or so it seemed to me. Staring at it for some time, I wondered if Emma had been beckoning me to her bed in London? I suddenly felt the urge to get on with the journey, but I had two more days in Leningrad and a lot more paintings to see.

There are two Leonardo da Vinci paintings, the more famous being *The Madonna and Child* or commonly known as *The Virgin Breastfeeding*. There are other Italians such as Raphael, Titian and Michelangelo, and a large Spanish collection including El Greco, de Goya and Velazquez. They also claim to have the largest collection of French Impressionists ever assembled. The Hermitage is much more than a magnificent museum; it is truly a monument to Russian history, reflecting its glory and vastness. That glory was recently celebrated, though not without a touch of melancholy, by the well-known Russian filmmaker Alexander Sokurov in his masterpiece *Russian Ark*. This film is remarkable not only because it blends the beauty of the museum's art with the glory of Russian history into a magnificent visual spectacle, but also because it was made in a single ninety-six minute shot, a first in cinematographic technology.

I returned to Moscow the following day and took the train to Warsaw for a short visit before heading to Belgium and my home town of Gent.

Red Square, Moscow.
Next page: Russian Orthodoxy inside the Kremlin.

Emma and I taking photos of each other inside the Kremlin.

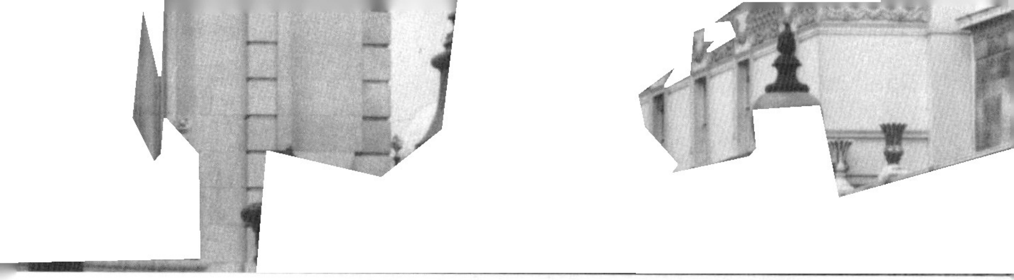

2.
Escape from London
1966

THE initial excitement of reunions with family and friends and being the focus of attention was short-lived. I had been away in Australia and New Guinea for three years to the month, but *I* had changed, and therefore *my world* had changed. Yet here, everything seemed the same and the gulf between my past and my present was both wide and deep. I felt like a tourist in my own town, and an intruder and voyeur into my own family. Apart from wanting to visit Emma in London, two incidents helped me decide not to stay in Belgium.

Waiting for a tram in Gent one day, I overheard a conversation between two men in their thirties. One said he had just come back from a holiday in Algiers, just across the Mediterranean. The other replied *'Why would you want to go there? There are much nicer places near here without all those black bastards.'* Of course, not all Belgians have these sentiments nor do they have a monopoly on racism – Australia has its share as well.

The other incident occurred while visiting an uncle and aunt

Brussels. After they had shown lukewarm interest in my travels, my uncle said: *'All right, well, you've had your fling now, got the wild adventurer out of your system, now it's time to settle down and get married.'* Getting married, me? *Never!* That was the last time I went to visit them. Two days later I left for London.

I had written to Emma that I was coming and she offered to meet me at the station in London. That's when I met Peter, her husband. They took me to a small hotel somewhere near the edge of the city and Emma and I arranged to meet the following day.

She was much more talkative then and explained what was going on. She and Peter had been separated before she went to Kabul. As they were still good friends, they had been meeting for the day to catch up and he wanted to come to meet me. So far so good, but what about the good doctor? Where had he disappeared to? It turned out that he was in London too, visiting family before returning to the States. More importantly to me, she now revealed that she was very ambivalent about her relationship with Bill and did not know whether to break it off, let it cool down, or go with him to the US and work at improving it. I suspect she had not really anticipated that I would come to London. I pointed out to her now she had an additional choice. We had enjoyed our flirtations across Russia, which may well have been the beginning of her signal to Bill that she was not as committed as he thought. I, on the other hand, had come to London exclusively on the basis of her invitation. I was old enough to realise that inviting someone to visit you is not the same as a strong desire for a deep relationship. Still, now that I was here and found that she was no longer married to Peter nor fully committed to Bill, I was more than ready to enjoy her company whenever she was available.

I liked London immediately. It has so much life, culture and vibrancy, and my three years in Australia had given me a reasonably good understanding of the English language, which made it much easier to deal with people. While in Brussels I had made enquires about the possibility of emigrating to South America Brazil, Chile, or Argentina. Having migrated once (to Australia) I knew I could do it again, but nothing positive had come of it. A few days after arriving in London I wondered where I would go next or if I would stay there. I decided to let the future unfold by itself and just wait and see what happened. Two days later, the unfolding occurred. Strolling along in the warm summer sunshine, I saw a placement agency dedicated to helping *'guest workers'* find jobs. To my surprise, one of the professions they specialised in was, yes, hairdressing. I went in to ask some questions and discovered that if I had a job it was possible for me, as a Belgian national, to work in Britain even though Europe was not yet *'unified'* as it is now. My continental hairdressing training had worked well for me in Australia so I thought I'd give it a go here. It took them less than a week to find a job for me in a Hyde Park salon that was part of a London-wide chain. I went for a short interview, with no test to show what I could do, (which is uncommon in our trade) and I got the job, just like that. I rented a furnished room nearby in Montague Place with a charming retired actress. She looked like Miss Marple, was destitute and an alcoholic, but was also very funny and generous. One day a plumber was fixing something in the bathroom. Coming home early from work, I caught her peeing in a bucket in our shared kitchen. She laughed so much she had to sit down again and filled the bucket some more.

While the salon was located in the posh Marble Arch area, it was not a high-class place. The clientele was a mixture of tourists and working people from the surrounding businesses. The salon receptionist doubled up as manageress, but as she was not a hairdresser we had practically no professional supervision. The owner of the chain popped his head in once a week for two minutes and that was it. Staff turnover was phenomenal.

For the rest of that year I soaked up the pleasures of London. I saw plays by George Bernard Shaw and Oscar Wilde, amongst others, and admired stage performances by Ralph Richardson and John Gielgud. I did all the tourist attractions, from the Crown Jewels and the Tower of London to Madame Tussaud's. I saw Swan Lake again at Covent Garden and learned to appreciate the music of Elgar and Walton during my many visits to the Royal Festival Hall. I learned to appreciate the smell of English beer and the water of the Thames. Emma came to visit me whenever she was in the area, either at the salon for a haircut or at night in my room. We went out for dinner to many exotic places, Biagi's, a superb Italian restaurant, being our favourite. Our friendship gradually blossomed into a fully erotically-satisfying relationship, at least for me. While Emma was not much older than I was, she was much more sophisticated and world-wise, especially in the area of sexuality. I came to see her more as a tutor or a coach than a lover, which may have been less satisfying for her in the long run and I suspect she may have found the conquest more fulfilling than the consummation.

Although I was twenty-three, Emma was my first proper sexual relationship. When I was at hairdressing school I had plenty of crushes, but was far too shy to say or do anything about them. One of my classmates looked so much like the teenage Elizabeth Taylor that I could hardly stop staring at her. A few years later in Sydney I had a severe crush on one of the manicurists at a salon where I worked, but without results. In Port Moresby I had what I regarded as a girlfriend, but there too I never got to taste the so-called *'forbidden fruit'*. My only other experience of actual sex before Emma, not counting boarding school games, was in Taiwan.

While in Taipei, on the way to Japan from New Guinea, my travel agent suggested hiring a guide because of the language problem. My Chinese guide was middle-aged, very charming and took a somewhat paternal liking to me. One night after a taste of Chinese Opera, which was visually exciting but not exactly soothing to my Western ears, and a delicious feast of fine Chinese cuisine, he suggested it was too early to go back to the hotel and asked me if I would like to have some *'more pleasure'*. I wondered what he had in mind. On the outskirts of the city there was a health resort called Peitou, famous for its natural warm sulphur spas. *'Additional services can be provided, like girl giving you massage,'* he said. That sounded fine to me. I had some suspicion that there was more to getting a massage than he was letting on. I was naïve for my age, but not so naïve that I didn't see what was coming. Since the *'forbidden fruit'* had not up till then been offered to me freely, buying it seemed not such a terrible thing. Some of Taiwan's *'fruit'* looked very attractive to me and given my age I was well and truly ripe for it.

When my guide came back to pick me up, he was chatting in Chinese with the girl who had *'served'* me. Her name was Lina and he translated that she liked me very much and wanted to thank me for my kindness and could I please come again the following day because she really would like to see me again? I replied, via my guide, that I too was thankful for her kindness but unfortunately I was due to leave for Japan the following day and could not come back. I am sure that her feelings for me were, at least in part, because I had given her a large tip. She had also been flattered by my choosing her over three other girls who had been presented to me at the beginning, a situation that was more embarrassing to me than to them. It now emerged that she was new to this business and had found her very first client to be particularly kind and gentle. Little did she know that this was due to my complete lack of experience. Whatever else I had learned that night, I now knew that sulphur water baths are very relaxing.

A recently published tourist pamphlet tells me that Peitou was once notorious as a destination for large groups of male tourists from Japan and other countries because prostitution was legal there. Ah, so that's what it was? The publication continues to explain that in 1979, Taipei City Council finally passed a resolution to prohibit the practice of the world's oldest profession. Just as well I went before that time!

When I was in Warsaw a few weeks later, again I had a guide. She was a young university student who spoke very good English. Showing me around, she took every opportunity to tell me about the oppressive Polish system and how difficult it was to escape it, while all the while I was waiting for her to tell me about the local sulphur baths. On our visit to Chopin's birthplace, a short drive from Warsaw, she became rather emotional. At first I thought it was due to her love for Chopin's music. On the way back to Warsaw, sitting close to me in the back of a large black Russian limousine, (I was still travelling first class) she begged me to write to her and keep in touch. It was important for her intellectual development, she tried to persuade me, to stay in contact with the rest of the Western world. I promised I would write.

I did actually write to her once I had an address in London. She replied to my first letter declaring her genuine love and asking would I please marry her. She desperately wanted to get out of Poland. If my Taiwanese guide had contributed to my sexual education, my Polish guide made a serious contribution to my political education. While I empathised with her plight, I desperately did not want to get married under any circumstances and I was not ready to break the law for her freedom. My awareness of the political world was slowly awakening through first-hand experience.

Emma was my first relationship including sex, as opposed to a 'one-off' incident. I had no idea about the nature of her involvement with Bill or Peter during that time and I deliberately avoided asking about it. One evening I went to see the recently launched multi Academy Award winning film *Doctor Zhivago* by David Lean, starring the wonderful Omar Sharif. Walking home afterwards, I wondered if one person could genuinely love two others at the same time as Pasternak seemed to suggest in this story. Zhivago is happily married to Tanya but falls in love with Lara, all the while insisting he loves both equally well. While I could see that it would be difficult to accept this proposition emotionally, I was intrigued and attracted by the probability of it being possible. I wondered if that was what Emma was doing and would that make her more emotionally mature than people who could only be attracted to one person at a time?

I noticed a certain uneasiness about Emma on occasions. Mostly she was intensely present to our interactions, but she could be far away and moody also and I never managed to work out what caused the difference. Her visits were erratic, two days in a row and then not again for a few weeks. I was patient and naïve, but I tried to observe and learn and understand what was going on. Where was this leading to? I experienced an odd mixture of curiosity as an interested but detached observer, yet suffering the pain of being played with like a toy as well. Many more questions than answers arose from all this and I did a lot of mulling over this in my diary. Towards the end of June I wrote in my diary (which I had been keeping since my first day in Australia in 1963):

'Emma is in the most mixed-up situation I have ever known. Her ex-husband has invited her to accompany him on a business trip to Monaco; Bill has asked her to go with him to the US; I could ask her to go with me to South America. Do I really want to do this? I have enough problems looking after myself, not to look after her as well. I must do something to sort my relationship out with Emma.'

I was only mildly surprised when a few months later she told me, with some hesitation, she had decided to go back to Kabul with Bill on another term of duty. I was more surprised when she suggested I should visit her in Kabul some day. Was that a strategy to soften the blow of rejection and did she again anticipate that surely I wouldn't go that far? Did she invite me on the assumption that I would have learned my lesson by now and would certainly not follow her to Kabul? Probably. On our last meeting before she left London to go back to Kabul, in a moment of sentimentality Emma told me she actually liked me better than Bill and that I was a nicer person, but she added: *'You are not old enough for me'*. I did not know what she meant by that and was too stunned to ask. I was left to guess. Had she been using me as a mere toyboy? Or was her relationship with me only to tease or torture Bill? Or was she simply 'collecting' men? Peter, Bill, me, and who else? Being a ladies hairdresser, I thought that I had a better understanding of women than most men, but this was my first encounter with this degree of complexity and I was lost and confused. A few days later walking around Piccadilly Circus, Eros reminded me that it is his bow and arrow that cause such pain in the heart of the sentimental lover. I should have known.

Having been well and truly bitten by the travel bug by then, the idea of going to Afghanistan immediately appealed to me, despite Emma's ambiguous behaviour. And where was Afghanistan anyway?

A week or two after Emma left for Kabul, an Iranian tourist came to have her hair done at the salon. Discovering where she was from I told her I had an aunt living in Teheran. When I told her my aunt's name she said '*She lives two doors from us, I know her well*'. Small world. I did not know at that time the word 'synchronicity' as used by Jung. When I shared with her that I might even visit her part of the world one day, she said she would tell my aunt to expect me. Suddenly it seemed as if I had made a decision to go that way if for no other reason than to visit my aunt. I didn't know then that seven months later I would actually visit her.

Looking back on my time in London, I notice the increasing usage of what I now call 'positive self-talk'. My diary had many self-encouraging phrases. I was beginning to reassure myself:

'not to worry about the troubles at work'

'it was probably for the better if Emma chose Bill over me'.

To some extent it was a way of rationalising things, but it helped me to cope with some of the uncertainties, some of the underlying fears and ever-present need for security. It was self-help therapy and on-the-job training, which had started at the age of six to cope with a life of not depending on other people. I was gradually coming to grips with the challenges of relationships, independence and self-respect.

The notions of 'relationship, independence and self-respect' were violently thrust into my face when, that year, I came across Jean Genet's *The Thief's Journal*, which was, according to Sartre, 'the most beautiful book Genet has written'. I had been interested in Existentialism for some time and had read a little around the subject without really understanding what it was all about. I was seduced into fascination with Existentialism in the early sixties by the flagrant and public display of the de-facto relationship between Jean-Paul Sartre and Simone de Beauvoir, the two most popular authors in the field of Existentialism at the time. Instantly, they became my heroes, not because I agreed with what they said, which came later, but with what they did. They vigorously denied marriage, stood up for what they believed, sympathised with communism and, most shocking of all, they championed Jean Genet.

Born in Paris in 1910, Genet was abandoned to the state welfare services by his prostitute mother, never knew his father and became a beggar, a compulsive thief, a cheat and con-man. He spent time in prison in many European countries and was eventually condemned to life imprisonment in France in 1947. By then he had already been published and many leading artists and writers were so captured by his 'artistry' that they organised a public appeal, led by Jean Cocteau and, incredibly, he was pardoned by the President himself, who invited him to dinner. To be an advocate of homosexuality and to elevate begging, theft and robbery to a form of mysticism would have been sufficient to assure him some notoriety at that time, but to write about it with such brutal honesty so as to be regarded a poet and a martyr assured him a special place in Existentialist literature. Reading Genet had been an exploration into a world entirely foreign to me and was a challenge to my own self-respect and honesty. Already then I asked myself in my diary:

'Could I ever write with the same degree of honesty as Genet?'

Before leaving Port Moresby on my Trans-Siberian journey, my best friend, Sylvia, whom I had considered my 'girlfriend' had mentioned that one day she would like to visit the UK and Europe as she had family in the UK on her father's side and in Switzerland on her mother's side. During my time in London I had been in correspondence with her and, shortly after Emma left for Afghanistan, I received word from Sylvia that, as she had finished her studies, she planned to arrive in London in January 1967. She asked if she could stay with me, at least initially. It was early December 1966.

After six months in London I was ready to spread my wings again. Suddenly, and regardless of Emma's invitation, the Middle East became an attractive destination. However, I was not in a rush to leave and I could easily wait until Sylvia came. It then occurred to me that when she arrived I would have to tell her that I was about to leave for Afghanistan.

'Why Afghanistan?' she would ask.

'Because a separated woman, who wants to be with her boyfriend more than with me, invited me, though she probably does not expect me to go there.'

No, maybe that's not what I would say. By now I had planned to buy a car and travel to Afghanistan overland. The journey, they say, can be more fun than the destination. Little did I know what was coming. The logical thing to do would be to invite Sylvia to come with me. She could see parts of Europe on the way and get off wherever she wanted to, or come all the way. Either she came or she didn't, that would be her choice, not mine. I decided it was far too early to worry about what would happen once we got to Kabul. Waiting to cross bridges till you come to them seemed like good advice at the time. I simply wrote back saying she was welcome to stay and that I looked forward to seeing her again.

About two months after I had started the Marble Arch job the receptionist-manager left. I mentioned to the owner that it is better for the manager of a hairdressing salon to be a hairdresser and I told him that, since I had managed my own business in Port Moresby, I knew what to do. To my astonishment he appointed me manager there and then. Over the course of the following few months I became increasingly uncomfortable with his attitude towards staff and his constant demands for more revenue. Looking back over my entire working life he was undoubtedly the worst boss I have ever worked for. Two of the other senior stylists were also very unhappy and threatened to leave if I didn't get them an increase of their measly salary. There was no way the boss was going to give them more money even though I told him they might leave.

He said '*Let them, there are plenty of hairdressers looking for jobs.*'

One night in early December the two senior stylists and I were having dinner together, as we often did, when Tony, who was from Spain, said he was thinking of leaving and going home for Christmas. The other one, Eric, a Scottish lad, thought he might do the same. When I told them that I was thinking of leaving in January myself we all looked at each other and laughed. What if we all left at once *before* Christmas?

Christmas that year was on a Sunday. The week before Christmas, from the Monday to the Saturday inclusive, the salon was heavily booked. The Saturday of the week before that, after we got paid, the three of us went to the pub to say goodbye to each other with a few excellent British ales. We felt a bit like a group of thieves planning the heist of our lives. By the Monday before Christmas all three of us had left the country, leaving the salon to the two juniors. The handwriting in my diary for that day is bigger and stronger than usual:

'Teach the greedy bastard a lesson, treating us like scum!'

Maybe my travels through Russia and insights into the revolution had activated dormant anti-capitalist sentiments in me, or maybe I could no longer tolerate being exploited. Either way, the Friday of that week, 24 December 1966, was my 24th birthday and the first Christmas Eve in four years with my brothers in Belgium.

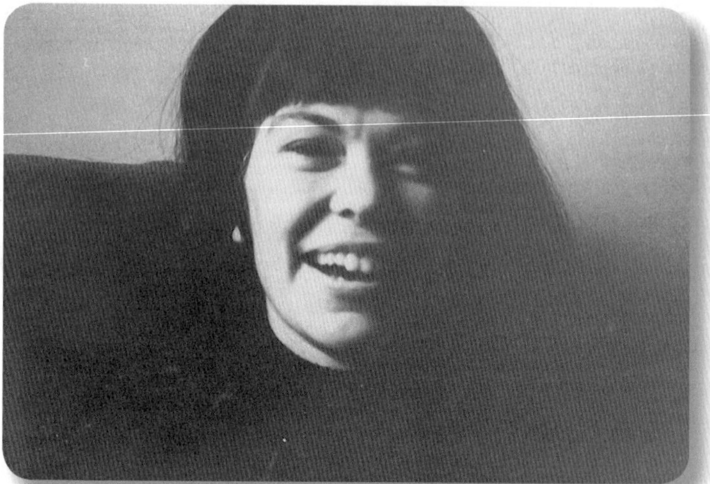

12th June, 1966: I arrive in London.
Emma meets me and I stay for the rest of the year.

Below: The recently renovated Atomium in Brussels.

Eros aiming his arrow at my heart.

3.

The early days: not a good start

SYLVIA didn't arrive in London until late January 1967 and I went back from Belgium to meet her. I had kept my room with the actress. She, of course, had copped the brunt of my boss's anger. After he had learned what had happened, he went there and shouted at her, demanding she tell him where I was, threatening he would be back with the police if she didn't tell. Before leaving I had paid a few weeks rent in advance and I had told her I was going on holidays without specifying where and that I would be back later.

Sylvia arrived on a cold and windy January evening, jet-lagged but in good spirits. Apart from a large ladies handbag and a briefcase, her only luggage consisted of an enormous bright-red crocodile-skin suitcase with bulging pockets on all sides. Nowadays she would have passed for *Mrs Crocodile Dundee*. We cabbed to my room in one of those famous black square boxes on wheels they call taxis in London. Too excited to go to sleep, we talked. She had completed her kindergarten qualifications and had spent the holidays in Bougainville where she grew up. I gave her a short version of my Trans-Siberian trip and finally came to the topic of Emma. I explained that I had been invited to Kabul and asked her to join me on a Trans-European overland journey to Afghanistan. We had shared no commitment to each other in the past and there was none implied for the future at this time either. When she realised she could still visit her family, both in England and in Switzerland, and be a tourist in London, she found the offer too good to refuse. She spent a couple of weeks in London and I returned home to Belgium to get ready for our journey.

After a bit of shopping around I bought a brand new Opel station wagon, tax-free since I was taking it out of the country. It was sandy beige with brown trimmings, a combination that now would look positively old-fashioned. When Sylvia came to Belgium in late February we took it for a run on a day trip across the Dutch border before finally setting out on Sunday 5 March 1967 on what was to become the adventure of a lifetime. The car contained practically all we owned between us. I took a large wad of traveller's cheques, the safest way to carry money everyone had told me, and I left some money with my brother Freddy in case I needed it later, which turned out to be one of the wisest decisions I ever made.

As it was on the way from Gent to Paris, I went to see my father in the old people's home he had been in for some time. He had lost his speech completely after his second stroke and walked with a stick, dragging his right leg. His right hand was clutched into a tight fist held close to his body so I had to shake his left. No hug. He was only sixty-five but looked more like seventy-five. His white hair was very thin and his cheeks slightly hollow. I am sure he recognised me, I could tell from looking straight into his eyes. Within a few minutes tears were streaming down his cheeks. He knew who I was alright. I wondered how he felt. He couldn't tell me since he couldn't speak or write. Was he sad to see me? Was he sad that he couldn't speak? Was he sorry for some of the things he had put me through when I was little? I don't know and, frankly, at the time I didn't care much.

I experienced an odd mixture of compassion for a person so badly afflicted and a cold disregard for the father I didn't know or understand. By now I had began to see that putting me into boarding school may well have been the only thing he could have done and my anger towards him had considerably diminished. I think I went to see him more out of curiosity and I did not think of how my visit could have been of any benefit to him. There may have been some gratification on my part to actually see him reduced to practically nothing after having been the dominant repressive force in my early life. I did not experience it as a victory on my part though, perhaps more as some measure of 'divine justice'. We didn't know it then, of course, but he would live another seven years like this, about the same duration I had suffered in that terrible boarding school where he had so ungraciously put me during my youth. Visiting both my brothers and my mother and father before leaving brought back a lot of early childhood memories.

By the time I was born, my parents' twenty-year-old marriage was already on shaky ground and probably had been for some time. I was the third boy in our family. Alfred, though we always called him Freddy, is ten years older than I; Andre is five years older. My father used to joke, in one of his better moods, that he was only 'allowed' every five years. It took me some time to understand the joke and once I did it wasn't funny any more.

It has only slowly dawned on me over the years that my mother might well have preferred to have a girl to redress the gender balance in the family. I have old photos where as a young child I was wearing what looks very much like a silk blouse and my blond curly hair was long enough for most people to think I was a girl. I was so sweet and angelic at the age of six that I was asked by the local Catholic nuns at the convent to be Jesus in the Easter procession. As a young boy I always felt inadequate, weak, and girlish. I had a pretty face, curly blond hair and was below average in size. In later years at school I was certainly treated as a weakling by the other children.

My father told me that he was in the middle of shaving, getting ready to go to work, when my mother yelled out that it was time to go to the hospital as the baby was coming. The actual time of birth was not part of that story but it was probably sometime that morning. The date, however, was 24 December 1942. Yes, the day before Christmas. That event, Christmas, the celebration of the birth of one of the most revered religious leaders in Western history, has always overshadowed my own birthday. Growing up in a traditionally strong Catholic environment certainly did not make it easy for me to resent this. In many European Catholic countries, Christmas celebrations start on the 24 December by having Christmas dinner that night and going on to midnight mass afterwards. The chaos of getting last minute Christmas presents, for me doubling up as birthday presents, preparations for the Christmas dinner and all the practicalities of getting the event ready would have taken away the focus from the birthday boy. I say *would have* because I cannot actually remember a birthday in my early childhood any more than I can remember an elaborate family Christmas dinner. Maybe neither occurred or they were relatively uneventful. Come to think of it, I cannot remember any dinners at home where all five of us, mum and dad and the three sons, sat down together. I am sure it must have happened, I just can't remember. Things were not all that flash in Belgium in 1942. After all, it was the middle of WWII in Europe. Food was not always easy to get and luxuries were unheard of in our household. What I do remember is meeting at a neighbour's house a man in a soldier's uniform smoking a pipe smelling like a sweet shop on fire and speaking a language I didn't understand. Almost certainly an English officer billeting with civilians. This memory came back to me one day when watching an episode of *Dad's Army*.

I also remember that as a young child I spent more time with my godmother, my mother's sister, who lived next door to us, than at home with my mother. On the face of it that was because my mother worked part-time as a manicurist in a beauty salon. Apart from my mother working, the other reason I spent more time next door was because there was already a good deal of tension between my parents. They quibbled if they spoke at all and often messages would be sent to each other via the children. There are images in my mind of being secretly reprimanded by my mother for doing things with my father. Yet there are few memories of having fun with my father as he was always away at work and when he was home mother took us visiting to her relatives. Both my mother and father came from very large families, not unusual in predominantly Catholic countries. The Catholic Church's prohibition of contraception is a crime against humanity that persists today but has as yet not been identified as such by the international court. Surely it is no less cruel to force unwanted children into life than it is to force wanted ones into death?

My parents had ten siblings each, so there were lots of aunts and uncles and cousins and nieces. Not that we spent much time with them as they were scattered around the country and into France, where our family originally came from. When we did visit family, most of the energy seemed to be taken up with gossip, arguments over money and scheming instead of having fun. There may well have been some fun but, again, I cannot recall a family visit or any sort of occasion where all of us were together enjoying the outing.

I did have fun with my brothers, at least on some occasions, but being five and ten years older than I am they were mostly not available for my companionship. My main memories of my brothers are of heroes, people I looked up to and admired, probably even envied.

Freddy was, in my eyes, a clever, intelligent and practical person who became a fitter and turner and already worked in Paris at a time when I didn't even know where that city was located. He had an officer's rank in the army and married the daughter of a shoe factory owner. Once he applied for a job with the Belgian *Gendarmerie* and I was impressed, even though it turned out he was not tall enough to qualify. Andre, a much more outgoing character, entered an apprenticeship as a pastry cook before I had time to settle in at boarding school. He became a paracommando in the army and went to the Congo for part of his compulsory military service. They nicknamed him Tarzan for his bravery, strength and good looks. He moved to Brussels and married a woman who already had a child. These were real men who did important things, some of which were seriously disapproved of and others which were offered to me as models to follow. I often felt small, left behind and pretty much useless compared to them. My clearest memory of an early interaction with them was a pillow fight the three of us had in Freddy's room and me accidentally pulling Andre's pyjama pants down. We laughed ourselves silly, an experience I was later to relive under hypnosis.

They were the big boys in my life but they were outside my reach, so I turned inward. (I didn't really get to know them as people until we were adults many years later.) I developed a liking for drawing and watercolour painting, solitary activities suitable for a shy boy. I regularly suffered from laryngitis, stomach cramps, tension headaches, and felt restricted chest movements, all probably symptoms of anxiety. Drawing, reading and playing solitaire with cards were my favourite activities. I still like playing solitaire, even if it is on a computer now, and reading continues to be my all-time favourite activity.

One day when I was about five or six years old, I was drawing at the living room table when I saw my parents having an animated conversation, which was rare since they hardly talked at all. But when an argument developed, they began actually shouting at each other. I had never seen anything like this before and I had no idea what it was about. Then, suddenly, I saw my father with his hands around my mother's neck and her yelling at the top of her voice. She managed to wriggle herself free from his hold and ran from the house.

Rather than follow, he ran upstairs to their bedroom and I heard him rummage around in a wardrobe or chest of drawers, but I had no idea what he was doing. I stayed sitting at the table, stunned, frozen and alone for what felt like a very long time before she returned. As soon as she came in, he again started shouting at her, demanding to know where she had been. She wouldn't say. He grabbed her again and as she yelled out, two police officers entered the house. I did not understand at the time how such a coincidence could have occurred. She had, of course, gone to the police and they had probably suggested that they come back with her and wait outside ready to enter the door which she had left open upon the slightest sign of disturbance. My father had worked it out immediately and was furious.

Statements were taken, things written down, all in front of me still sitting at the table. At one time, one of the police officers sitting next to me made a remark about my drawing, which suddenly made me feel terribly important. I had been acknowledged as part of the household. It left me with a strange mixture of fear and excitement. I knew that what was happening was not very good but at least something out of the ordinary had occurred. I have always been able to visualise this scene and, of the early memories of my childhood is one that has the most impact. Many years later when a woman I shared a house with physically attacked me, I had my hands near her neck in self-defence. Suddenly, I saw that scene of my father's hands around my mother's throat flash in front of me and I let go immediately. I was more shaken by the sudden and vivid recall than by the minor scuffle with the woman.

I do recall some good times from my early childhood, such as when I went to a nearby kindergarten run by Catholic nuns. My parents were not particularly devout Catholics but it was normal in our family, as it was and still is in the rest of Belgium, to go to church on Sundays and send the children to Catholic schools. The nuns wore big puffy habits all the way down to the ground with white starched caps on their heads, never showing any hair at all. Once I saw a small strand of hair protruding from one of these caps and I remember being surprised. I am not sure whether I expected them to be bald or more holy than the rest of us hairy creatures. The nuns were kind, warm, motherly, and mostly elderly and smelling of soap. I liked going there. I think they gave me something I didn't get at home, a safe place to play with children my own age. I remember playing with bright strips of paper, weaving them through slits in pages of glossy coloured paper producing a sort of woven mat which looked very pretty and appealed to my early sense of aesthetics. We walked from our house to kindergarten, we had no car then, and I can still see the small brown shoes I wore at the time with fat laces which I couldn't do up.

A less pleasant memory was the arrival at my preschool of St Nicolas on December 5 when children were given what English-speaking people call Christmas presents, supposedly from a Spanish Bishop, the patron saint of children. Unfortunately, he had an assistant who was referred to as *Zwarte Piet* (black Peter), who had a different bag from St. Nick's toy-filled one. In his bag he put the children who had not been 'good' that year and he would take them with him, goodness knows where, possibly never to come back. This was my first taste, and there was much more to come, of the use of fear by Catholic educators to control children's behaviour. All I need to do is close my eyes to see the face of the blackened, angry-looking man to feel the fear it evoked in me. Does this mean that deep inside me I knew I had not been a good boy and might have been taken away? Or was I the cause of my parent's arguments and the origin of my mother's disappointments? Surely that would have been enough to end up in the bag?

All this completely drowned out the pleasure and excitement of looking forward to getting presents. Maybe it is not surprising that for me, my birthday apart, Christmas has never held the excitement it seems to generate in others. Today, if it wasn't for my own children, not being a Christian anymore and repulsed by its commercialism, Christmas would be a complete non-event for me. And maybe it is also not surprising that such early experiences of frightening authority figures created a problem for me with authority generally. There are many instances where I was both afraid and wanting to rebel against these authority figures, my father being the main one.

Only ten minutes further from the kindergarten was the 'big' school. St Josef's primary school for boys was attached to a local teacher's college so that student teachers could come and practise there. It was actually called *Oefen School* meaning *Practice School*. Religious brothers, Catholics of course, ran this school. There were some lay-teachers also but on the whole black-robed men with white collars administered the whole complex. I remember getting ready for school, showing my new schoolbag to my godmother and being very excited about it all. My teacher in the first year was a handsome, tall and very friendly Brother. He was a relatively young man and had a great way with kids and occasionally played the violin in the classroom, which made a great impression on me, and I took to him immediately. He may well have been responsible for my subsequent ability to respond positively to classical music. Later he went to the Belgian Congo as a missionary and I was sad to see him go. I think that it was my first conscious experience of loss.

In my second year I had an older lay-teacher who was very formal, strict and traditional. He may have had a sense of humour but never showed it. My troubles, both intellectually and interpersonally, started to come to the fore here. In spite of having had a reasonably good first year, the second was not very pleasant, to say the least. Maybe things had gotten worse at home, but I remember clearly not being well grounded, feeling anxious and afraid. I became easy prey for the 'real' boys. Learning became a struggle. I was told that I was not very good at almost everything. Reading was difficult, maths almost impossible and my handwriting was atrocious. I have very clear recollections of spending recesses in the classroom staring at the inkwell through tears, trying to avoid making more smears than I had already made just trying to write. (Most of us had our right hand thumb, index and middle fingers permanently blue with ink stains). Many other recesses were spent standing in the corner of the large concrete square that was our playground, hoping no one would bump into me. I was the victim of occasional bullying. I had no skills to deal with this and all I could do was cry. I remember my brothers trying to help me with my homework, no doubt at the insistence of my mother, but often expressing the hopelessness of my situation, albeit in a good-natured way.

One of the contributing causes of my school problems could have been an accident which occurred early that year. My brother Andre, who was still at the same school then, would often take me on the cross bar of his bike held in balance between his arms. Most of the way was unpaved and littered with big potholes, which he would aim for rather than avoid. One of them must have been bigger than he judged safe and down we went, me first then the crossbar on my leg and then he on top of that, crunching my right leg bone. Why I wasn't taken to hospital immediately I don't know, but I cried continuously for what seems now like more than a day before an x-ray finally revealed that my leg was splintered in several places and needed to be put in a cast. A makeshift bed was made up in the living room as I couldn't get up the steps to the upstairs bedrooms. When the pain went away and I didn't have to go to school for about six weeks, I distinctly remember enjoying the event, even though it was a further blow to my educational achievements. To make matters infinitely worse, the major drama of my childhood happened later that same year.

My father was the personal chauffeur for one of the city's main administrators and had the use of the car during his lunch hour. The car was a big black Chevrolet, replaced every second year, and always the latest model. It was one of my little joys in life to get a ride in this big American car, the likes of which we didn't often see in our working-class neighbourhood. Few people had cars in our street and only one of the houses had a garage. Our street, *Karel van de Woestijne Straat,* was named after a bohemian Flemish poet. Our house was a slice in a row of houses all built from the same plan. There were three bedrooms upstairs and an attic serving as workshop; downstairs there was a dining room and a small kitchen and a narrow backyard about ten metres long, with a toilet off the kitchen but no bathroom. Years later when my father bought a second-hand Volkswagen, he had the lounge room converted into a garage.

One day he came home for lunch, as he often did, only to get the biggest surprise of his life. My mother had taken a good deal of the furniture, most household items, and all her personal belongings and disappeared. In the middle of the dining table, which for some reason she had not taken, she had carefully placed a small statue of an owl. The word *uil* (meaning owl) in Flemish is used to call someone a stupid person. I often wondered what made her rub the salt in like this.

As we found out much later, in her own words she '*... couldn't stand it any more.*' Her plan was to claim custody of the children afterwards on the grounds that my father would be unable to look after us and that he was a violent man, unfit to be a parent. She was right about the violence. His reaction after realising what had happened was to take his revolver, a World War II leftover, and drive around looking for her wherever he thought he might find her. As he later admitted in telling the story with some pride, '*Luckily I didn't find her,*' by which he meant lucky for him because otherwise he would have been in prison for murder. Some years later he showed me his revolver and actually fired it against the far wall of his work garage, the bullet ricocheting and landing about a metre from where I stood. I was never sure whether he was trying to impress me with his marksmanship or scare the hell out of me. He may have been violent in a number of ways, but he never actually hit or shouted at my brothers or me as far as I know. His own anger and frustration may have been repressed to the extent that they only revealed themselves in bursts directed mainly at my mother. Oh the blessings of married life.

When he calmed down, he went to a niece, the daughter of one of his sisters, who lived in the city, for some immediate support and to help him decide what to do next. They came and got my brother Andre and me from school and brought us home immediately. To be taken out of school by my father in the middle of the day when the other boys had to stay there gave me a sense of being special in a way I had never experienced before. The intention was less to look after us than to show us what a terrible thing our mother had done. I remember standing around on the footpath outside the house with my father, his niece and some neighbours, all trying to figure out what had happened and what to do next. It must have been summer as I distinctly remember the sun was out and it felt nice and it was exciting to be part of a real-life drama, not realising the impact and gravity of the situation. I can't remember crying, not on that day anyway. I was barely six or seven years old.

I ended up being carted off to an elderly aunt, my father's older sister, who lived in a small country town called Ieper, famous for World War I battles, some fifty kilometres away from where we lived. Her own children had grown up and left home; her husband had retired from the fire brigade. They lived in a house with room enough to take me in and look after me. She was very kind and good to me, though somewhat formal and old fashioned. Her husband had an enormous hernia between his legs which caused him to be a grumpy old sod. Luckily he was very much in the background of the small household, although he did impress me enormously when he showed me how to kill one of their chickens for Sunday dinner. He had a small but very sharp knife and, holding the chicken's body between his legs, stuck it right through the creature's neck, letting the blood drip, till it became still. I was allowed to help with plucking the feathers, a job much more difficult than I had imagined.

I was given homegrown free-range eggs for breakfast every day, which I usually collected myself from the coop. This was because I was supposedly malnourished, at least according to my father, since it suited him well to paint my mother as black as he could. The doctor we had consulted to establish my condition had prescribed oxen-blood extract to 'beef' me up. This came in small glass tubes, which I had to break the head off, often cutting my fingers in the process.

Probably the most memorable feature of staying with my aunt was that she gave me a lolly every night just before going to bed. Dental hygiene was obviously not considered to be as important then as we think it to be today. I quite enjoyed being there and felt like I received special treatment, being the guest in this house. The main problem was having to go to school there as well. Being shy, under-confident, academically woeful and a stranger with no friends (I don't remember having any friends in my other school either) was bad enough. What was worse was that the regional dialect in this town was so different from my own that I was treated as a foreigner, an intruder, a weirdo and I had no skills to adapt to new circumstances. I developed tonsillitis and had my tonsils promptly removed in a doctor's surgery.

The ice cream remedy as well as having some days off school was ample compensation.

I was there for the rest of that year. Staying with my aunt and uncle gave me some security and time to find some balance, at least in the short term. The change of scene itself was a welcome distraction. I was not sure what would happen next and I had some anxiety about the future, which was not surprising for there was much worse to come.

I don't know whether it was because my aunt and uncle were too old to look after me indefinitely or because Ieper was too far away for my father to visit regularly, but at the beginning of the new school year instead of going back to my aunt and uncle's place I was unceremoniously shoved into a boarding school that was attached to the primary school I once attended as a day boy. Now, not only had I lost my kind mother-substituting aunt, I also had to go to what turned out to be a 'dump' for state wards. We went home only every second weekend, from Saturday after lunch (as we had school on Saturday mornings) till Sunday afternoon, back in time for six o'clock dinner.

Academically I had not achieved anything at the school in Ieper and I was fearful of going into Year Three. All my available energy was needed to cope with just being there, my attention diverted by emotional upsets and anger at having to be locked up in that place. Learning anything was the last thing on my mind. I wanted to get out of there. But that, it seemed, was impossible. My father needed to go to work, my mother was no longer there and my oldest brother was now working in Paris, staying with friends. Even though he was unable to look after us, as my mother had anticipated, my father had won custody of all the children and that was that. I guess his lawyers were better trained than hers. I was supposed to go and spend half the holidays with my mother and she was allowed to visit me at school once a week.

Having been well-conditioned against her, receiving visits

from my mother was not something I was supposed to enjoy, even though she always brought something like biscuits or jam or a pair of socks. If she was as nasty as I had been led to believe, why would I be looking forward to seeing her? The time spent with her during the holidays was equally awkward. She tried very hard to make it special for me; I tried very hard not to enjoy it too much. Gradually my father found excuses for me not to go to her, such as the opportunity to go on a holiday camp by the seaside with some health insurance club to which he belonged. Her visits to school also decreased gradually and soon both visits and holidays stopped altogether. It was probably best for both of us.

Looking at my life as a whole, the period of being at that boarding school stands out as the blackest and most miserable time of all. Bullying and picking on the smaller kids goes on at all schools but bullies only have so much time to do it before they have to go home. At my boarding school they had all evening, every evening, and all day both days of every second weekend! As an overall memory, at least of the first few years, it seems to me that there was hardly a day I didn't cry, or get hit, bullied or shoved around. There must have been some but I certainly can't remember them.

Catholic Brothers ran the boarding school, the same order that ran the primary school. A few of them were nice and helpful, but most of them were there, it seemed to us, so they too could pick on little kids and push them around, no doubt to prop up their own inferiority complexes. One of them seemed to delight in flicking his long fingernails against our ears from behind so we would get a surprising sting, sending us running with tears in our eyes. Others had physical fights with the bigger boys, leaving the smaller ones of us shivering in our boots, but secretly hoping they would get knocked out.

A few of the brothers were there so they could play sex games with the boys. The fact that sexual abuse in the Christian world, especially the Catholic Church, is a secret revealed worldwide nowadays does not mean it didn't happen then. Luckily, I personally did not experience anything more than the odd overly enthusiastic hug and some patting on the leg just inside my shorts.

One of the brothers did take some special interest in me after a few years there. He had a harelip and was very tall and big, like a gentle giant it seemed to me at the time. It was probably towards the later part of my stay there that he took rather too much delight (I thought even then) in lending me, under the pretext of helping me with my education, rather explicit material about human reproductive plumbing. Sex education at our school was non-existent, so what was he thinking? I never did find out if he was concerned for our 'sex education' or in furthering his chances of approaching us to fulfil his own interests by arousing our curiosity. He also took me one day into the room of a dead brother who was laid out for burial. In order to demonstrate that bodies get stiff after death, he lifted the leg of the dead brother and achieved his purpose well to my amazement. Again, I was puzzled by the reason he would do this but of course could not make anything of it.

There was more going on than I was aware of at the time. Only a few years later there was a scandal with several of the brothers being sent away to another convent.

Today the sexual abuse scandal within the Roman Catholic Church has reached epidemic proportions. In one American Diocese alone, within one year, twenty-four priests were moved from one place to another, presumably so that they could continue practising their 'calling' on a new batch of children. One priest was convicted of 130 offences and over one billion dollars has been spent on legal defences and payouts to silence victims in one state of the US alone. One commentator was moved to say that we are not dealing with some rotten apples here but with deliberate secrecy of the barrel. (A few years ago in Australia, the incumbent of the highest office in the country, the representative of the Queen, stepped aside pending rape accusations against him, (which since have been quashed), while his own church found him guilty of allowing a priest sex-offender to continue working with children in a school. In the ten-year period between 1993 and 2003, fifty Catholic priests and thirty-two Brothers have been convicted of sexual crimes in Australia, not counting of course the ones that were not caught or got away for lack of evidence.[1]

When you think about it, the Roman Catholic Church is a dictatorship ruled by an office, which claims infallibility for its chief commander (a supreme act of arrogance in itself) but, worse still, which then seeks diplomatic immunity under international law. As former Catholic priest John Bartlett wrote in an Australian newspaper '*The doctrine of infallibility seeped into the everyday life of the church and became a justification for clerics to be a law unto themselves.*'

And many Catholics would probably agree with former Jesuit Ian Guthridge when he wrote that infallibility is 'difficult to take seriously'[2].

Of course, sex play is not confined to the religious priests or brothers. Some of the older boys at our boarding school and some of the domestic staff took liberties with the smaller ones as well. And not all of it was aggressive, but rather was for mutual comfort. Gentle genital fondling among early teenagers, same or mixed gender, may not be well regarded by those in authority, but if you are deprived of physical expression of warmth at home it's a damn sight better than a sharp clip on the ear. When you reach the age where the instinctive sex drive appears and you are told that it is 'evil', you want to taste it, don't you? It's a natural part of being human to want to find out what you are not supposed to know about. The use of fear, especially of eternal burning in hell, when used too often loses its grip after a while. I remember deliberately doing some of the things you are not supposed to do from a Catholic point of view, such as lying in confession, or taking communion in a state of so-called 'sin', to see what would happen. Nothing did, of course. I secretly delighted in taking my confirmation, which is supposed to be a sacrament, in a state of sin, having masturbated in the toilet that morning. So much for effective religious education. I would go so far as to say that, at that school, they made such a botch of it that they successfully put me off organised religion for life. Of course in the long run they did me a favour, but that was not their intention.

Apart from the social and religious oppression, the physical living conditions at our boarding school were also a challenge to our young bodies. We had to get up at six in the morning to attend church before breakfast two or three times a week. Even though there was a chapel in the complex of the convent, we had to go to a local church about fifteen minutes away. This was not a pleasant task in the freezing winter where Belgium has snow and temperatures remain in single digits for most days. The dormitory where all of us twenty-five to thirty 'inmates' slept had only one potbellied stove, no central heating and no hot water. We took a shower once a week in the basement of the sports building attached to the teachers' college across the street from our complex. When I first went there our main room was the size of an ordinary classroom. The only room we had, apart from the dormitory, was right next to the slaughterhouse where cattle were killed once a week. Some of us must have wondered at times when it would be our turn to go in there.

My first two years at boarding school were a scholastic disaster. I did so badly academically in my third year that I had to repeat it. The embarrassment for a smaller-than-average, vulnerable, somewhat effeminate boy to fail at early primary school is enough to make you feel inferior for the rest of your life. Little wonder I remember practically nothing of these years except emotional misery and sadness. The fourth and fifth year teachers were considerably more dynamic and enthusiastic or maybe I was able to see more of what they were doing, having less tears in my eyes by then. It wasn't until the final eighth year of primary school that I began to take interest in some of the subjects. I enjoyed French, probably because I was good at it, having been around family and places where it was spoken. I particularly liked painting and drawing. The Year Eight teacher, who was also the director of the school, was an art specialist and gave me personal encouragement, something I had rarely received before. I also discovered that, while we did not have sport as a subject, during physical education I was able to run well and for longer periods than most kids my age. It could have been because no one wanted me in their soccer teams or maybe it was because it was something I could do by myself, preferring solitary activity. I may well have felt subconsciously that the longer I could run, the further I would get away from circumstances I passionately detested. Wishful thinking at its best, without results.

By the time I was fourteen years old, my last year at school, I had finally developed some survival skills and managed to be there with some degree of comfort. I had a couple of friends by then and being one of the senior boys, I occasionally received some respect or admiration from the smaller ones. I guess they couldn't tell the difference between someone merely being older and genuine leadership.

I also realised around this time the implications of the fact that our house was within biking distance from the school, and while I had to be there when I was little, I could now be at home and attend day school. I was old enough to look after myself, so I argued to my father. But to no avail. While it was easier for me to be there in my last year, the thought of being able to be at home, so near yet unattainable, was an increasing source of frustration for me and generated a good deal of bitterness towards my father. During the fortnightly home visits I would be moody, internally angry, and resist getting ready to go back. Yet, at the same time, I wanted also to get away from the man who had locked me up in that miserable place. The many years of repression from both school and home were beginning to generate serious opposition. I was never openly violent or rude to my father, but internally the war was on. I remember vocalising to a friend one day that I wished my father was dead. He said I shouldn't say that, as if by saying it aloud it would come true. Hearing this, I was tempted even more.

Even though I would not have believed it at the time, in hindsight there have been some positive outcomes from having been incarcerated for seven long years in that 'hellhole'. My higher-than-average threshold for pain and suffering is a direct result of the training received there and has been useful in later life. My capacity for insight into the stupidity of narrow-minded organised religion and the atrocities committed under its guise were carefully nurtured in those early days. My Catholic upbringing at once provoked a strenuous reaction against it and yet at the same time formed a platform for my later inquiry and studies in philosophy, comparative esoteric religion and genuine spiritual traditions. And, perhaps best of all, the rigorous discipline imposed by the school rules, the boarding school regime, and the religious practices laid the foundation for a very useful self-discipline in later life. I discovered early on that self-discipline is one of the most fundamental characteristics of independence. And finally there is nothing like being caged in for years against your will to foster the desire to be free.

I also learned to lie. It is a very useful tool to avoid punishment when you cannot do what they want you to do. Research has discovered that the main reasons children lie is to protect themselves from hurt and embarrassment and to make themselves look better than they actually are to their peers and other people. Of course, these are the same reasons adults lie, especially if their ego is still so fragile that the truth would be too painful. It takes a lot of self-assurance and internal balance to allow the truth to become more important than personal comfort. So, as adults we continue to lie until we no longer need to.

When I eventually got out of boarding school I lived at home with my father and I took up a four-year apprenticeship as a ladies hairdresser. During the course of these years I learned to drive. My father had bought a second hand Volkswagen by then, a leap forward in our social status. Being a professional driver, he taught me efficiently and allowed me the use of our family car on occasions. Once I went to a party and backed it into a post. The damage was only a bent bumper bar and he fixed it himself without making too much of a fuss, to my great relief. Under the pretext of needing to practise hairdressing and study for college, I no longer went to church with my father on Sundays. He did not make a fuss about that either. I am sure he only went to church out of habit and to meet with friends at a church that was not anywhere near where we lived.

During my last year at boarding school, the senior boys were given two cigarettes on the weekend that we stayed there. Looking at it now, this was a rather criminal act, but smoking, especially in Europe, was very much the thing to do. As I didn't enjoy it at all, I traded mine for chocolate or other sweets. When later I started moving around socially as the peer pressure to smoke rose I smoked long, thin, little cigars instead. I believe this was my first conscious tactic to distinguish myself from the crowd. However, like most teenagers then and now, I conformed by drinking too much on occasions.

What I did not learn, peer pressure or not, was how to get myself a girlfriend. Not that I wasn't interested. There were several girls at the college I had a considerable crush on, had dreams about and would have loved to kiss, but my newly found intellectual self-confidence did not extend to the interpersonal domain. I did develop friendships, one of which still lasts today, and a group of us, mostly hairdressers, got together to have parties regularly. But nothing happened. Was I too shy? Was I still under the influence of my Roman Catholic upbringing? Or was I ambivalent about my own sexuality without knowing it? Probably all of the above.

1. *Sex, Power and the Clergy*, Muriel Porter, 2003.
2. *The rise and decline of the Christian Empire*, 1999.

My parents at their wedding, 1926.
As you can see this was no laughing matter.
It was to last for twenty-five years.

By age six I looked so angelic that I was selected by the sisters of the local convent to be 'sweet Jesus of Nasareth' in the Easter procession. As you can see from the concern of my face I was wondering what to do with all those followers behind me.

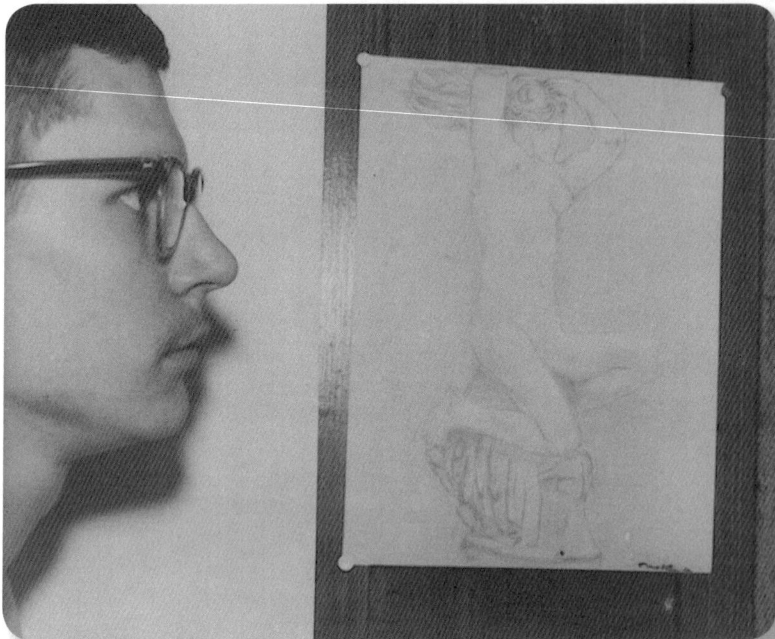

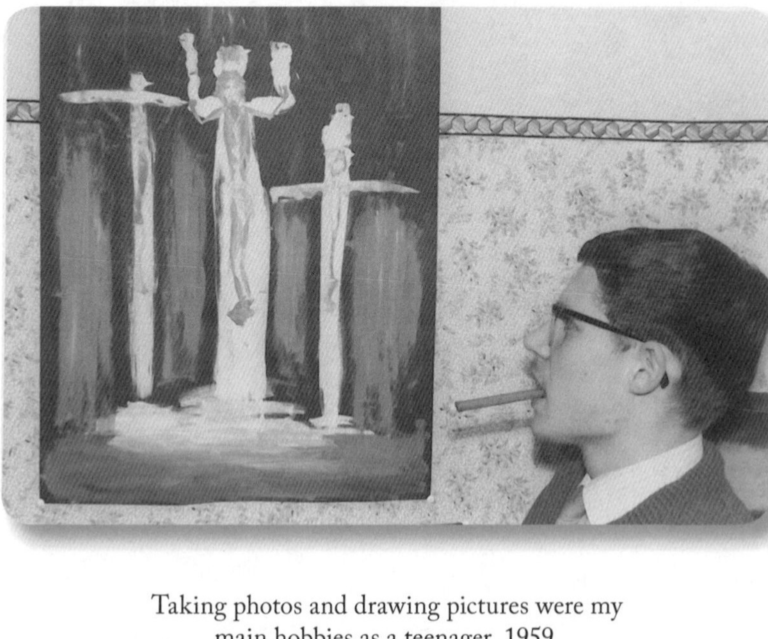

Taking photos and drawing pictures were my main hobbies as a teenager, 1959.

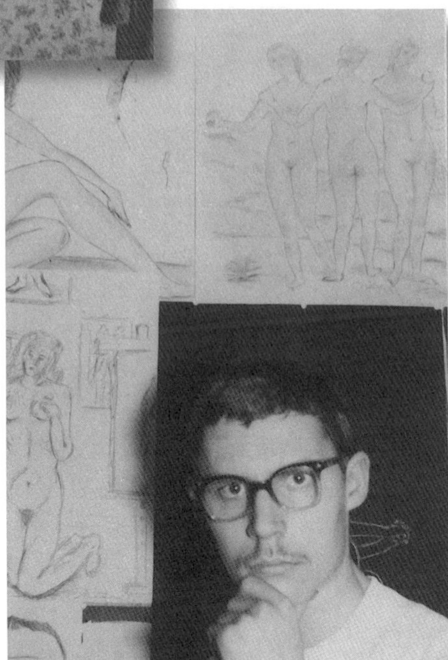

4.

Across Europe with Sylvia

1967

AFTER Sylvia and I left my father, we drove straight to Paris. Everybody loves Paris, the most romantic city in the world! Even growing up in Belgium I heard a lot about Paris. When I joined the world of hairdressing, like most other fashion-related industries we looked to Paris for the newest fashions and latest trends. This gave me the perfect excuse to go to Paris on my first unaccompanied holiday outside Belgium. It would be part of my professional education and give me a chance to test my wings and my independence. I was eighteen and even though I was still generally tentative and not very sure of myself, I was ready to step out into the world. I made my case to my father and to my surprise he agreed. I imagine that his objective of keeping his children away from their mother had been achieved. Her punishment for leaving having been imposed, he could now relax control and let us go to do our own thing.

The fantasies I had in my head about the romanticism of Paris stayed exactly what they were, fantasies. The two weeks I spent in Paris made no contribution to the fulfilment of my longing for romantic involvement, except with the city itself. I loved it and it remains one of my favourite cities.

I bravely ventured a walk around Pigalle one night, the prime red-light district, and while there were many invitations, I lacked the courage to accept any of them. My natural shyness and Catholic indoctrination were still dominating my behaviour even though I had abandoned going to church a few years earlier.

Whatever disappointment I might have felt about the lack of 'sexploration' on my part was very generously compensated by what Paris had to offer in cultural education. I had become interested in art and painting but I had seen nothing like what I discovered in Paris. I spent hours wandering around Montmartre looking at the street painters and two whole days in the Louvre Museum. Housed in a twelfth century Royal Palace, it claims to be the largest museum in the world. Its main claim to fame, of course, is none other than the Mona Lisa, a rather small but intriguing painting by Leonardo da Vinci, one of a total of eight of his at the Louvre. Tens of thousands of people file past it every year, with queues lasting over an hour, and this would have been even more so in the year 2003 when she turned 500 years old, and still smiling. After seeing some of da Vinci's drawings and learning about his life and personality, he immediately became and has remained one of my all-time heroes.

I was also enormously impressed by two gigantic white marble statues gracing the entrance hall to the museum. One is called the *Victoire de Samothrace*, a spectacularly elegantly draped wide-winged woman, and the other, equally larger than life, *Venus de Milo*, a naked Aphrodite without arms. Whoever the artist, apparently unknown, he or she certainly had an eye for beauty. Trapped as that beauty was in cold marble, I found these ladies considerably more erotic than any prostitute I saw in Pigalle.

In contrast, but equally impressive, were the sculptures of

Auguste Rodin at the Rodin Museum. Here was an earthy yet graceful quality shining through rough and ponderous rock speaking of humanity and pain rather than romantic love. Together with Henry Moore, his younger English contemporary, he dominated the world of sculpture and remains among the best-known and loved artists in that somewhat neglected field.

I was amused more than impressed by the tomb of Napoleon in *Les Invalide*. It is an enormous marble casket, which stands in the middle of a vast hall. However, the only way it can be viewed is from a gallery surrounding it about six metres above. In this way you inadvertently pay homage to his Imperial Highness by bowing your head to see his casket, whether you like it or not. His megalomania survived even in death!

Being my first time away from Belgium alone, I also encountered my own cultural dimension and differences which had not struck me till then. Looking at myself from a European perspective, I realised that ethnically I belonged to a group of people who had been persecuted and dominated by not only at least half a dozen other European nations but also by their own French speaking countrymen. As Bill Bryson aptly observed in his chapter on Belgium, in his book *Travels in Europe*, 'The Flemings', by which he means 'the Flemish' (Flemings makes us sound like lemmings) '*can't stand the Walloons and the Walloons can't stand the Flemings, but when you talk to them a little you realise that what holds them together is an even deeper disdain for the French and the Dutch*'.

As humorous observer Harry Pearson puts it in his book *A Tall Man in a Low Land: Some Time Among the Belgians*, Belgians generally '*suffer from low self esteem*' and '*are not given to self-promotion… [they are] so self-effacing as to make Michael Palin look like Mohamed Ali*'.

As I still speak English with a foreign accent today, I let

people guess its origin if they like to play that game. On most occasions they name many central European countries and principalities and even South Africa before they eventually stumble on Belgium. Belgium has such a low profile that many people in Australia don't know exactly where it is. The most internationally famous Belgian, on a par with the little pissing boy in Brussels, is Hercule Poirot, a figment of the imagination of an English woman!

Belgium as a country did not become an independent state until 1831, which is very late by European standards. It took another fifty years before the parliament heard a speech in Flemish. When I grew up in Gent and went to work in the city, people with a higher standard of living usually spoke French. I knew I came from a low-ranking, working class family, but it now turned out that I belonged to an inferior ethnic group as well. I learned much on that holiday in Paris.

So here we were, Sylvia and I, about to start a short few days in that same romantic Paris. We had been good friends in New Guinea but our relationship had remained platonic and had continued to be so during our few days together in London. Would Paris change all this? Having had some lessons from Emma in London, there was a certain expectation on my part that Paris would work its charm on me and Sylvia.

We booked into a small, inexpensive little hotel in Rue de Londres near the Gare Saint Lazare. Wanting to make the most of our time in Paris, (there was so much I wanted to show her), we decided to start early, managing two levels of the Eiffel tower on foot and walking most of the Champs Elysees to the Arc de Triomphe. We ate and drank too much and promptly went to sleep as soon as our heads hit our pillows. We spent a good deal of the next day queuing for the Louvre and then walked our legs silly trying to take it all in. The following day, we left early on our way to Switzerland, all of which goes to show that you can't depend on the charm of a city to change your luck. Of course, it could have been me who was lacking in charm rather than Paris and I should have known by then that it takes more than luck to change the nature of a relationship between a man and a woman.

Once we managed to find our way out of Paris, we meandered through Burgundy, the region not the wine, to Dijon, the city not the mustard, and reached Bern in Switzerland late that day. We spent the following two days in Gwatt, a small town south of Bern on the edge of Lake Thun, where Sylvia's niece lived. She was very Swiss: friendly, formal, plain but intelligent. Sylvia felt dutifully obliged to share all the gossip of the Australian contingent of the family and the niece showed polite interest.

On our way to Italy, we crossed the Grand Saint Bernard, the mountain not the dog although the dogs are named after the mountain. Unfortunately there was a lot of fog that day, spoiling the undoubtedly spectacular views. Once we came down from the Alps, the highway took us to Milan, which we bypassed. We slept in the car, for the first time, somewhere outside Verona. With the back seats folded down and our luggage on the front seats, there was plenty of room in the back of the station wagon. It's not what you call comfortable but it is a cheap form of accommodation. It was the first time we tried it and I thought it would help us relax after the rush in Paris and the formality of the family visit. It probably had the opposite effect and while Sylvia didn't complain she was not exactly enthralled by the experiment. Something wasn't working but at that time I had no idea what it was. My relationship with Emma had easily slipped into the sexual domain, but that was entirely due to her initiative and not to my skills as a Casanova, which were obviously still lacking.

Sylvia wanted to see Venice and as it was practically on our way, we decided we might as well stop and see it. I'm not sure if it was just a bad day or whether it is always like that, but my dominant memory of Venice is the all-pervading, slightly putrid smell of damp rotting wood, which completely overshadowed my enjoyment of the magnificent architecture. It wasn't until years later that I discovered Venice is built on small interconnected islands and is apparently very regularly flooded, one of the worst cases being in 1966, just the year before we were there, when the water rose to 1.83 m. Reading this restored my faith in the quality function of my nose. We had the car serviced during our walk and got out of there as soon as we could.

We camped by the beach near Trieste before moving on to Zagreb and Belgrade, in what was then known as Yugoslavia, which was still more or less in one piece, and then on to Sofia, the capital of Bulgaria. These cities and the way of life there reminded me of Russia. People walking in the streets at night, drinking in the cafes, the food in the shops, the architectural style, the way the people dressed – all had some Russian influence. I am not sure if the people were happy or not, but these cities looked dull and grey. Had the Russians really improved the lives of these people by bringing, or should that be 'imposing', communism to them? We didn't stop long enough to ask then, but I think we have our answer from recent history. The Russian flavour in those cities, in turn, reminded me of Emma, who, after all, we were on our way to visit, but as we were still a long way from Kabul I set the question of what to do when we got there well from my mind.

What was on my mind upon leaving Sofia was our next landmark, Istanbul, gateway to the East, bridge to other cultures. Ever since I saw the 1964 Oscar-winning film *Topkapi* with Peter Ustinov, Maximilian Schell and Melina Mercouri, I had wanted to visit Istanbul. Topkapi is the museum where, in the film, the robbers steal the emerald-studded dagger by being suspended from the ceiling, avoiding the security system embedded in the floor, a clever trick later repeated in the more recent *Mission Impossible.* It is also the place where 16th century Sultans hid their secret harem: a golden cage full of virgins ready for the plucking by the masters.

Istanbul, or Constantinopol as Constantine the Great (the Roman emperor who conquered the then Byzantium city in 324) modestly called it, was buzzing with Turkish charm, Oriental mystery and colourful people, not to mention the unmistakable omnipresent wail of Turkish music and Muslim prayer calls. Luis Baralt, in his book *Turkey*, put Istanbul into historical perspective when he wrote that '*when New York City was nothing more than a modest Dutch trading post, Istanbul was a thriving metropolis with well over two thousand years of history behind it*'.

We spent two days in Istanbul, window shopping in the Great Covered Bazaar, a walkway glittering with gold and silver and a bargainer's paradise, feasting on the smells of spices and unusual fruits and vegetables. We admired the famous Aya Sofya, the church that turned into a mosque which then turned into a museum, but found the diamond-and-emerald-rich Topkapi museum unfortunately closed. Yes, it is crowded and very dirty in some places, at least it was then, but Istanbul is alive with activity.

After crossing the Bosphorus by ferry, (the modern bridge connecting the European to the Asian part of Istanbul was built only in 1994,) we took another ferry from Kartal to Yalova, saving us going around the inlet via Izmit. We were on our way to Bergama to visit the nearby ancient Greek cities of Pergamum and Asklepieion. We stopped briefly at Bergama where the biblical St Henry is supposed to have established some of the early Christian communities. Interesting historically, but when we saw the collection of old stones we realised that you need to be somewhat of an archaeologist or maybe a devout Christian, or both, to appreciate their importance. We did not offend anybody by leaving soon after we arrived as there was nobody there to offend.

So we went south to Izmir which, by contrast to Asklepieion, was overcrowded but also very lively. We actually visited Izmir three times. Shortly after leaving it for the first time, a stone thrown up by a passing truck broke the windscreen of the car. We had to go back to town, our second visit, to have it replaced. Being a latest-model car, they did not have spares as yet and they had to have the glass blown to measure, which took most of that day. We had time to indulge in one of my favourite Turkish delights, 'halva', and stroll around town. Izmir, or Smyrna as it is also called, is Turkey's second largest port and a hive of commercial activity but still has a lot of traditional ways about it. There are sweet shops everywhere and street-side Turkish coffee sipping, in a glass of course. Large women in black dresses and old men with toothy smiles, wearing caps and squinting from the sun, (they don't seem to believe in sunglasses) are everywhere. By the afternoon of the following day we were about fifty kilometres out of Izmir when the new window cracked in half, courtesy of the bumpy road, so back we went for our third visit. More halva, tea and sunshine. I was beginning to like Izmir.

We enjoyed Turkey mainly because we were finally in a country that was completely different from the standard Western European culture and flavour, and we were far enough away from our own culture for it to be exciting just being there. We had been travelling for over two weeks now and were enjoying each other's company more than we had since we left London. Our forced stopover at Izmir enabled us to take a break from 'being on a trip' and to get back in touch with each other rather than looking outwards to the road and the buildings we passed.

Going east from Izmir, the road climbs into the densely wooded Toro Daglari mountain range. As we wound higher and higher, the weather became increasingly cold and the sky darker and darker. We were somewhere halfway between Konya and Adana in the middle of nowhere when it actually began to snow. With the road narrow and increasingly slippery, and the visibility rapidly deteriorating to practically nil, we decided to look for a place to stop and we easily agreed that we would not sleep in the car that night. But where instead? There was nothing in sight.

We persisted cautiously for about another hour when we finally saw what looked like a very small guesthouse. We had to walk around the old building to find the entrance and once inside it took a while to attract someone's attention. When eventually we did get to talk to an older, semi-deaf gentleman who spoke apparently no English, he made the universal sign for sleep by putting his palms together next to his cheek, and we enthusiastically nodded, '*Yes, yes!*', and showed him some money.

The place was very old and neither warm nor very clean; there was a faint whiff of urine in the air, but the price was very cheap. We hesitated but could not face going back into the snow and risk not finding anything else. The tiny room we were allocated had an oil lamp for light and a sheet for a door. The single bed had a skinny doona on top and a lumpy mattress under the doona. We didn't bother to ask where the bath was after he pointed to a very small room with nothing in it except for a hole in the floor, which we took to be the toilet. It was a most unromantic environment and yet as the cold night drove us into each other's arms, we finally gave Plato the flick from our friendship. Despite the weather, any remaining coolness had now well and truly melted. It was a rather comical event because we were interrupted several times by another old man who wanted to sell us some tea, presumably to warm us up, and then he brought some sweets and finally came back one more time to make us pay for the refreshments. We suspected that he just wanted to take a peep at this unusual pair of guests and we laughed our annoyance away as it did not matter any more. When we drove off the following morning with daylight providing a better view of the place, we suspected that this was not a guesthouse at all but a refuge for homeless men and that we had provided them some welcome entertainment, probably making their stay considerably more tolerable.

Looking back, I ask myself why it took so long for Sylvia and me to reach this point in our relationship. Was our pattern of relating in New Guinea still dominating our behaviour? Did we take our relationship too seriously, thinking it had potential for the future? It was certainly a very different type of relationship to that which I had experienced in London with Emma, which had been almost completely opportunistic and experimental. I wrote:

'Relationships are very much like chemistry; you get different results from differing combinations.'

I would ponder on the implications of sexuality on relationships between friends a lot more later in life, and whenever I did the difference between my experience with Emma and Sylvia would usually come to the fore. I became intrigued by the nature of the various components of that chemistry and tried to find out which are more important and how it all works and how I could keep it uncomplicated and balanced rather than twisted, tangled and fragile to the point of being counter-productive. My diary during those years is littered with observations and questions and gropings around this issue. Obviously much more experience and practice was necessary.

While we were both much more at ease, the fact that our relationship now had a sexual dimension would make matters more complicated in Kabul and beyond. But we still had Syria,

Iraq and Iran to cross so I was not letting that thought get hold of me just yet and tried to enjoy what was available as much as I knew how to. At any rate, what Paris had not been able to provide was brought to us by this tiny little hamlet, the name of which we never even found out, somewhere in the cold Turkish mountains.

The Eiffel Tower, Paris.

5.

The Coup at the Crack

1967

JUST over two weeks after setting out from Belgium, we reached the tiny Turkish-Syrian border post of Yayladagi on 19 March 1967. Before crossing the border we had spent a few moments in Antakya, better known by its former name of Antioch, at least by historians specialising in early Christianity. Already an important Roman military stronghold, it was also regarded as a commercial and cultural centre some sixty years before the birth of Jesus Christ. It was in Antioch, some twenty or thirty years after the death of Jesus, where Peter and Paul preached what was later to become known as Christianity. The early establishment of so-called Christian communities before the existence of the Christian Church as we now know it was not without its infighting, and Antioch was one of the main arenas of the early battles for power, followers, and succession rights, particularly given its potential for recruitment from an estimated 200,000 inhabitants. Of course, there still is tension within the Roman Catholic Church today, as in most power-driven organisations, especially between the fundamentalists and the progressives.

At the border we were glad to get out of the car and stretch our legs. It was midmorning and the springtime sun was warming up. A small shed-like wooden structure, one door and two windows, served as a customs office. One officer dressed in military-style uniform stood outside the shed and very faintly smiled as he nudged us into the 'office'. Inside, behind an old-fashioned shop counter, was another officer in uniform. He simply said, *'Passport'*. We gave him our passports and watched him paging through them. As we waited, a man of European appearance in his late twenties came in behind us. He was well dressed and of the friendly type that starts chatting to anybody they encounter. In this out-of-the-way, small place with nobody else around, meeting two other Europeans was a good enough reason to strike up a conversation. With an indistinguishable accent, at least to me at that time, but in a jovial tone he said: *'Ah, iemand van Belgie, spreekt u Vlaams of Frans?'* [Ah, someone from Belgium, do you speak Flemish or French?]

He had noticed the 'B' for Belgium on the back of my car and smiled broadly as if to seek applause for his clever deduction. I replied that I spoke both Flemish and French but preferred English these days. He said he could speak that too. It is not unusual for Europeans to speak several languages, so I did not feel the need to be impressed. He kept on chatting while he had his passport checked after we had ours returned. We politely responded.

As we walked out of the office, in good English but with what sounded now more like a Germanic accent, he introduced himself as '*Gunther, my father is the German Ambassador in Israel.*' He was on his way to Tel Aviv to join his family for the Easter holiday. After some more pleasantries he suggested that, since we were going in the same direction, we should have lunch together in a rather special little restaurant he knew just past Lattakya, only fifty kilometres south. We were somewhat more impressed by now – it's not every day that one gets invited to have lunch with the son of an Ambassador. After we saw his expensive sports car, Sylvia and I looked at each other and we both thought, 'why not?' He jumped in his red Fiat and led the way, driving very fast. When you don't know exactly what is happening, you can be suspicious and back off, play it safe and miss out. Or, you can be open to what is coming, wait and see, and give it a go. We unquestioningly gave it a go as there seemed no reason not to. Having lunch with an interesting-sounding person could be more fun than looking at a pile of old stones.

Latakya is a coastal city dating back to the second century BC, with a very Mediterranean flavour. It is one of the few port cities Syria has along its 150 km stretch of coastline between Turkey and Lebanon, just across the water from Cyprus. There were many small restaurants right on the waterfront, but we drove past them all. We thought he was going to keep on driving, that maybe he had forgotten about us following him. Soon enough, he stopped by a small, rather isolated, very old-looking little building with a few tables, shaded by Cinzano umbrellas. Gunther indeed knew the proprietor of the restaurant and they chatted in Arabic for a few minutes. Then, a small Syrian boy of about eight or nine appeared from inside the house and bantered with our host. They displayed a genuine fondness for each other. He was obviously familiar with both the region and the people. We felt much more relaxed now and enjoyed all the attention of being special guests. We had several dishes of delicious Syrian food, generously accompanied by local white wine, and relaxed even further. We chatted about our travels and the countries we had been to and exchanged stories and experiences, as travellers do. When Gunther discovered that we did not have a particular itinerary but wanted eventually to end up in Kabul, he suddenly came up with what he thought was a great idea. '*Vy don't you join my vamily and me for Easter, it's a very special time in Israel.'*

Now we were very impressed as well as very relaxed. It took only a few seconds for Sylvia and me to confer and agree that this was too good an opportunity to miss. It wasn't Easter in Israel that attracted us as much as the stay in an ambassadorial residence. Kabul would still be there later and this side trip was not all that much out of the way. Emma was not exactly waiting for us either.

There was one problem. I had made plans to visit the 'Krack des Chevalier', or as they call it in English, 'Crack of the Knights', one of the oldest medieval castles in Syria, dating from the times of the crusades. It was near here and it would be a pity to miss out. Gunther smiled and said: '*Ve can go zere on ze vay, not a problem at ool.*' We could go there and he would hang around waiting for us because, he explained, there isn't much there and it wouldn't take us long to see it. He was now, it seemed, our tourist guide as well. To top it all off, he paid the bill, categorically refusing any contribution from us, which we had offered rather weakly. It is easy, of course, to be generous when you have plenty of money to throw around. Why he was aiming it at us, we as yet had no idea.

So the plan was that he would lead us to the castle and there wait for us, before driving through Lebanon and on to Israel. Just as we were about to go he suggested we swap cars, since he had not yet driven '*one of those new Opel cars.*' He was obviously a car enthusiast, driving a late Fiat sports model, and his curiosity seemed only natural. I would have had no hesitation swapping cars with him except for my own lack of confidence in my ability to drive his sports machine safely in an environment with which I was not familiar. I explained that, as I didn't know the roads or his car, this was a risk I preferred not to take. '*I'd hate to damage such a beautiful car,*' I told him. He seemed disappointed but accepted my concern and off we went. Most of the one-hour drive was along the beautiful Mediterranean coast, but when we swung inland I was increasingly glad he was taking us there. There were many unmarked turns and our map would have been totally inadequate to lead us to the castle. As he had before, he again drove fast, and I was glad I didn't have to do this in his car.

When we got to the castle, Gunther said he didn't want to come in with us because he had seen it many times before. While we walked around he would go into the small village nearby and call his family, letting his mother know that he was bringing two visitors. We had no mobile phones then and there were no public phones at this 'dead' castle. We thought nothing of it and to notify his mother seemed like the decent thing to do. As Sylvia and I started out from the car park to the entrance to the castle, he spontaneously asked with a bit of a coy smile if he could drive my car to go to the village and back. Since I wouldn't need to drive his, there was no reason now not to let him. He was leaving his car, approximately twice the value of mine and containing several pieces of expensive looking luggage, in the car park, so it seemed perfectly safe. Without giving it a second thought, I threw him my car keys and Sylvia and I walked into the castle.

Walking around this vast castle empty of people, apart from Sylvia and me, empty of artefacts or displays, we wondered why this castle was here: why it was called 'Crack des Chevalier' and what had happened in those huge halls on cold mountain nights and hot summer days. The answers to all our questions, and many more, all led straight to the eleventh century Pope Urban II. At that time political Europe was fragmented and unstable. The Turks were advancing on Eastern Europe and the then so-called Mohammedans behind them were conquering slabs of Asia Minor, already having taken charge of the Holy City of Jerusalem. Urban II must have been a shrewd strategist as he thought the need to defend Europe could be combined with the recapture of Jerusalem, and in the process would strengthen Christian unity and the papal authority. Very clever indeed.

So the castle relates to the Crusades? Yes, but there is more. My brain did an electro-magnetic search and came up with the name of Godfrey of Boullion. Primary school history lessons? Godfrey of Boullion? What has he got to do with it all? And where is Bouillon anyway? I knew that. The castle of Bouillon is in the Belgian Ardennes, which then was French territory. I had been there during a holiday with my uncle and aunt from Brussels when I was about twelve.

Later research revealed that indeed Godfrey of Bouillon, Duke of Lorraine, (or Duke of Bouillon, depending which website you hit) was in fact the heroic leader of the first crusade. Godfrey was born on 18 July 1061, of noble parentage; his father was the Duke of Boulogne, his mother a particularly devout Catholic and philanthropist and no doubt the inspiration to her sons to go on the Crusades. So when Urban II sent out his call to arms, Godfrey responded positively and in the summer of 1095, aged thirty-four set out from Bouillon Castle accompanied by his brothers Tancred and Baldwin, and a few hundred men, destination Jerusalem.

Reading all this it occurred to me that they undertook a journey very similar to the one Sylvia and I had taken, basically from Belgium to the Middle East via Constantinopol, or Istanbul in our case. Of course they had no travel guides to read before they left and probably no detailed maps as we had, and who knows what they expected to find on the way. As one commentator put it, '*The first Crusade was an act of faith and hope and of ignorance.*' Did they believe that this would earn them a guaranteed place in heaven? Or were some of them going mainly for the sake of the adventure, to explore the world, as Sylvia and I were doing?

By the time they got to Syria, many other armies from all over Europe had converged on the area, some arriving by sea. Reaching Jerusalem mid-July 1099, Godfrey led a huge band of Christians all willing to die for their faith. They slaughtered practically all the human beings living in Jerusalem at the time, women and children included, in the name of Jesus Christ. I wonder what He would have had to say about that?! Godfrey was recognised for his murderous 'bravery' and was proclaimed 'Defender of the Holy Sepulchre'. He did not enjoy his glory very long, dying one year later, and was buried at Mount Calvary. His brother Baldwin succeeded him and was crowned King of Jerusalem, a title the more humble Godfrey had refused.

Many years after Sylvia and I had completed our adventure, I came across Tim Severin's account[3] of how he retraced the journey of Godfrey on horseback, taking three months to complete it. Godfrey took three years, having had to fight many battles on the way. Sylvia and I had taken three weeks, enjoying the comforts of a brand new Opel stationwagon, which was now driving off into the distance, leaving a trail of dust behind it.

During the hour or so that we were in the castle, we did not meet a single soul anywhere, not even a ghost. We took lots of photos, including one of Sylvia in the pulpit of the chapel. We cavorted around like children, running here and there; playing with the echo in those vast, empty rooms, wondering what might have gone on in those halls on cold nights, what games they played and how they managed without women. A contemporary travel guide to Jordan and Syria tells me that now one of the halls inside the castle is converted into a cafe, calling it '*a shameless rip-off joint*'.

When Sylvia and I strolled out of the castle's entrance we wondered why Gunther had not yet come back. He had told us the village was only ten minutes away. Maybe there was a queue at the phone booth? We walked along the base of the castle for a while followed by a half dozen children trying to sell us what they claimed were antique coins and American chewing gum. We took a few photos of the outside of the castle and settled near the car park, happy to rest for a while. The children expressed some interest in the sports car and, thinking it was mine, asked in gesture language if they could sit in it. Unfortunately, we could not oblige them as it was locked, but we told them to wait for a while and when Gunther came we would ask him if they could take a pretend ride.

T. E. Lawrence, better known as Lawrence of Arabia, labelled the 'Crack Des Chevalier' as '*the best preserved and most admirable castle in the world*' so our guidebook told us as we continued waiting for Gunther. It was built by the later Crusaders from about 1150 and took them almost 100 years to complete. At the base of the outer structure it measures some 180 x 120 metres. Fully occupied, it could hold 4,000 troops. It came complete with baths, ovens, courts, huge reception halls, chapel and a well and latrines, apparently uncommon in those days. Its location, in one of the few gaps through a mountain range stretching 250 km, is purely strategic. It is sufficiently elevated to see approaching enemies for miles before they could surprise the castle. After defeating several attempts by the Muslims to take the castle, the Crusaders finally lost it to Sultan Baibars in 1271. The Muslims converted the Christian chapel into a mosque, but the pulpit remained. The whole structure is very impressive and the views from the top are spectacular. Interestingly, the Castle received a place in Philip Wilkinson's 1993 book *Amazing Buildings*.

It was now about five o'clock in the afternoon and the sun was gradually sinking. The old man who had sold us a ticket to get into the castle came to talk to us. I guess he found it strange we were still hanging around instead of getting into our car and driving off. He told us, in poor English, that the castle would close soon and asked if we wanted to go in again.

'*No, we are just waiting for our friend,*' we told him, '*the one driving the sports car.*'

Maybe he was a little suspicious about something or thought we might damage 'his' castle, so he decided to hang around for a while as well. By about six o'clock Gunther had still not returned. The ticket man was now decidedly anxious about the fact that we were not leaving. We tried to reassure him our friend would be here soon because he had left his car here and needed to return mine before we could resume our journey together to visit his family. We suggested that he must have encountered a small problem with the car.

Then suddenly, the old man turned to one of the children who were also still hanging around and asked them a number of questions. When he finally understood I had actually given

Gunther the keys to my car he became rather agitated and tried to explain in his very broken English that one should never give one's car keys to anyone, not even one's brother. We felt somewhat reprimanded by his tone as if we had done something which one should have known not to do. When by seven Gunther still had not returned, we tried to tell the ticket man that there must have been some accident and asked him if there was a way we could find out from the local ambulance or police. He simply said, '*Yes, come, me!*' Relieved that we were at last prepared to leave the castle and happy to be of some practical help to us, he marched ahead with Sylvia and I and a handful of children skipping around us following him. We couldn't even take Gunther's car as he had naturally locked it before leaving.

We walked what felt like a couple of kilometres to his house, a modest abode without electricity but filled with the spirit of hospitality. He called the police from a neighbour's house and while waiting for them he tried to convince us that the man who had driven off with my car was a 'bandit'. I wonder where he had learned that word. We said no, he is the son of the German Ambassador in Israel and that we were on our way to his family home in Tel Aviv for the Easter holiday weekend. He didn't argue and simply shook his head as if he knew better. He gave us some flat bread and tea and tried very hard to entertain us.

Two hours later a couple of policemen came to interview us. It was hard to communicate with regional police who spoke less English than the ticket collector, so he now also served as interpreter. They got the story somehow and, after checking with our host, told us to wait there. The castle-keeper now turned innkeeper said we could stay there and pay him later, not wasting an opportunity to add to his meagre income. We had some more food and drank something strongly alcoholic and went to sleep on floor mats that had been brought in from another neighbour's house. It was well past midnight when the local police came back. They told us that a vehicle corresponding to the description of my Opel had crossed into Lebanon at the border town of Dabousieh. We simply could not believe it. Sylvia and I had no way of explaining what seemed a set of indisputable facts. Maybe he had been kidnapped and the perpetrators would by now be asking a ransom from the German ambassador? Yes, that seemed possible. A plot by the Jewish people to take revenge against the Germans for the holocaust?

Another scenario was that the police could have made a mistake: it could have been a car very similar to ours, but not actually mine. That was not the case, the police told us, as the registration plate numbers were also the same. We were trying very hard to invent any explanation, however incredible, for what had happened except to believe that the car had been stolen by this person who had been kind enough to take us to lunch. That Gunther had stolen our car seemed to us utterly impossible. In retrospect this was an excellent example of people not believing what they don't want to believe, in the face of overwhelming evidence. Why would he steal our car, which was of much less value than his, with our personal luggage in it and leave his car and his luggage at the castle? Surely this must be a practical joke, albeit in very bad taste?

The police officers, probably tired of our naïve unwillingness to accept the facts, told us firmly that there was only one possible explanation: the red sports car wasn't his and neither was the expensive looking luggage in it because both had been stolen, probably in the same manner as he had stolen our car. We found that very difficult to believe simply because we didn't want to accept that we had been duped. I didn't know then that denial is the initial response to tragedy. The police recommended that we go to Dabousieh immediately to make a statement to the customs officers and identify the description of my car. So the two big police officers and Sylvia and I took off in their small police car, braving the dark cold night.

At Dabousieh we were met by the Homs regional chief of police, who took charge of the case from there on. His English was very good and we finally got a better picture of the situation. It was now clear that the vehicle which had entered Lebanon was not one exactly like mine but indeed was mine, confirmed by the registration number. Not only that, the driver of this car had used my passport to cross the border even though Gunther, if that was his name, did not look anything like me. '*How could a person who does not look like me use my passport to cross the border?*' I wanted to know. We were told that it had been dark and that there is very little traffic at this time of the night and security may have been a little lax. A little? It was hard enough to believe that our car had been stolen – it was even harder to believe that border police had been so careless as to let him go by without recognising that he was clearly not me as I appeared on my passport photo.

After some apologetic mutterings, the police chief recommended that we go to Damascus to make an official declaration of our situation to a special branch of police dealing with foreigners. It now dawned on me that not only had my car and passport been stolen but, together with practically all of my other belongings, I had also lost all my traveller's cheques. We had very little money on us, so how could we get to Damascus? The regional chief of police said he would take us back to Homs and after we had lunch with him in his flat, he took us the two-and-a-half-hour drive south to Damascus, the capital of Syria.

Damascus is supposed to be the oldest inhabited city in the world. It was the capital of the Aramaean Kingdom as far back as 3,000 years ago and was later conquered by Alexander the Great, at which time it became an important Greek city. Given our predicament, we had no time or interest in the historical or architectural curiosities of the great city. Our minds were on getting our car back as soon as possible.

It now began to become clear to us that our situation was in one way rather comical while in another way very desperate. Sylvia, who had her small shoulder bag on her when we entered the castle, had her passport in it and some money. I, on the other hand, had my camera on my shoulder, my wallet with a small amount of money in my back pocket, a handkerchief and nothing else. My passport, fourteen thousand US dollars' worth of traveller's cheques and our entire luggage was in the car, and the car was gone. So, I was in a foreign country without money, without identity, and in the hands of the police. In fact, officially from the Syrian point of view, I did not exist. There was no way that I could prove to them who I was or that I was somebody at all. It is in moments like these that you need a friend. The value of the moral, psychological and physical support Sylvia and I were to each other was immeasurable. Fortunately for us, the regional chief of police, a man old enough to be my father, was also very understanding and supportive. Not all officials we had to deal with later were that kind.

In Damascus, the lack of money again forced us to be at the mercy of the regional chief of police. He took us to his elderly sister's place, which had a spare room. She was willing to let us stay there for the night and see what our needs were after that. We had enough money to buy ourselves new toothbrushes and some food and a bottle of 'arak', a potent local drink sometimes referred to as 'fire water', with which we had become familiar in Turkey.

The following day the regional chief of police took us to the Chief of State Security in Damascus. This was now officially an 'international incident' and had to be handled by the appropriate authorities. Again we had to tell our entire story, explain the circumstances in which all this had happened and suffer the humiliation of having been so stupid as to give the keys of our car to a complete stranger in an area of the world riddled with con-artists. Humility is a hard lesson to learn. We were clearly a trivial annoyance to these people, but being foreigners we had to be treated with some degree of respect. The whole of that day was spent waiting around for telephone calls, telegrams and meetings between all sorts of people who had differing opinions as to what they should do with us.

Finally, a senior looking uniformed man told us that we should go to Lebanon, since that was where our car was now. The Syrians could not do anything about it from here except let the Lebanese police know about our situation and that we were on our way there. He expressed his regret that he could do no more and wished us speedy recovery of our car. While this was disappointing in a way, at least we knew where to go for the next step in this increasingly frustrating process.

After we had gone back to our room to collect our new toothbrushes and thank our hostess profusely for her hospitality, we set out to find the bus station with the help of some teenagers wishing to practise their English in the process. The bus journey from Damascus to Beirut, the capital of Lebanon where my car now was, is less than a hundred kilometres and leaves several times a day, the fare luckily just within our means. At the Syrian border near Riyar we were waved through once they had seen the letter I had been given by the Damascus Security Police explaining my situation to the Syrian customs officers.

Entering Lebanon, however, without a passport and despite my letter, was not possible. The Syrian police had told us that they would notify the Lebanese customs people and maybe they had, but I could not go into Lebanon without a valid passport. Sylvia could go if she wanted to because she still had her passport. Fortunately for me she chose to stay with me.

So we were stuck in a no-man's land, out of Syria but not into Lebanon, floating in political limbo. It was dark by now and no one had any suggestions as to what to do. A short walk from the border there was a small shop that served as cafe and bar, mostly used by the customs officers during their breaks. One of the customs officers who had taken some pity on us took us there and, over a dinner generously washed down with arak, chatted to us about all sorts of things, including the differences between European and Arab treatment of women. To my shame, the next thing I knew I was waking up with a monstrous hangover in a dark and smelly storeroom behind the shop. Sylvia, who had evidently consumed much less arak than I had, had instead been chased by the lusty Arab customs officers to whom a single young good-looking European woman (whose boyfriend is drunk and passed out) was fair prey. Fortunately Sylvia was sufficiently resourceful and managed to save herself. My embarrassment, however, was as big and painful as my hangover. We must have provided sufficient entertainment that night for some of the Syrian border guards to take pity on us the following day. They phoned Damascus and the advice was to return to the Security Police there. We decided to hitchhike and, with the recommendation of a customs officer, a Bulgarian businessman gave us a lift back to Damascus in his black Russian limo.

This time, another official, after more questioning and consulting my file, suggested that since I was a Belgian National it was up to the Belgian representative in Syria to provide me with papers that would allow me to enter Lebanon. Having been unsuccessful in fobbing us off to Lebanon they now handballed us to the Belgian delegation in Syria to cope with my non-identity problem. We went straight to the Belgian Embassy, fortunately not far away.

Once again I had to tell my whole story, explain how I was in this embarrassing situation, and endure the faint smile of amusement on the face of the *charge d'affaire* at having been as naive as of give the keys to my car to a complete stranger. He also told me that if I had come here in the first place it would have saved a lot of time. Fortunately, he was sympathetic as well as amused and issued me with what is called a *laisee-passe*, a document temporarily replacing a lost passport. A new passport could not be issued just like that – confirmation had to be obtained from Belgium to prove that I was me. Unfortunately, the *laisee-passe* required a photo and as no instant passport photo machine was available, I had to go to a photography studio and ask them to develop it immediately. It was now the day before Good Friday and, if things did not proceed that day, we would be stuck in Damascus for the whole of the Easter weekend. Running all the way from the Embassy to the studio and from the studio to the Embassy, we got back just before closing time and I was given my papers.

As we walked away from the Embassy, one of the young men we had met before turned up and invited us to his uncle's place, a small hotel restaurant. We provided the entertainment with our story and they provided a wonderful meal and, since it was too late to go to Lebanon, a room for the night as well. Their generosity was a humbling experience, but we were getting used to receiving handouts and enjoyed their company and the distraction from our own anxiety.

The following morning, walking us to the bus station, our host gave Sylvia and me each a set of what the Arabs call 'worry-beads' for good luck. I still have them today and they bring back memories of the helpfulness and kindness that those Syrian people showed us in our time of need.

It may have been Good Friday, but at least the buses were running. We waved our friends goodbye and off we went to Lebanon. At least that's what we thought until the Lebanese customs officers, different ones from two days ago, decided that this piece of paper, even though it had been issued by the Belgian Embassy and had my photo on it, was not a passport and, since you can't enter Lebanon without a passport, I couldn't go in. For some officials, rules are rules and they don't know the difference between a genuine exception and a request to bend those rules. I thought we clearly had a legitimate exception, whereas they thought we were asking them for a favour. As we were not offering anything in return, since we had nothing to offer (and even if we had it would not have occurred to me that we might have got through that way) no favour came.

Once again we had to let the bus go without us and again Sylvia chose to stay with me. It took several telephone calls to the customs headquarters in Beirut and over an hour waiting for replies, consultations and checking with the officer in charge before the customs officers were finally told to give me a one-day visa, provided I report immediately to the police headquarters upon arriving in Beirut. As we got ready to hitchhike, this time inside the Lebanese border, who should pull up but our Bulgarian friend, smiling in disbelief. After we convinced him that we hadn't simply walked all the way from Damascus, he took us straight to the Beirut Central Police station.

And yes, once more I had to explain (to the Lebanese authorities this time) the whole of my story and, once again, but more so than before they found it very amusing. One police officer openly laughed and called me a fool. I guess he was right. They called other officers over to tell them the story, which spread like wildfire throughout the police station. I felt humiliated but there was little to do except hope they would help us find the car.

After much discussion and indecision among the officers, it was eventually decided to assign a case officer to look after us until my passport was either recovered or renewed. Amal, the officer who got the task of looking after us, was a softly spoken man in his fifties and to our relief he immediately took us seriously. His English was fairly good and he treated us like his children. He took us to a small pension hotel called "Home Sweet Home" (a home at last) where Sylvia and I were given a room each since it was against the law to rent rooms to people of the opposite sex who are not married, so Amal told us. (Since those days we all have learned much more about Muslim rules, but then we didn't understand why this was so.) The police would take care of all costs until they retrieved our car and possessions which, they guaranteed us would be a matter of days only. Amal explained to us that Lebanon is a small country, not like Australia, and that all the border posts had already been notified with the details of our car and my passport and that very soon we would be able to resume our journey. That news, delivered with paternal reassurance, and the pleasant surroundings of the hotel, not to mention the lovely city itself, made us feel a lot better, at least on that day. It was also Easter now which meant that nothing official could be done with regards to getting my new passport for at least three days. The Belgian Embassy in Damascus had telegraphed the city registry in Gent to have a copy of my birth certificate sent to the Belgian Embassy in Beirut, by diplomatic mail presumably, so they could issue me with a new passport after the Easter break.

The son of the hotel manager, who called himself Richard, came to talk to us when he discovered that we were from Australia. He had family there and hoped to migrate himself one day. He asked many questions, wanted to spend time with us, and brought us food and drink in return. We were happy to help and found his curiosity a nice distraction from our own miserable situation. There was also much time and opportunity, despite our *chambre separé*, for the new dimension of our relationship to blossom. The release of tension, in every form, was very welcome.

Over the next few days, despite the distractions from Amal, Richard and the magnificent city of Beirut, which had not yet been destroyed by war, the seriousness of our situation began to settle in and the question *'What if they don't find the car?'* emerged to the foreground. Every day on his obligatory visits, Amal assured us that they would find it and Richard brought more arak to help us cope. Sylvia, however, began to show some signs of strain. She was beginning to think of calling it a day and going back to London.

Two days later, Amal still had no news of our car but announced he had found better accommodation for us. We were transferred to a one-room serviced apartment in a hostel closer to the police station where I had to report every day. It was a nicer place but the boost to our morale was short lived. We went for walks around Beirut, enjoyed the city to some extent and chatted some more with Richard and some of his friends. We saw the kindly Amal every day but our hope waned as time went by.

It was Tuesday 4 April, over a week since our arrival there, when some of my spare money arrived, which I had asked my brother to transfer to Beirut. We both bought some clothes and I felt like a person again. But still no car. Amal remained hopeful but we had given up; we finally had to accept we had been conned and would probably not see our car again.

Sylvia had by now decided she would return to London, which was what she had come over to Europe for in the first place. She booked herself on a ship from Beirut to Marseille from where she would take the train to London. She had become rather disappointed with this journey and was sick of being chased by Arabs. While we had got on very well, considering the challenge, and had enjoyed some great times comforting each other, being with me was not a sufficient attraction for Sylvia to stay. At the same time, it has to be said that being with her was not a sufficient attraction for me to go with her back to London.

As it turned out, my presence would have been very useful to her but I was not to know what further calamity was about to strike her. My mind had been set on going to Afghanistan and

I was now so close to it that I didn't feel like abandoning the project. My options were either to find work in Lebanon or to push on to Kabul. I was told that it would be difficult to obtain a working permit in Lebanon, whereas at least I had a contact in Kabul. That evening I took Sylvia to the famous 'Casino du Liban', sometimes compared to the Paris Moulin Rouge, to express my gratitude for her support and to celebrate the restoration of some comfort and to say goodbye or, hopefully, 'au revoir'. The show was absolutely spectacular, with entertainers from all over the world. Beirut lived up to its sometime name of the 'Paris of the Middle East'. It was an eerie experience switching from being a 'non-person' supervised daily by police like a criminal and living in cheap accommodation, to enjoying some champagne in the company of some of the richest holiday-makers in Lebanon.

When I saw her off at the boat the following afternoon, Sylvia felt apprehensive and said she had butterflies in the stomach. She was a little sad to leave me behind but also relieved to get out of this mess I had gotten her into. She never blamed me and she knew I had not deliberately done anything wrong, but her actions clearly said: *'I've had enough of this'*. I certainly could not blame her either.

I am sure that I did not clearly understand it nor articulate it at the time, but I had begun to appreciate the benefits of what certainly had been a disaster. Yes, I had lost all my possessions, most of my money and my brand new car. I probably had also lost a friend in the process. I certainly would not have reproached Sylvia for not being impressed with my travel arrangements, or me.

Yet there was a curious sense of relief in not having anything.

The burden and responsibility of looking after one's possessions was lifted, the risk of losing anything disappeared and a certain lightness and freedom was taking its place. I know that this will sound unbelievable to most people, but there was a certain sense of relief in this situation and a humbling sense of privilege that I had been able to experience this unique state of affairs. I had also experienced that, when you are a 'nobody' legally because you cannot prove who you are, you are still a person and people are still willing to help you even if you are from a different country, from a different ethnic group or even a different religion. My humanity and my selfhood did not depend on who I was officially, how many possessions I had, or to what group of people I belonged. I was simply a human person taken care of by a number of other human persons because *I was in need of being taken care of.*

I did not know at the time that all this was having a positive personal growth effect on me any more than I had realised in my youth that boarding school would have some beneficial consequences on my character development, but I am certain of it now and I have often reflected on it since. All those humiliating experiences of having to tell so many people what a silly thing I had done were superb contributions to the development of my humility, something I had not yet started to work on consciously at that time in my life. Whenever I am aware of my need for more humility today, I am often reminded of the generous dose of grounding I was given in the Middle East.

Three days later, after collecting my new passport, I had to travel back to the 'Crack des Chevalier' to pay the ticket collector and get my camera back, which I had left behind as a deposit and as reassurance I would return as soon as I could. When I told him that they still had not found the car he smiled an '*I told you so*' and again I had to swallow my Western-educated pride and ignorance in the face of this simple but wiser Syrian peasant. He welcomed my generous payment for his hospitality, which I considered payment for the lesson he had taught me to never lend my car keys to anybody.

After I had all the various inoculations required to travel to Afghanistan, I bought my Air Ariana ticket and the next day, with a very sore arm, I arrived in Kabul airport.

3. *Crusader: By Horse to Jerusalem*, 1989.

Crack des Chevalier from the tower.
Opposite page, top: outer wall seen from inside;
bottom: Sylvia inside the pulpit at the chapel.

6.

Pacific beauty

Australia & New Guinea 1964

DURING my last few days in Beirut, after Sylvia had left, I pondered on the future of my relationship with her. Where would we go from here if ever we got another chance? I also recalled the first opportunity I'd had with Sylvia and how it had all started. Australia and New Guinea felt a long way away from Lebanon, both in time and space.

I arrived in Australia as a migrant from Belgium in 1963. In those days the immigration rules dictated that if you took the assisted passage, the Australian government would pay most of your fare on the condition that you stay for at least two years. If you left sooner, you had to repay the amount they contributed to the inbound journey. By the end of the first year, while I was having a great time in Australia, I had not yet decided that I would stay indefinitely. If per chance I was to go back to Europe after two years I wanted to see as much as possible of this region. I had been on a holiday to Lord Howe Island and explored the Red Centre, so what else was there to see? My sense of adventure drew me to Papua and New Guinea, at that time still a territory of Australia. I was curious, having heard it described as one of the most primitive societies in the world and very tropical. A travel agent told me that the only way you could go there and stay for a while was if you had a job to go to. A ladies hairdresser among the 'fuzzy-wuzzys' of Papua, as they were referred to then by Australians? Maybe not. But then again, who knew? There were many Australian public servants there, and they would need their hair done, wouldn't they?

I had been talking to one of my clients at the salon where I was working at the time about my hope to visit New Guinea when she told me her sister lived there. She offered to write to her to find out about the state of the ladies hairdressing industry in Port Moresby. (Now, of course, she would just send a text message. The world of communication has changed a bit in the last forty-five years!) Not only did she get a prompt reply, but against all expectations the owner of the only ladies hairdressing salon in Port Moresby was looking for a person to manage the salon on her behalf as she wanted to retire. I wrote to them immediately, explaining my qualifications and experience. They were delighted and asked me to go over as soon as possible. Life takes sharp turns sometimes but I was ready and willing to explore. Of course I had no idea what to expect. It was with some regret that I left my job and the many people I had come to appreciate, but such is the nature of adventure – you have to let go of the known to explore the unknown.

It was 19 July 1964, two days before Belgium's national day, when I landed at Port Moresby airport. I was met by a Dutch couple well in their fifties. They had lived in Indonesia and, when the Indonesians became less friendly towards the Dutch, had spilled into the Australian territory. They took me to their house and, almost immediately after we had dinner and before dessert had time to settle, told me what they really wanted to do. They wanted to sell the salon so they could return to Holland to be with their aging parents. As far as I was concerned, there was an easy answer to this proposal; I neither had the money to buy a salon nor did I particularly want to be owner of a business. I had never been in business before and I didn't know what that would involve, especially here in this 'primitive' country. They had obviously thought about the possibility of this response and had their answers ready, proposing that I would not need to buy the salon outright, but pay it off in instalments via a fixed amount of the weekly income over a period of time. When they showed me their books and what would be left after those payments, and given the cost of living in Port Moresby then (not to mention the absence of income tax), it looked not only financially feasible but an attractive proposition. They did not press for an answer and invited me to sleep on it.

I did not get much sleep that night for two reasons. One was that my mind was mulling over this unexpected business proposal, which was a very exciting but new situation for me. The other was that the husband had a malaria attack and, sleeping in a room next to mine divided by paper-thin walls, I could hear him moan and groan all night. I had been warned about malaria and I was ready with my quinine tablets.

We went to see the salon the following day, drove around town for a while and then they offered me their blue Peugeot 404 on the same financial scheme as the salon. The car seduced me more than the salon, but I was also charmed by the smallness of the city and its Pacific beauty and peacefulness. We found a lawyer and signed the deal.

Coincidentally, the lawyer was looking for someone to share a house with by the beach just at the edge of town. His name was Jonathan and he had arrived there a few weeks ago to take over a small legal practice. We ended up sharing a rented house on Ella Beach for the three years I was there. It had no hot water, toilet flush or glass in the windows, none of which we needed anyway given the hot and humid climate. It did, however, have plenty of geckos, those small almost-transparent little lizard-like creatures that love showing off their ability to walk on the ceiling. We had a houseboy who did the cleaning, ironing and cooking and swept the garden path with dried palm leaves. He had a constant semi-grin on his face and when he laughed, which he did in response to most of what we asked of him, he revealed betel-nut-red stained teeth. I don't remember him saying anything much except '*Yes sir*' and '*No sir*', but he was happy since we paid him more than some of his friends.

The salon had an established clientele, but soon many more flocked to my door: now that they had a Continentally trained young male to do their hair, where else would any Australian woman go? Even some indigenous and half-caste ladies ventured to try my straightening technique. As a matter of historical interest, I was told that I was the first white male ladies hairdresser to operate a salon in Port Moresby, not that this will get me into the history books of that now-independent nation!

There were times I worked from seven in the morning till seven at night. On Saturday I worked till mid-afternoon and slept till Sunday morning to get over the week. I took Mondays off to take care of my personal needs and employed both an assistant hairdresser and apprentice to help. I was now the 'boss', with two employees. Business was good and the salon was paid off in half the time we had anticipated.

Having staff is, of course, always a potential for trouble and I had my share of it. The first apprentice I had was a good worker but completely possessed by her search for a husband, even though she was only sixteen. After a few months she married and left to go back to the 'mainland', as people living there referred to Australia. The second apprentice was so arrogant and unmannered that it was an embarrassment. I was about to have words with her parents when they rang to say she had another job. I had another who took my focus off work because she was just too pretty and sexy in a Lolita-like manner, but was incapable of doing the work. My not being able to work because of her, and her not being able to work because of her as well, was obviously not going to work at all. She realised this herself, fortunately, and within a week or two she left, so I didn't have to let her go either.

I then thought it would be a responsible thing to do to give an indigenous girl a chance. There was an indigenous assistant in the dress shop next door, which gave me the idea. Many were keen but most were totally unsuited from a number of points of view. The cultural gap was too big in most cases and their English, not to mention their language, was not quite up to scratch. I tried but did not succeed. Finally, I had a young man who really did want to become a hairdresser and who, with a lot of patience, eventually fitted in well. It was my first taste of trying to teach something to other people and it felt rewarding, if at times rather challenging.

Running even a small business is a lot of work. However, I made sure there was time for other things as well. I did a good deal of oil painting and pastel sketches on the weekends. I took some art lessons at a local college, although what I learned most is that I preferred experimenting by myself. Together with a couple of friends I went on a crocodile hunting expedition to a small river south of Port Moresby. We had to charter a small four-seater aeroplane to get there and then roam along the river in a dugout canoe. Fortunately we didn't see any crocodiles, but we did see many interesting people in what must be one of the most primitive but beautiful environments on earth. We had turtle soup and lots of exotic fish and some funny fermented coconut juice. It was completely unspoilt. I often wonder what it might be like now in that little village. Could it still be the same?

Social life in Port Moresby consisted mainly of private parties and dinners, for me mostly with clients from the salon. It was an excellent way to meet people. And then there was the theatre. My interest in art and music drew me to the local Amateur Dramatic Society. I offered my services as a make-up artist, since it had been part of my training at the hairdressing college in Belgium. They were doing *Maria Martin or Murder in the Red Barn*, a musical melodrama. Lots of make-up was needed. Later they did *Lock up your Daughters*, which also was a lot of fun. When they were doing *South Pacific*, the musical set on a Pacific island, apart from doing the make-up and hair of the main actors, I ended up with a small singing part as well. The main character in the play, Monsieur Le Beck, has two children whose French-speaking Polynesian female nurse teaches them the song *Dite moi pourquois*, one of the minor songs in the musical. The director changed the gender of the character, I applied some tan make-up to myself and, '*voila*', I got the part, as there wasn't anybody else with fluent French. That was my debut of a very short career in theatre.

That part gave me a taste for the 'boards' and I soon became involved in play reading sessions. I even had dreams of directing Arthur Miller's *After the Fall*, but it proved just a little too ambitious. Before long I took a part in a one-act play mainly because the director wanted someone with a foreign accent. The play, *The Sky is Overcast*, by Anthony Booth, is set in France during the German occupation. I could certainly do the French accent but few could do the German as well as I could. So I ended up being the SS officer while the rest of the cast members had at least an equally fake French accent. In one scene, the SS officer was to interrogate a French family about their suspected harbouring of a British paratrooper. When the daughter of the family was being uncooperative, I was to insult her, upon which she was to spit in my face and, in return, I was to strike her down to the floor. The girl playing the daughter, despite our on-stage antagonism, or maybe because of it, became my best friend while living in Moresby.

She was none other than Sylvia.

We got to know each other well after that and started going out together. We both liked dancing, a skill I seemed to have developed on the spot, and many a Friday and Saturday night were spent in the local dance halls or at the drive-in. We went on daytrips and picnics in my Peugeot and generally saw a good deal of each other.

She was studying to be a kindergarten teacher and had an inquiring, somewhat serious approach to life, very much like me. It was she who introduced me to Krishnamurti, the person who more than any other would influence my thinking later on in life. She had an old '78 long-play record of one of his talks, which she played for me one Sunday afternoon in her room at the college. However, at that time it seemed I was not ready for it and dismissed him as merely 'interesting'.

Sylvia was not only beautiful and charming but also intelligent and sensitive. Though we became good friends, unfortunately I am sure I did not meet her needs. I still had so many unsatisfied emotional needs of my own that I could not see hers. Despite our many enjoyable times, our friendship remained entirely platonic and I suspect that she may well have wondered about my sexual orientation. I even wondered about it myself at times. Apart from that, I took myself very seriously in those days. I was very intense and not very comfortable with many people. Sylvia was one of the few exceptions.

My own struggles to project what I thought I wanted to be

prevented me from meeting people as they were. One way to cover up low self-esteem and an inferiority complex is to present yourself as better than other people. Of course that may result in them seeing you as '*a bit of a snob*' and '*having a superior attitude*'. At the time I would have resented suggestions of this applying to me and probably would have vigorously denied it. But looking back more closely now I can see that it probably did apply. My personality was formed in a dysfunctional working-class marriage where closeness was unheard of and interpersonal charisma non-existent. I was overshadowed by two older brothers who were not really there and I had a mother who probably wanted me to be a girl. My early education was in the context of strict Catholicism in an all-boys boarding school where I was an easy target for bullying, mainly because of my effeminate appearance. I was afraid of authority, people who might hurt me and, probably (if subconsciously), of women in general.

So, was it surprising that I might have tried to project an image of superiority to protect myself from all those internal, and some external, dragons? Not really. To complicate matters further, while struggling to become more than just good friends with Sylvia, Jonathan my housemate was having a sexual relationship with a young man from a well-to-do business family. Living with Jonathan must have had some repercussions on the public perception of my own sexual preferences because I was 'approached' by men on several occasions. One of them was a guest director, from Sydney, to our Amateur Dramatic Society. One night after a rehearsal I offered him a lift to his hotel. On the way he reached out and touched me, assuming I was gay. I told him to stop but he protested that I should not deny my sexuality and that I was perfectly safe with him. I was gripped by a wave of assertiveness. I stopped the car and told him in an uncharacteristically angry voice to get out. He was shocked and probably insulted. I was shocked too at my own behaviour, but I was much clearer about my own sexual preference after that.

After nearly three years in Port Moresby, with a business paid off and some savings in the bank, I was getting tired of the climate, not to mention the long hours of work. Port Moresby is very humid most of the time and things get mouldy, including your mind. The choice was to return to Australia or go back to Europe. I chose Europe. The choice was not based on my desire to go back to Belgium as I had a clear feeling that this was not what I wanted to do. But since I now had the financial means, I wanted to travel and see more of the world, and going from New Guinea to Europe was a much more appealing journey than simply going back to Australia. Back in Europe I would decide where to go next and I could always come back to Australia if other places didn't work out. The travel bug had me firmly in its jaws.

I sold my business to my assistant in the same way I had bought it. She was delighted. That would provide me with at least some income for the next year or so while I enjoyed my travels. Sylvia was still finishing her studies and we kissed goodbye (more passionate than ever) with the promise that she might come to Europe one day when she was ready and we would meet up again.

And now she had come and gone already, leaving me feeling that I had missed out again. *What lesson was it that I hadn't learned yet?*

I have always regretted that I didn't get closer to Sylvia, not only in a sexual way but also as a person. We do what we can with what we have, but at that stage of my life, self-mastery had not been high on my agenda, if at all.

Now, here in Beirut having had a second chance and having managed to get a great deal closer, I regretted that our relationship again had fallen apart, not so much because of what I had done than due to what I hadn't done. I had not taken care of her in the way she clearly needed at that time. Would I get yet another chance at another time? We hadn't closed the door on each other, so time would tell.

19th July 1964.
I arrive in Port Moresby, Papua and New Guinea.
(No not by car, I got it afterwards!)

7.

North to the Far East

From New Guinea to Japan 1966

THE *Taiyuan* was part freight and part passenger ship, ferrying people and goods between Australia and Taiwan, stopping in Port Moresby and Manila on the way. My parting celebrations with my friends in Moresby were extended due to the Taiyuan arriving late by two days. I was no longer working so we continued partying until the ship finally left on 24 February 1966, just ten days after 'Decimal Conversion Day' when Australia switched from pounds to dollars.

I was the only occupant of a four-birth cabin and thus enjoyed more room than those who had a single cabin to themselves. A steward brought coffee in the morning and the whole set up was rather more comfortable than I had anticipated. There were not many people on the voyage and for the first day or two I mostly slept, relaxed and read Simone de Beauvoir's first instalment of her autobiography *Memoirs of a Dutiful Daughter.*

On Friday 25 February we passed Thursday Island and stopped to let an Australian pilot off the ship, and on Monday we passed

Seram a rather bigger landmass. Then there were cocktails with the Captain before dinner:

'When he [the Captain] learned that I was planning to travel through Russia after Japan, he became very interested as he had been there himself and had written his impression which he gave me to read. He must have told other passengers as people started staring at me and others engaged me in conversation – I wonder what they are thinking – he must be a communist?'

A day or two later when I finished my book, an interesting passage in my diary reminded me of something I had completely forgotten until I researched this chapter:

'I just realised that one day I could do what de Beauvoir has done here and tell all. Given what has happened to me so far it could be quite interesting. I would dedicate it to all the children from broken homes. Of course it would take a great deal of courage to do this but possibly worthwhile.'

When I discovered this recently I was astonished that so many years ago at such young age I already had the thought of doing what I have only got around to doing now.

We finally arrived in Manila the following Friday, 4 March.

An Australian civil servant from Moresby (I'll call him Jim) I had gotten to know on the ship asked if I wanted to go with him to visit friends he had met on a previous visit to Manila. Sure, why not?

'First we went to see a cock-fight, the sort that people bet on heavily. It only lasts a couple of minutes and some bet thousands of pesos. (Australia has recently converted to dollars and I have trouble doing it to dollars instead of pounds) then to a 'Jai-Alai' game – again heavy betting – what is it with those Filipinos? – then to a nightclub where his friend worked as a singer.'

Her name was Lolita, no kidding – I had not read the book yet. She was in her forties but younger looking, typical Filipino beauty. We ended up taking the dance floor over – I was not usually that extraverted and I blame the amount of alcohol I must have consumed by then. My diary explains:

'She asked me to dance, and of course I did – I had enjoyed it with Sylvia in Moresby – especially with a few drinks in me it is hard to stop, (I must have had half a dozen Filipino rums in me) so we became the 'floor show'. I don't know who took me to the ship and when but I got there. Headache this morning.'

When I met Jim over late breakfast the following day, he explained that Lolita was expecting us for lunch. I wondered what had happened and why she was inviting us. When we got there it became clear. She introduced me to her daughter Joyce, a gorgeous eighteen-year-old, who was studying French and she wanted me to give her some practice; speaking French that is. So I did, all afternoon. She turned out to be a very impressive young lady; we talked about so many different topics and political issues, more than I could handle at that time. We finally agreed to correspond, for the sake of her French, which we did for some time when I lived in London.

We arrived in Kaohsiung, southern Taiwan, two days later. Before disembarking, customs officers came on board to administer a venereal diseases test to all passengers who had gone on land in the Philippines. I wonder if they still do this today? A young archaeology student helped me find a hotel and buy a train ticket to Taipei, the capital of Taiwan, the following day. After walking around for a while that evening I wrote (in Flemish for some reason):

'Kaohsiung is rather drab and grey. Had dinner in a small restaurant – very different from Chinese restaurant in Moresby. Lots of uninviting prostitutes walking on the streets.'

The six-hour train ride from the south to Taipei in the very north of Taiwan revealed mostly rice fields and vegetable gardens kept green by intricate irrigation systems. Probably on the assumption that all people who speak English are Americans, the taxi driver took me to the American Consulate, completely ignoring what I tried to tell him. Next he took me to a Tourist Bureau where someone spoke some English. Eventually I found a hotel and a guide who called himself William, I guess to make it easier for non-Chinese speakers. During the next two days he took me to the modern arts museum (rather poorly supplied), a Chinese opera performance (visually exciting but strange to western ears), a huge restaurant (almost exclusively patronised by men) and a nightclub with a floor show (which included an Australian trio). And of course the hot sulphur spa resort in Pei-Tao where I met the lovely Lina. Taipei is a much bigger and busier city than Kaohsiung but the flavour was equally drab in most places, at least the little I saw of it.

On the *George Anson*, the ship that took us from Taipei to Yokohama, I shared a three berth cabin with an Australian who worked in New Guinea and who I later met up with in Tokyo. He had travelled to Japan a few times before and was very helpful when we arrived there. I also befriended three young Chinese students who lived in Osaka and Kyoto who invited me to contact them when I told them I was planning to visit there. The three-day trip was fairly uneventful and again I suffered from a mild dose of sea sickness. We arrived in Yokohama on 15 March, and after a half-hour train trip and a short taxi ride I was in the enormously big and busy Dai Ichi Hotel in central Tokyo.

I had been looking forward to visiting Japan, fascinated by a culture that is so different from anything I was familiar with. When I first lived in Sydney, I had met a Japanese naval officer called Minoru, who gave me his address and told me that if ever I want to visit Japan I should contact him.

The first thing that struck me on setting foot on Japanese soil was the cold wind. I then realised that I was in the northern hemisphere and that it was still winter here. As I had not needed warm clothes in Moresby, I now needed to do some urgent shopping.

I spent a busy three days in Tokyo, making arrangements for my travel around Japan and seeing some of the museums in that big sprawling city. Getting around in Tokyo was a challenge, not only because many people don't speak English, but because, even though I had a good map of the city, all the street signs are in Japanese and they don't seem to have street numbers on the buildings. I asked directions from a policeman and he took me to the International Press Club nearby looking for someone who spoke English. A kind bell boy escorted me all the way to the place I was looking for.

'The train trip from Tokyo to Kyoto on the new Tokaido line, is first class by world standards with an average speed of 200 km an hour – it only took three hours and was extremely comfortable, with a good look at Mount Fuji en-route.'

While Tokyo is very westernised, Kyoto looks mainly Japanese. Mr. Tang, whom I had met on the *Taiyuan*, had arranged for me to stay in a traditional Japanese inn – a guesthouse rather than a hotel. While it was interesting and cheap, the building was very old and somewhat dilapidated: comfort was not its main feature. The following day, 20 March, was a Sunday and Tang escorted me to some of the 'must-see' places around Kyoto. One was a large cultural centre where they performed some of the traditional Japanese crafts like flower arrangements, koto playing, Geisha dancing, and puppet plays. At lunch time…

'We went to a small restaurant where everybody sits at a counter rather than at tables and they eat little rolls of rice with seaweed around it.' (Now, of course, sushi bars are everywhere in my home town of Melbourne.)

Almost everything in Kyoto is photogenic; not only the temples and shrines but ordinary houses and even the walls around them have aesthetic features.

'In the evening we went to what Tang said was the best Sukiyaki restaurant in Kyoto. The décor was tradition Japanese, sliding doors,

tatami floors, sitting on cushions around a low square table. A girl dressed like a geisha brings in a small cabinet containing all the food including the cooking tools and proceeds to prepare the meal there and then in from of us, a fascinating spectacle in itself. In small china cups we drink warm sake and every time we took a sip she would replenish it. The meal was interesting and different from what I was used to but tasted delicious. After hot towels the girl packed everything up and went out backwards bowing.'

Hiroshima, my next stop, was in stark contrast to Kyoto, entirely modern and almost completely devoid of character. Of course, it had to be completely rebuilt after the atom bomb was dropped. I may not have gone there if it hadn't been on the way to visit Minoru, but since I was there I decided to go and visit the Memorial Peace Museum. That one-hour visit was probably one of my most unpleasant experiences ever, not only because of what you see there (lots of photos of burnt people and items distorted from the heat of the blast), but also because of how it makes you feel. It is something I will never forget. The mixture of sadness and outrage I felt at this barbaric event is something that I am unable to put into words.

I finally met up with Minoru and he took me to his house in Miyajima, a small island near Hiroshima. The opportunity to stay with people rather than in a hotel is always welcome when travelling in foreign countries and allows for a much closer and richer contact with the culture. I enjoyed that opportunity for three days and it remains one of the highlights of my visit to Japan. Minoru's family hospitality was exceptional; their generosity almost overwhelming and their kindness was gentle and unpretentious. I was given several presents which it would have been bad manners not to accept. The only real awkward moment was at bath time. The communal bath shared by the whole family was so hot that I could not possibly go in it, so I had to invent another way of washing myself.

On the way back to Yokohama, where I was to join the *Khabarovsk* to go to the USSR, I briefly visited Osaka and its International Trade Fair with a large representation from Australia but none from Belgium.

On the whole, Japan was as different to me as Kabul turned out to be later.

The Golden Pagoda near Kyoto, Japan.

The Golden Pagoda near Kyoto.
Practising my reflective photography.

8.

Three months in Kabul

1967

THE Afghan airline, *Ariana*, has probably never won major industry awards, even though it has survived to this day, despite the lack of tourism in recent years. The flight from Beirut to Kabul was long and rather bumpy. There was a short stopover in Teheran and a longer one in Kandahar for 'technical reasons'. While waiting to resume our flight, passengers speculated among themselves whether Afghan technicians had the expertise to fix whatever was the matter with the aircraft. I heard a lady mutter to herself in French what an 'inconvenience' this was and I agreed, in French, leading to further conversation. Her husband worked at the French Embassy in Kabul and she had just taken a little holiday in Beirut, mainly to get away from the Afghan '*merde*', as she called it. When we arrived in Kabul, she helped me find the people I was looking for and I would get to see her regularly during my stay there.

My first encounter with Afghan bureaucracy was going through customs at the airport. For some reason my brand new passport, which I had been so happy to obtain only days ago, was confiscated. Was it because I didn't have a visa? I had been told I did not need one. Maybe because I came in on a one-way ticket and didn't have enough money to leave? Was it because my passport was so new and issued in Lebanon? They didn't explain why and only told me I would get it back when leaving. I had gone through so much bureaucratic entanglement over the last few weeks in Syria and Lebanon that this minor matter was not going to upset me. Still, being in a foreign country without my passport after all I had gone through recently left me a little unsettled.

Emma and Bill lived in a small three-storey brick apartment building of obvious Western design, built exclusively for guest workers. Neither of them was home, but their male servant, named Alan because his real name was too difficult for non-Afghans to pronounce, invited me in. Almost all foreigners living in Kabul had Afghan male servants, or 'bacha', as they are called, which reminded me of Port Moresby where we also had indigenous servants. Afghanistan has been colonised by a number of foreign powers and the colonial way of life for 'ex-pats' was typical there.

Even though Emma had written to me a few weeks before that there might be a work opportunity for me in Kabul, she didn't know I was actually on my way, now earlier than anticipated, since that decision had only been made recently. So the surprise on her face when she arrived home later that afternoon was not unexpected. It should also not have been surprising to me when her surprise quickly turned to embarrassment. Surely she knew I was coming, or didn't she tell Bill and if not what would we tell him when he got home?

The moment of truth had arrived. I had been putting it off but now it was here. At least Sylvia was not here to witness this. It is easy for a young male infatuated with a woman to imagine that she is also infatuated with him and that all she wants is for him to be near her. In this situation, nothing could have been further from the truth. If she had given me the impression that she wanted me to come to Kabul for her then that was as much part of my imagination as it was part of her perverse little game with Bill. I knew that the situation was not a clear and simple matter between them, but I had no idea what was awaiting me in Kabul. It is painful to admit that at the age of twenty-four I was so naïve that I couldn't see clearly what was going on. When you are there, twenty-four feels very adult, but when you are sixty, in retrospect, it looks embarrassingly immature.

However, I was here now and we had to make the best of it. When Bill came home, after the initial awkwardness, the ice melted quickly as I told them my story of the last few weeks. The incident was a convenient deflection from the situation at hand. The fact that by now I had very little money left (most of what my brother had sent having gone on the airfare) helped them decide that I could stay there and that they would help me look for a job. I was grateful for their civility and compassion. They could have told me to leave, but they didn't.

Emma had been having her hair cut by the only European hairdresser in town at that time and she knew that they were very busy because of the sizeable diplomatic population in Kabul. In the afternoon of the following day, Emma and I went by push-bike, a common form of transport in Kabul, to visit the salon. It was about the same size as the one I had owned in Port Moresby. The owner, an English woman called Doreen, agreed that two days per week help would be very useful to her. She suggested Thursdays and Saturdays as Friday is the Muslim holy day of the week and since she had converted to her Afghan husband's religion, she could not open the salon on that day. I accepted immediately.

However, since her husband worked in the government, she

could not risk employing me illegally and I would have to obtain a work permit. After talking with him about it, she discovered that he might be able to help me in this matter. The first thing to do would be to get my passport back and go to Peshawar, in Pakistan at the other side of the famous Khyber Pass, to obtain a proper entry visa, because work permits could only be issued to people with a visa. As I had already made a formal application for such a work permit, and as long as the Afghan authorities had my passport, I was authorised to wait for it and could start work in the meantime.

With a place to stay and a part-time job, basic security was restored and I could now look at the bigger picture. After all the effort, adventure and expense to get here, not to mention the calamity on the way, it was clear that this was not really the place for me to be. (I had not yet come across the phrase '*Be careful what you want because you might get it!*', but this was a typical example.) Even though it would be cheap to live here, income from a part-time job was not exactly extravagant and it would take time to accumulate enough money to get out of Kabul. I still had some money left in Belgium (as well as some regular income from selling the salon in Moresby) and I asked my brother to send some more now that I had an address, at least for the time being. It took four weeks for the money to arrive. Not that it mattered because by that time I still did not have my passport back and could not have left even if I had wanted to. '*Why was it taking so long?*', I asked my employer. She asked her husband. He asked people in the relevant department. Waiting for the answer took weeks and when it came it provided no explanation. More waiting. In all it would be nearly three months before I was finally able to leave. Bureaucracy at its most magnificently ineffective.

Three months in Kabul is a long time, especially when all you really want to do is leave. But there was plenty to do. At the salon I got to know the many Western women coming every week, as much for something to do as to have their hair done. We swapped stories of countries we had lived in and others we had visited. Madame Lefevre, the French lady I had met at the Kandahar airport, told me all about diplomatic life in general and the duties of a diplomatic wife. This was their fifth post, the most primitive of the lot she assured me. Emma and I went to the American Film Society and saw many old movies and we rode around on our bikes.

Given my theatrical experience in Port Moresby I joined the British Society's production of Eugene Ionesco's *The Rhinoceros*. The play, an example of the 'theatre of the absurd' genre (as are the plays by Jean Genet) is the story of a group of village people gradually changing into rhinoceroses. My part, that of the cafe proprietor, appears only in the first act and had no more than about twenty-five lines, which suited me well since my mind was really on other matters, not to mention that I had enough absurdity in my life already. I did however enjoy being part of the process, including making papier-macher rhino heads. At least ten nationalities were involved in staging the play, including the daughter of the Japanese Ambassador. It was truly an international production.

I learned to play bridge at some of the dinner parties we went to, providing a welcome temporary distraction. What diverted me most from my own personal situation however was the rise and fall of the tension between Emma and Bill. I was never sure what made it go up or what brought it down, but it became increasingly clear that it wasn't just my presence.

When the latest Middle East war broke out on 6 June that year it provided another distraction from my waiting.

King Zahir Shah was still on the throne and Kabul was relatively peaceful then by Afghan standards, at least on the surface. Under the surface, the communist party had established itself and was waiting for an opportunity to enter politics. The rise and fall, if not of political tensions than of outright war, has been one of the hallmarks of the area of land we now call Afghanistan. Its geographical location may well have something to do with that. Trade routes through Afghanistan have been traced back as far as 2000 BC. The city of Kabul was established around 1500 BC, give or take a few hundred years, and may well have been a centre of religious developments with influences from Zoroaster, early Hindus and Buddhists.

Its Western neighbour, Persia, or Iran as we now call it, had been trying to annex Afghanistan since as early as 500 BC. Alexander the Great had his eye on it at one time and Genghis Khan at another and the Huns took a big swipe at it in 400 AD. Around the time the Crusades were happening, Islam flourished in Afghanistan and became an important center of Islamic scholarship. It wasn't until the 1700s that Kandahar became an independent city and later was the first capital of Afghanistan until it was transferred to Kabul in the 1780s. On three occasions, in 1839, 1878 and 1921, the British thought they should sort out the eternally internal-fighting and restore order in Afghanistan. They should have learned the lesson that the Afghans are fiercely independent fighters the first time they were there when *all but one* of their 15,000 soldiers died on the battlefield. The Russians also discovered Afghan tenacity when they had to withdraw after ten years of trying to take control. In 1973, a coup removed the monarchy and the internal struggles for power flared again. In turn, the Mujahideen and the Taliban, not to mention the ethnic tribal factions, to this day continue to flex their muscles for control. And now the Americans, amongst others including Australians, are having a go at it. Each time I see news about

Afghanistan, which is almost daily, I think of my interesting time there.

On the domestic front, life settled into a routine. Emma worked part-time at the childcare centre of the British Council. Whenever I was not at my part-time job, which seemed to coincide often with Emma being at home too, we would spend a pleasant and companionable time together. Emma was kind, generous and helpful, but no more. She was not cold to me, but whatever passion we had shared in London might never have happened. She had come back here to be with Bill, not me, and I respected that. My being here made life distinctly awkward for her, not to mention Bill. The awkwardness often accumulated into tensions between them. They never accused me of being the cause of this and I assumed that there was more to this situation than my being there. There were other occasions when the three of us went out together, visiting some of their friends or to see a film, and we got along just fine.

It was against this domestic background that the saga of my own adventure took a new turn. The new chapter started with a telegram from Sylvia which I received via the British Embassy barely two weeks after arriving in Kabul, the text of which read: '*Caught Gunther Marseille fly here immediately*'. I knew she had gone from Beirut to Marseille on a Turkish vessel, but how does this explain that 'Gunther' was caught there? He was supposed to be somewhere in Lebanon. I answered by telegram, addressed to Sylvia care of the French police in Marseille. '*Inform if absolutely necessary. Long way from Kabul. Low finance. Await cable.*' And wait I did.

Three weeks later the plot thickened considerably when a letter arrived from my brother in Belgium who had been advised by Interpol Europe that my car had been traced to Libya. Libya? Where was Libya? I thought he had been caught in Marseille and now he is in Libya? Does that mean he escaped from custody?

I was confused and frustrated by the conflicting information from different people in differing countries who each, it seemed, had only partial information. What I needed was more accurate information about what exactly was going on.

My immediate reaction was that if my car was in Libya, all I needed to do was to go to Libya and get it. I wrote to my brother to ask for more details from Interpol. I wrote to the Belgian Embassy in Libya to ask if they knew anything about the recovery of my stolen car. I visited the French Embassy in Kabul and had lunch with Madame Lefevre and her husband to see if they had connections in the Marseille judiciary to find out if Gunther was indeed caught there. All of this occurred at the same time as me trying to get my passport back and obtaining a visa to work in Afghanistan. None of my enquires resulted in any answers at all, let alone useful information. More waiting. It was May by now and spring had sprung upon Kabul. The mountains surrounding the city turned green and flowers appeared everywhere. Rehearsals for the *Rhinoceros* were in full swing but my mind was not really focussed on it.

Then came the news that my application for a work permit had been denied. Why? Who knows, they didn't tell me. So now officially I was supposed to leave the country. That was fine by me since I really wanted to go and find my car wherever it was, except I didn't have enough money yet. Doreen's husband was able to get me an application form to ask for an extension to my tourist visa. If it took as long to grant that, or to refuse it, as it had taken to refuse my work permit, I would be fine for the next several weeks. Eventually I heard from my brother saying he could not obtain any further information from Interpol and Sylvia seemed to have gone mute. No reply from Marseille. More waiting.

7th April, 1967. I board an (Afghan) Ariana flight in Beirut with stopovers in Teheran and Kandahar, arriving in Kabul twelve hours later.

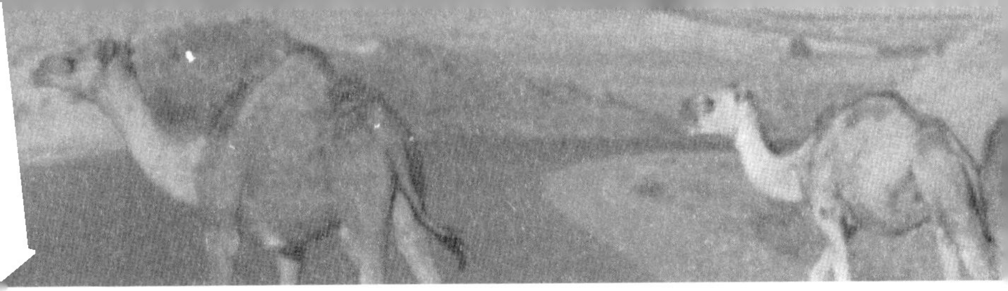

9.

Art with hair

Kabul 1967

HAVING my part-time hairdressing job in Kabul was useful not only as a financial contribution to my eventual return to Europe, but also took care of two days a week, which made waiting much less of a burden.

I became friendly with the regular clients and the time went by pleasantly enough. Doreen had a young girl helping out with general non-professional tasks at the salon. She was interested in becoming a hairdresser and so Doreen asked me if I would teach her some of the basics of the trade whenever there was nothing else to do. Carmel was not Afghan or she would not have been allowed to work there, let alone be in the presence of a Western man, without a veil. Her father was an Iranian Christian and her mother was Greek, both working for an aid organisation.

Carmel was as sweet as a rose and as beautiful as a dark pearl. She was no more than sixteen and bursting with fresh womanhood. Teaching someone hairdressing requires close proximity and sometimes, for instance, you have to hold the person's hands to show them how to cut hair. I also demonstrated how to put long hair into a chignon using her own gleaming dark hair. Carmel and I never spoke a single word we would not have wanted her mother to hear, but our eyes and smiles revealed a subtle if entirely innocent flirtation of the most exquisite kind. I continued to enjoy Emma's mature and intelligent company, but it was Carmel I saw when going to sleep at night, with Vladimir Nabokov lurking in the shadows.

It was after one of our 'training sessions' that Carmel asked me why I had become a hairdresser. Her innocent but sincere question sparked a flood of memories and the following day I kept going back to it. I wondered how indeed had I ended up earning a living fiddling with women's hair, a profession for which, I was beginning to discover, I had a rapidly decreasing interest.

During my final year at boarding school, thoughts about what to do with me next must have preoccupied my father's mind. As for me, all I could think of was getting out of there. I liked drawing and painting and had some flair for art in general. One of the trades taught at the trade school, attached to this educational complex, was house painting. I thought that this would be the trade for me since I believed that was where you graduated from to become a painter of pictures. This illustrates rather dramatically how naïve I was at that age. I suppose someone must have told me that this was not the case so I did not become an apprentice house painter. This prospect gone, I had absolutely no idea not only of what I wanted to do, but also of what was available and what I was capable of doing. As I remember it, I thought I could do practically nothing and had learned very little at school. At one stage I thought that what the brothers do at boarding school seemed easy, requiring no qualifications, and with the benefit of free board and lodging, so maybe I would do that. That thought must have lasted only a very short time since, luckily for me; it never went any further than a passing consideration.

Finally, after seven eternal-seeming years, the long awaited day of release from incarceration arrived. I was fifteen and a half and the very thought of no longer being at school was intoxicating. Unfortunately, with it came apprehension about the big unknown world out there and my uncertain future in it. Like a prisoner who has been inside too long, I wondered whether I would be able to cope on the outside.

One of my father's sisters (my aunt Alida) had been talking to her hairdresser about her nephew who didn't know what to do and I assume he could not think of anything else to suggest except hairdressing. This, my aunt must have thought, would be the perfect occupation for a physically weak, intellectually underachieving, somewhat effeminate boy who did not know what he wanted to do except draw pictures. Maybe, not unreasonably, she equated wanting to draw pictures with the artistry in hairdressing. My father agreed with her, not knowing what else to do with me and in fact not knowing much about me at all. So, a four-year ladies hairdressing apprenticeship was entered into. I worked full-time in a city salon and went to Hairdressing College four nights a week, my brand new bicycle my mode of transportation.

The transition from an all-boys Catholic boarding school to working in a ladies hair salon and going to evening college, where two-thirds of the students were girls my age and older, was not without physical and emotional problems. However, the euphoria of release from boarding school and at the same time not needing to spend much time with my father, buoyed me on, and self-discipline began to come to the fore.

The first few months were a struggle but I survived. Shampooing women's hair without splashing water all over their faces and sweeping up the floor after haircuts was not so difficult. Talking with people was more of a challenge. I didn't know what to say and I had nothing to talk about. What was I going to tell them? How terrible my boarding school was and what an appalling student I had been? How my mum had left me when I was six? Many of the clients were from that social stratum that preferred to speak French, even though Gent is in the heart of the Flemish-speaking part of Belgium. Despite being reasonably familiar with French, I was not at the level of fluent conversation, so I felt appropriately inferior from that point of view as well. The ability to talk elegantly about nothing, in any language, did not come easily to me and is still not one of my strengths today. Today, as my language skills have improved and my assertiveness has increased since then, I explain to people that I have a distinct antipathy to meaninglessness.

During the quiet times in the salon, having done the daily chores of polishing the mirrors, dusting the benches, filling the shampoo bottles and generally cleaning the place, there was time to chat with the other staff and read the beauty magazines that were available to the clients. The world of women – the world full stop – was beginning to reveal itself to me. These magazines told me some of the things women do to their bodies in order to make them more attractive and keep them looking young and sexy. They also told me some of the things they do with men, which I was sure were exaggerated or pure fantasy. Some of the conversations between clients and the hairdressers, within earshot of the young apprentices, made me think that either the magazines were right after all or that people made up stories to impress their hairdresser. It turned out that both were the case at different times. Many of the conversations I overheard in the salon while handing rollers and pins to the senior hairdressers brought to my notice aspects of life of which I was completely unaware. People talked about film-noir, contemporary theatre and symphonic concerts. They discussed international politics, the stockmarket and overseas travel on business. They shared sordid details of their private life, which at the time I thought they would not have told even their father confessor, if they had one that is. Gossip galore!

I was learning a lot, a lot more about other things than hairdressing, but I had so much more to learn. If anyone had looked they would have seen large green patches behind my ears. I became painfully aware of my inadequacy as a person in the adult world and the poverty in knowledge and experience with which my working-class background and boarding school upbringing had left me.

In those days, the salon closed at lunchtime for an hour and I had time to roam the city. I spent many lunch hours in bookshops, art material supply stores and record shops. I became interested in films and music. We had an old wind-up phonograph at home and the first record I bought for myself was by Helmut Zacharias and his orchestra. He was popular at the time and his slight 'swing' treatment of standards was easy to listen to for my uneducated ear. One day my older brother took me to a concert featuring Lionel Hampton, the vibraphonist, and instantly I was hooked on jazz. I started reading novels and detective stories, George Simenon and Agatha Christie being my favourites. I wanted to know everything as eagerly as a person who had not been fed for weeks would want to eat the proverbial horse.

At the Hairdressing College I discovered that I had the dexterity to do the work of hairdressing and intellectually could deal with the theoretical aspects of the course, not that this was anything complex by academic standards. Apart from the standard topics you would expect, the curriculum included stage make-up, wig-making, facial massage and the history of hairstyles.

It was very comprehensive professional training which would stand me in good stead later on. I was neither amongst the best nor dragging at the rear of the class as I used to do at school. I could also understand most of what I read and what I heard. Maybe I wasn't so dumb after all. That was a revelation to me. My self-confidence received a much-needed boost from the fact that, both intellectually and practically, I was holding my head well above water.

During the holiday in my second year of study, I went to stay with my aunt and uncle in Brussels where the international Expo was held that year. Its main icon, the Atomium, was a four-storey-high model of the atom. I spent several days wandering around looking at all the pavilions from countries around the world, probably laying the seeds of my later lust for travel and adventure. The Atomium has recently been restored and was as impressive as ever when I went to take another look at it in 2007, during a brief visit to Belgium for the first time in fifteen years.

For the last few years at boarding school my mother had not come to visit and I, persuaded by my father, had not gone to her. So I had not seen my mother for about five years when one day, standing in the reception area of the salon looking out at the street, I saw her walking past. A tidal wave of emotion swept over me. I wanted to run out and say hello to her and, at the same time, I hoped she would not see me. She didn't look like a bad person to me; she was just a woman, appearing very sad and aged. I had by now begun to know my father better, put him more into perspective, and begun to understand why she may well have been unable to stay any longer. Yet the many years of strong conditioning by my father's propaganda against her made me unable to walk up to her, at least then. I would however be able to do it a couple of years later.

By the time my ladies hairdressing apprenticeship came to an end, compulsory military service knocked on my door. Though not politically active in any way, I had developed a negative reaction to violence, military or otherwise, no doubt from being pushed around at school. My inadequate assertiveness was still dominating my responses to the outside world. I also knew of the bullying that goes on in the army and the thought of going back into another repressive situation like the one at boarding school did not enthral me. I also knew there would be little scope to practise ladies hairdressing in the army.

As it turned out, my time in the service was not as bad as it could have been. After the initial three months of general instruction, I was sent to Aken in Germany as part of the so-called occupation troops and later assigned to Seigen to work in the Military Post division, distributing mail to the various stations in the country. Since the postal service was a semi-civil part of the army, I was exempt from many of the drudgeries of everyday army life. I had a tiny room of my own next to the post office from which I ran a small business cutting hair for some of the officers who wanted better service than the barber dished out at the officer's mess.

And now here I was, doing it in Afghanistan of all places. I gave Carmel only a very short version of how I came to be hairdresser not wanting to shatter her dreams about her own future.

The Rolls Royce is a magnificent car (even the 1926 model) but not built to drive in the desert.

In Afghanistan there are rugged mountains and camels and lots of emptiness and dust.

10.

Going back in style

Kabul to Brussels 1967

ONE sunny afternoon Emma and I were playing chess, one of the activities we had enjoyed together on the Trans-Siberian train, when the front door bell of her Kabul apartment rang. Emma went to answer the door and I heard her shout: '*Oh, Peter, what are you doing here?*' Peter, her ex-husband turning up in Kabul as well?!? Is this situation turning 'surreal' or 'absurd'? Did Ionesco write this play? Fortunately it turned out to be a different Peter, one I had not yet met, and after the excitement of the surprise settled, he explained why he was there.

Peter Watson was a friend of Emma's family and worked for a London antique-car dealer. He had been sent to India to buy up old Rolls Royces that the Maharajas were selling off due to a change in Indian law proclaiming them no longer eligible for the generous pensions they had been entitled to from the Indian government up until now. As their fathers and grandfathers had been feathering their nests with British cars, their heirs could now cash in their savings.

Rolls Royce cars, if well maintained, increase in value after a certain age and become a good investment, so they are always sought after in England. Some of these cars were driven north to Russia and shipped by train back to the UK. The other way to get them back to Britain was to drive them from India to London, saving on plane fares for the drivers. Peter had simply dropped in to visit Emma as they had known each other for a long time. When he said he was looking for a co-driver to take a 1926 Rolls Royce convertible back to London (via Brussels), he could not have come at a more opportune time as far as I was concerned. I put my hand up in application and got the job. We agreed that if I did not charge him for my driving, he would not charge me for the lift and we would share the cost of petrol. The delay in getting all the paperwork to drive the cars out of Afghanistan and into Iran coincided with the time it took for me to get my passport back, as I would no longer need my extension. During that week we just fitted in the two performances of the *Rhinoceros* before leaving. The comic absurdity of the play was ironically reflecting some of the weirdness of my own situation.

I went to say goodbye to Doreen and Carmel who were sad to lose me, especially Carmel who had hoped that I might have finished training her to be a hairdresser. I kissed Carmel on the cheek as softly as I could and she blushed like a pink rose. I would have liked to take her with me but, alas, that was impossible. So I kept on dreaming.

We left behind us an increasingly frustrated Emma, unsure of what to do about her on-again-off-again relationship with Bill. Bill himself had gone to the States the week before on some urgent family business, and she would now be all by herself. Although my infatuation with Emma had well and truly dissipated, I was still fond of her and felt bad leaving. She had been very gracious in helping me and I was thankful, but did not know how to express it beyond mere words. It was time to go, I had business to attend to in other places and I simply did not know how to help her.

Peter, who was considerably more street-smart than I was, suspected some sexual perversion going on between Emma and Bill and explained it as the reason Emma wanted to get away from him while at the same time missed him when he wasn't there. In retrospect, having studied some psychosexual pathology in the context of counselling, he may well have been right. I had absolutely no insight into such matters at the time.

Either way I had to let it go.

We finally set off from Kabul in the late afternoon on 29 June. There was Peter, myself and Daisy, an English girl in her twenties who Peter had met in the local backpackers joint and who wanted a ride to Teheran.

Rolls Royce is probably the most prestigious mark of car in the world. It stands for quality, class and reliability. To drive one, even if it isn't your own, is probably the dream of many motoring enthusiasts. I am not a motoring enthusiast by a long shot, but I have brought a number of them to salivation when telling them of my opportunity to drive a Rolls for thousands of kilometres.

My first chance came early in the afternoon of our second day on the road after leaving Kabul. I had explained to Peter that I had been instructed to drive double clutch Bedford trucks in the army, whereupon he answered, '*In that case you'll be fine driving this beauty.*' We stopped shortly before reaching Kandahar, Afghanistan's second largest city and former capital. Peter slept beside the Rolls while Daisy and I took the front and back seats respectively. Being a very valuable article and not being able to lock it up like any other car (it being a convertible with a part of the hood missing) we always had to sleep in and/or next to it. We breakfasted on a can of corned beef and billy tea.

In Kandahar, Peter had some shopping to do. *Kandahar Gold*, so Peter explained to me, was one of the highest grades of hashish you could buy and, passing right through the place itself, it would be a shame not to buy some '*for on the way*'. He had obviously been a consumer before and seemed to know all about it. What was more surprising to me than all this information about something which I knew practically nothing about was the ease with which Peter found the 'stuff'. We spent less than two hours in the city, which included asking around, the actual transaction and buying some provisions. Of course, smoking hashish is still a common practice in those countries and therefore easily available.

We left mid-afternoon and not long after Peter said he wanted to have a smoke of what he had just bought, so would I mind driving? It was surprisingly easy – just like the army Bedfords, except much more comfortable. After half an hour of getting used to it, I thoroughly enjoyed it. After that we shared the driving more or less half each, all the way to Brussels. We had admirers wherever we went, some people offering money just to sit in it or be photographed next to it. Swarms of children always seemed to appear whenever we stopped.

Rolls Royce quality not withstanding, the trip was not without mechanical troubles. Apart from several minor issues, the main problem was the tyres. In 1929 the tyres for these cars were large in circumference but skinny in volume. We had two spares, but the surface of the roads in India and Afghanistan were mostly unsealed and very wearing on the old rubber. By the time we got near Herat on the Western side of Afghanistan, two of the tyres had holes big enough to let the inner tubes blow balloons on the outside. We could not risk going any further without spares. From Herat Peter contacted Rolls Royce in London and was told that it would take at least two weeks to find suitable tyres and ship them to Herat. Another solution had to be found. Peter held discussions with several mechanics in a variety of garages in Herat, complicated by both linguistic and mechanical differences, but eventually came up with a solution both cheap and practical. They would cut the spokes of the Rolls wheels and weld contemporary truck wheels to the hubs so that whenever we wore down tires we could get replacement sizes in any country. Later, after returning to England, they could weld back the Rolls wheels and restore the car to its original glory. It worked beautifully and we only lost two days from our schedule.

The other main inconvenience on this journey was the dust. The combination of an open car, hot-sweaty-mid-summer weather and the dust from unsealed roads made for a crusty skin that felt like sandpaper.

Sleeping in the Afghan desert, looking at the stars, is a beautiful experience. Looking at those stars while smoking some *Kandahar Gold*, courtesy of Peter, made them even shinier. It was a new experience for me and I am glad I tried it, but it is not something that developed into a habit. The following night without the '*Gold*' the stars were still pretty shiny. I have come across natural and more permanent consciousness-changing processes since and I have never returned to '*Kandahar Gold*'.

In Teheran, after dropping Daisy off at a backpackers hostel, we visited my father's sisters who had married an Iranian businessman many years ago. She had received the message from the neighbour I had met in London, so my appearance was not entirely a surprise. We made it clear immediately before they felt obliged to invite us in that we could not stay with them because we had to take the car out of the city and be on our way. By Iranian standards they were extremely well-off and lived in a very nice house. So, as a compromise, and still fulfilling some familial duty, they took us to an outer-suburban restaurant for dinner, which would have saved their furniture being smeared with desert dust. Their twenty-or-so-year-old daughter declined to take the ride to the restaurant in our Rolls, her excuse being she worked at the Shah's imperial palace (he was still in power then) and public behaviour protocol was very strict. They coped very well with this runaway nephew they only knew by name.

Iran was not any less dusty than Afghanistan and was just as hot. On the road from Teheran to Tabriz, we took a detour to have a beautifully refreshing swim in the Caspian Sea. The Afghan and Iranian corrugations and potholes had been a challenge to the old shock absorbers and in Tabriz we had modern ones put on. We entered Turkey on 10 July and spent the night just outside Ersurum. The mountain range in that area is stunning and reminded me of the trip Sylvia and I had taken through southern Turkey just before meeting Gunther only a few months ago. And now, at last, I was on my way to solve the mystery of the stolen car. We made a point of having a swim in the Black Sea, which of course isn't black at all.

We crossed Turkey in three days and reached Istanbul by the 13th. The only noteworthy event on the next stretch of the journey was the border crossing into Bulgaria. Peter had ingeniously stored his '*Kandahar shopping*' in the large car battery holder that came with the Rolls. A modern battery takes up much less room, so the leftover space was just perfect. The lid was fastened back on and it looked untouched. The sight of the car itself had been a distraction to most customs officers at the borders we had crossed – they were more often than not interested in having a good look at this unusual vehicle than checking what we had in it. The Bulgarians, however, must have had the idea that this car was designed to distract them and therefore proceeded to make us take everything out of it to inspect it all. The entire car was searched and one of the officers used a gadget that looked like a very big dentist mirror to look under it.

Peter was so confident of his handiwork that he didn't blink an eyelid. It must be said that we both felt much more comfortable when eventually we were grudgingly waved through after at least an hour of searching. There is something satisfying about avoiding rules imposed by authorities who behave like bullies. As the roads dramatically improved from then on, it only took another three days before we arrived in Brussels.

In Brussels, the welcome home fun at my brother Andre's place was overshadowed by his marriage breakdown being in full swing. While I felt sorry for him, there was little I could do. I was certainly not in a position to give advice on relationships at that time given my record in that department. We were able to park the car in a nearby garage for the night and had our first comfortable sleep away from it for seventeen days. In Gent it was school holidays and the next day we took Freddy's children for a ride in the Rolls, much to their delight.

While we were getting the car ready to put on the ferry from Oostende to Dover, Peter asked me if I would do him a favour. Since I was going to London to find Sylvia, he asked if I could bring his '*Kandahar shopping*' across to England, travelling separately on my Belgian ID card. That way the customs officers wouldn't see from my passport that I had been in all those supplier countries. He explained that for me the risk was practically non-existent. For him, on the other hand, having come from Afghanistan and having previously been busted (I later found out), taking the stuff with him was a considerable danger. Mathematically speaking he was right. Peter sealed his shopping in two small plastic bags so it could not be sniffed and guaranteed me that he would back me if anything happened.

I celebrated Belgium's national day, 21 July, with my brother Freddy and his family and left for London on the night ferry the following day. I never thought about what I was doing very much and just did it. It wasn't until I got into a cab in London after passing through customs at the station that I felt a tension slipping away which I had not felt before. Peter was enormously grateful for my help and I spent the day with his lovely family at his country home.

Back in London, I found the flat where Sylvia was staying. At last the mystery of the stolen car and the events of capturing the thief would be revealed. I became increasingly anxious and curious as I was getting closer to the moment of meeting with Sylvia once more. I wanted desperately to know what had happened and how she was herself. I was also eager to find out how she now felt about the whole debacle. When I got to the address I had received from her in Kabul about a month ago, a young woman who had just moved into the flat answered the door. She told me that Sylvia had left to go back to Australia only a week ago. '*What?*' I had just missed her! She said she had heard that Sylvia had been ill and that was the reason she had gone back home to Australia, but didn't know anything else. I felt very disappointed at missing her so narrowly, but more so that she had suffered physically and become sick, presumably because of what happened. But what had happened? I still did not know by then and neither did I know where to contact her in Australia because she had not left a forwarding address.

I went to see my actress landlady in Marble Arch and told her my story. She was interested to hear about my theatrical debut in Kabul, and told me that she had not been hassled any more by my former employer, and hadn't seen him since. As my mission for Peter was completed, but having failed to meet my own objective, there was nothing for me to do but go back home to Belgium and try to sort things out from there.

After three months in Kabul, on June 30th, I catch a ride with Peter in a 1926 Rolls Royce back to Europe.

We had dinner at a local tea house and then sixteen days later we arrive in Brussels at my brother Andre's, below with adopted daughter Chantal and son Alain.

11.

Discovering sunny Sydney

Belgium – Australia 1963

RETURNING home from London I contacted Belgian Interpol, but no further information about my case was available. Local police were of no help at all. So where to from here? I was beginning to consider going to Libya to retrieve my car, if that was what it would take. Although Libya is in North Africa, that's not too far from Belgium when you have been living in Australia and travelled overland from Afghanistan. Going to Libya was not the problem – what I would do when I got there was. I needed a few days to think about what steps to take next.

One night we were sitting around drinking one of my favourite Belgian beers, reminiscing about the time my brother Freddy and his family had seen me off to Australia. I had been staying with them when my travelling had started. It seemed such a long time ago now and much had happened since and here I was, back again. It reminded me of my early days in Australia and how I got to go there in the first place.

It is usual when men come home from their compulsory military service, even in peacetime, to hold a big celebration. Families greet their 'returnees' at the station and some get drunk for days before they even reach their homes. In my case, no one was there to welcome me home. I took the tram to our house and no one was there either. My brother Freddy was married by then and had a job with the Port Authority of the city of Gent. My brother Andre had gone to live and work in Brussels. During my absence in Germany my father had a stroke and was now being taken care of in a home. Mother, of course, had left years ago. The place was cold and empty and I didn't even feel like putting down my kitbag and changing into 'civvies'. I felt much more like running out of there, but where to? Standing in the middle of our living room and looking around at the emptiness, an overwhelming feeling of sadness and loneliness, of being once again abandoned by both my parents, gripped me by the throat, squeezing tears from my eyes. A strong voice inside me said, '*That's it! You are all on your own now. You wanted to be free, well now you are. Your life is now up to you. You can either cry about being alone or get on with being free. Your choice.*' I wiped my tears away and chose to get on with it. Writing this, more than forty years later, tears welling in my eyes, again I wipe them away and get on with it.

As soon as I got hold of myself, it occurred to me in a blinding flash that I was at the beginning of my life – my life as an adult – and that up till now it had only been a shabby and poorly organised introduction, with the real thing yet to come. I felt like a butterfly just out of the restrictive cocoon but not yet sure how to fly. And where would I fly to, even if I could? The idea of complete freedom was still new to me then and it felt strange, and yet the possibilities were almost endless. I knew it was up to me, but the time needed to be right and I was not quite ready. I wanted to gather some experience in my newly acquired profession and test my wings. I felt confident that out of this holding pattern something would come and when it eventually did I would be ready.

By now I also had become somewhat more at ease with myself. I was nineteen going on twenty and had survived boarding school, the army and a professional apprenticeship. I could drive a car, drink, smoke and talk to people. I still didn't have a girlfriend, something I was beginning to be a little concerned about. In the army, men talked about little else and I had nothing to show off with in this respect. A hairdresser friend and I regularly visited a girl called Rose who worked at a bar, she was there to drink with the patrons and flirt a little, but strictly nothing else. We became friendly and often spent a few hours drinking there on weekends.

Rose was very good at her job but also very honest and the more we got to know her the more she treated us like friends and took us into her confidence. She genuinely liked meeting people, chatting about anything and everything and having a fun time. Rose was at least ten years older than I was and our relationship had no sexual connotations. She reminded us of that often enough, lest we should forget it. I was an enthusiastic amateur photographer at that time and I wanted to extend my repertoire. Because I felt safe with her, one day I asked if she would pose nude for a photographic session. It was a testimony to our friendship that she immediately agreed and an indication of her sense of humour when she added, smiling and narrowing her eyes, '*But if you have any funny business in mind you're dead!*' She smiled less when I replied '*I don't go for older women.*'

It was not until I she took her clothes off and started taking on some provocative poses that my camera lens began to fog up and my hands became unsteady. I wish I hadn't said anything about older women. My sex education would have to wait, but I learned something about impulse control that day, an aspect of that all-important skill 'self-discipline'. She was pleased with the photos and I was pleased with my self-control.

Soon after returning from the army, I got a job in one of the most prestigious salons in the city. It was part of a chain of salons in France and Belgium. This made me feel more confident professionally. After about six months in this job I heard word from head office that they were opening two salons in America, one in New York and one in Boston, and were looking for stylists to go there. My hand shot up in the air before I had time to think about what I was doing. To my disappointment I did not qualify on two counts – I was neither a *senior* stylist nor had I been with the company for the required three years. It did occur to me now however that continental training in ladies hairdressing was an export commodity. There was nothing holding me back. Who was there to say I couldn't go? I felt ready to fly and see the world and I desperately wanted to get away from my Catholic-soaked, narrow-minded environment. I was free and wanted to take full advantage of it. All I needed was a destination and a ticket.

I took the first step via a summer season job for three months by the seaside with a new hairdressing chain. It was my first experience of living alone and taking care of myself. I rented a room, learned to cook, and earned enough money to buy books and go to the cinema. I felt grown up and in charge of my life, or at least of the material necessities. It was a big first step for me and I felt terrific having taken it. Afterwards I went to their main salon in Brussels and worked there a while. I stayed with my brother Andre and got to know him better too. This salon was even more prestigious. They drove special clients to and from the salon in a black Rolls Royce, a brilliant marketing stunt.

While working there I came into contact with two gay Greek hairdressers. They were by far the best hairdressers I had ever seen in action. The talent oozed from their pores. Their charm, friendliness and supreme self-confidence made me want to be like them. Did I want to be gay also? I don't think so, but by now I still had not had any confirmation that I was capable of acquiring a girlfriend, and still being more effeminate than your average bloke, I guess some doubt may well have crept into the minds of some people, not to mention my own subconscious. It certainly was clear to me now that to be gay in the world of hairdressing is not a disadvantage. I was to meet many gay men and women in the world of coiffure as time went on. In the meantime, I was sitting firmly on the fence, or should that be on the shelf?

Then, one fine day I was at Freddy's place in Gent when a niece of his wife came to visit. She had come to say goodbye because she was leaving to go and join her boyfriend in Australia. '*Australia? Where is that?*' we all asked.

When she explained that the Australian government was encouraging people to go there and that they generously assisted financially with the voyage, my interest was immediately sparked and before I had found out where exactly Australia was, I asked her what one had to do to sign up. After she left we got an atlas out and discovered that it was more or less on the other side of the world, we all laughed, but it made no difference to my immediate intention to go there.

Belgian law required me to have completed my military service before they would let me go, which I had. Australian law required me not to have a criminal record before they would let me come, which I hadn't. I had enough savings to pay the small amount required to go there and enough to live on for a while if I had to. The charter flight was leaving from Frankfurt and Freddy and his family took me there to see me off. His three boys, Noël (who was born on Christmas day and hence inherited my name), Marc and Luc shared the back seat of their Volkswagen with me. Migrating to Australia at that time was as simple as that. I had no hesitations then and I have no regrets today.

Precisely three months after the niece's visit, on 20 May 1963, seven months before my twenty-first birthday, I landed at Sydney airport. I was one of a party of about forty immigrants. We were bussed to Central Station and taken by train to a migrant reception centre near Albury-Wodonga, called Bonegilla. It felt as if the train journey was as long as the flight from Europe – it took ages. The accommodation was primitive, but as I was only there for four days it didn't matter. The Dutch-speaking immigration officer 'processing' people at the centre advised me there wouldn't be much work for a continentally-trained ladies hairdresser in Bonegilla and that if I could sustain myself for a short time I'd be better off in Sydney.

My arrival back at Sydney Central Station on the eve of the 25 May 1963 is the first entry in a diary I started on that day. It was a little skinny A5 notebook, now yellowed around the edges by time. It faithfully reminds me that I struggled to explain to the taxi driver what I wanted. I had the address of the Belgian Consulate in Woollahra and I wanted to go to a cheap hotel nearby. However it wasn't until we got to the consulate, located in the middle of the upper-class residential suburb of Woollahra, that I was able to tell him I really needed a place to stay that was preferably nearby and cheap. He had difficulty telling me that there was no such thing as a cheap hotel here, so we had to return to the city. Eventually we did find a place at two pounds and five shillings a night. The room was tiny, just enough space to squeeze in between the bed and the wall.

After writing this first entry into my diary, I felt like my 'real' life was now beginning and the future was here and now, wide open. I was ready for anything to happen and to start living my own life, free from the old restraints and restrictions of the past. That is, until I bumped into some of them which I had brought over with me in my own head.

Once I had been accepted to migrate to Australia, I had about two months to wait, during which time I reflected on my relationship with my mother and father. Father had suffered a second stroke by now and was left speechless. I felt there was not much to say, so I decided not to even visit him before going away.

Mother was another kettle of fish. By now she had not seen me for nearly fifteen years. I, in the meantime, had the opportunity to get my own opinion about what had happened in the past and how I felt about it. I knew that my father had conditioned us to believe that because she had left us, she was the 'bad' parent. I also knew from living with him since leaving boarding school that he was a difficult person to be with and certainly no model parent either. By that time I was no longer actively resenting either of them and my intense anger of a few years ago had dissipated. While there was no particular urgency in me to see her, I felt a certain sense of duty. In all fairness, she deserved recognition as a person and some sign of reconciliation from me, especially as I would be away for at least two years, probably longer, and she might not see me again, ever.

About a week before leaving I found out where she lived and went there. I rang the doorbell. She had not seen me for so long that she did not recognise me at all until I spoke and said my name. It then hit her like a severe blow to the head and I thought she was going to have a heart attack. She literally could not speak for what seemed at least ten minutes. She cried profusely, holding my hands, and could not stop looking at me in disbelief. Her little boy, who she had lost at such tender age, yanked from her hope by ruthless lawyers, had returned to her just like that. Surely she must have thought that she was dreaming? But no, here I was, in the flesh. As she was struggling to regain her balance, I was wondering if she was going to survive the moment, especially knowing that it would be me this time who would soon tear her precious little son from her again by announcing that I was leaving for the other side of the world, possibly never to return. This is what I had come for and now I could not get out of doing it. I felt brutal, cruel and heartless, but in the end I had to be free and be my own person. Having survived more than ten years without the care of a mother, I could not contemplate returning to live with her, though that is what she had hoped for.

She survived the second blow – my telling her that I was leaving for Australia – and found solace in my promise of continued contact. I reassured her that it was only for two years and that now that we had made contact I would write to her regularly. She recovered sufficiently to tell me that all those years ago before leaving home she had been assured by her lawyer that she would be granted custody of the children, at least the youngest because he still needed a mother most, and that there was no way she would lose out. She explained that 'he' (my father, who she could not call by his name after all these years) had more money and connections and had found more aggressive lawyers and told many lies about her in court, including that she was having an affair with a family friend. She fought for years, prayed and prayed, and finally gave up. She learned to live with the pain of having left her children and knowing she would probably never see them again.

And now this. She didn't know whether to be happy or sad. I felt uneasy and didn't know how to end this visit. Finally I invented a reason why it was time for me to go, because I could no longer stand the pain I saw in front of me. I also feared that she would be clingy, begging me to stay, but she was brave. She must have known she had no hope of changing things as they were now. It was much too late for that.

When I got up to leave, I could see that she desperately wanted to end our reunion on a positive note. She wanted to give me something, but she didn't know what – she didn't know what I'd like, she didn't know me at all. She was not prepared for this. She fumbled in her purse and gave me a small amount of money. Refusal was out of the question. Accepting was the least I could do, offering a small easing of her guilt and suffering.

I felt queasy walking along the footpath leaving her house. In one sense I felt I had done the right thing, but at what price to her? Would it have been better to let sleeping dogs lie? As it turned out, in time, she did enjoy our being in contact and when years later I returned for some time, she was able to see me again under much better circumstances. More importantly, as a result of my visit, her two other sons, Freddy and Andre also approached her later on. While that didn't work out the way she would have liked it, in the end she did see all of her children and some of her grandchildren again before she passed away.

Sunday 26 May, my second day in Sydney, I walked right across the Harbour Bridge. What a view! The Opera House was still under construction but its basic shape was already visible. I did a brief tour of both the Australian Museum and the Art Gallery of New South Wales and lay on the grass in the Domain, something not permitted in many European parks.

The Belgian Consular staff, when I eventually got to the Consulate the following Monday, were very helpful. They wrote a letter of recommendation, introducing me and explaining my qualifications since I was as yet unable to do so myself in English. I meandered through the streets with my letter, showing it to any ladies hairdressing salon I encountered. Some just shook their head negatively. Others simply said: '*No English, no job. Come back later.*' It was in the middle of my second week that the receptionist of a city salon pointed to a seat and asked me to wait there. A suave-looking young man in his mid-twenties came out, speaking fluent French with a Swiss and English accent. He told me that if I was free the following day, I could meet with him and his partner for an interview and gave me an address.

Double Bay in 1963 was nothing like it is today, but it was already the most cosmopolitan suburb in Sydney, boasting a Chinese, Italian and French restaurant, all in the same street. It was in that same street that a new salon was to be opened. The young man introduced me to another broadly smiling young man, his partner, both in business and in life as it turned out. He asked me a few questions and I was asked to demonstrate the special way of cutting hair in which I had been trained.

After some more questions and a chat between the two Swiss partners, they decided to offer me the job. It would be at least two weeks before the official opening. Having been migrants themselves they were sensitive to my situation and asked if I had enough money to live on till then, offering help if I needed it.

I was ecstatic. It was the most exciting day in my life so far, by a mile. Not only had I scored myself a job in the newest, most luxurious salon in Sydney at the time within ten days of arriving in this country, to top it all off I had also two weeks holiday to begin with. This came in very handy because I wanted to find some lodgings not too far away and settle in before starting work. I also wanted to explore this magnificent city and quickly learn some English.

Even though it was mid-winter, it was more like a summer where I came from. They were two fabulous weeks. Not speaking English was an inconvenience, but I soon learned since I had no other option but to do so. I found a room in a guesthouse in Darling Point overlooking Rushcutters Bay, a twenty-minute walk from work.

I explored Bondi beach, went to the zoo and visited all the galleries and concert halls. I wrote in my diary that it was:

'...like being born again into a different world, and being a different person. I have to remind myself that this is real – that I am not dreaming this – it's true – it's true.'

A new person with his own thoughts, experiencing freedom to think, freedom from family and religious oppression, and no strings attached from any puppeteers. Never in my wildest dreams had I hoped I would wake up one day in a paradise, with the sun shining most days, free to be me. The experience was simply intoxicating. Only if one has been in any form of prison, either physically or psychologically – and I had been in both – can one appreciate fully what it is like to be free.

That year in Sydney is one I remember with great fondness. My employers not only took me into their business, but also into their home and hearts. We became friends as well as colleagues, and often went out together. They liked the beach, dining out and going to concerts, and I often enjoyed evenings listening to classical music at their home. I was becoming aware of culture as something you participate in rather than hear other people talk about.

I was not unaware of the gay subculture in hairdressing and it was therefore no surprise when they also took me to *The Jewel Box*, *Les Girls* and *The Purple Onion*, my first experience of drag shows. It was a puzzle to me at first as to how people who enjoyed classical music, the theatre and fine furniture could also enjoy rather cheap-looking entertainment. I didn't see it as all that funny at the time. I think they saw it as entertainment and no more. There was never any impropriety on their part and I felt completely comfortable with them, which is more than could be said about my boarding school years.

Being young and unattached and, as yet, totally lacking in experience with women, I was far from blind to the attractive Australian girls. When I started working at the salon, there was a young manicurist of exquisite beauty also starting at the same time. She had the body of a nymph and walked like a ballerina. She would smile innocently, revealing perfect white teeth and look straight at you with her big brown eyes. One day when there was a drop of blood on my lip she asked if someone had kissed me too hard. I shyly replied that it wasn't from a kiss since no one ever kisses me. She smiled brightly and said '*I might have to then*.' I was naïve enough to think that this is what she really wanted to do and she sent my imagination into a dizzy spin. She went as far as to invite me to dinner at her home to meet her parents. Why she did this I couldn't work out. Did she feel pity for this poor lonely little migrant, or did she need her parents' opinion? I wasn't invited again, so I took it that either I didn't meet the family expectations or that she had done her duty to make a migrant feel welcome in Australia.

Not meeting expectations had been the curse of my childhood. A few days after this event I wrote in my diary:

'"G" is very beautiful and I admired her very much, but I think she is not very intelligent.'

It seems that at the tender age of twenty I needed a girl to have more than a good-looking body to be serious about her. Or was I just rationalising my disappointment?

That July I was invited to the reception at the Belgian Consulate to mark Belgium's national day. I duly attended. Just as well I went because I met a young woman with whom I could talk in French and have a conversation about more than just the weather. She was born in Belgium but had spent most of her life in France and had now lived in Australia for a few years.

She was a little older than I, a good deal taller, and not what I would have called attractive, but neither was she ugly. We went out to dinner a few times. My diary records the rather whimsical observation that if the Belgian woman only had the body of 'G', serious friendship might have a better chance. It seems I wanted more than just intelligence as well. Seemingly wanting to explain to myself better what I was really after, I wrote further:

'I am longing for tender companionship and understanding. I am too young for so-called love and at any rate I don't believe in it.'

Whatever my confused idea about 'love' at the time and whatever that thing was that I didn't believe in, I desperately wanted to be understood and taken seriously.

I was free but alone.

Enter Rafael Saldaña! Rafael, a Spaniard, came to work as a general help at the salon where I was working. We had lots in common and together we explored almost every subject under the sun. He introduced me to paella, his theory of sex (get as much of it as you can), and boiled condensed milk in a can, which tastes like toffee. It turned out he was a painter and later became a well-known exponent of the Australian 'naïve' school. I was also painting at the time and he gave me many useful tips on brush technique and colour mixing.

He told me, sitting under a palm tree in Centennial Park, in one of our many conversations, that the most satisfying part about painting was visualising the compositions on the canvas. Once you have seen it in your mind's eye, the job of creation is done. The rest is technique and hard work. '*And*,' he added in his laconic Spanish way, '*sometimes I can't be bothered. I am very lazy.*' We became life-long friends. I attended a retrospective exhibition of his work in February 2001, a few months after he died unexpectedly and suddenly from a myocardiac infarction aged seventy. Maria, his wife, gave me a personalised running commentary of some of the stories behind the paintings and brought him back to life for me. It was a very moving experience.

My twenty-first birthday dinner in a nice Italian restaurant in Kings Cross on the 24 December 1963, was a party of one. Partly because I didn't want to intrude on other people's Christmas Eve and partly because there was no one who would have rather been with me than spending Christmas Eve with their family. As for me, I was glad I wasn't with my family that Christmas and the loneliness of that evening was a small price to pay for the freedom from familial oppression and the choking of religion around my neck. I was here to be me and the joy of it far outweighed the solitude. There would be many more times that I would have to pay the price for freedom.

Freedom doesn't come cheap.

I arrived in Sydney by plane on the 25th May 1963. In December of that year I would be twenty-one. They are still building the Opera House but I am already reading Sigmund Freud.

12. From a blue lagoon to the red heart

Australia 1964

AFTER settling in at work and having found a place to live, my initial explorations were in and around Sydney, my first expedition being to Kuring-gai Chase National Park, just north of Sydney. My image of a 'park' was based on well-laid-out paths among mowed grass and flowerbeds. It turned out that Kuring-gai Chase was much more like a large forest. Whatever path there was, I soon got off it and worked my way through the bush as best I could, not realising the potential danger. At first it was exciting to be lost and I had confidence that I would soon reach a road or a path and be back on track. It must have been at least two hours after I had left the path that I started getting a little concerned. It was a hot day and, inexperienced migrant that I was, I had not brought anything to drink.

To my relief, I encountered a dry creek bed and while I could have done with the water, I knew it would lead me to some place where I could orient myself. I followed it for what felt like another hour when at last I found a sign of life. A young boy and his dog were just sitting there in the middle of a clearing on the edge of the creek bed. I told him I was lost, and asked if he could help me to the nearest road to Bobbin Head. I could see from the somewhat bemused expression on his face that he must have thought me an idiot adult, as the road was just over the hill. He guided me for a short five-minute walk and we reached the station from where I had started out. I will never know whether I went around in circles or in a straight line and back, but it taught me to be better prepared for the Australian bush in the future.

I also had to learn about the dangers of the Australian sun from experience. One weekend when I lived in a flat in Double Bay, I went to the beach about mid-morning with a particularly interesting book. I went home for lunch and had arranged to meet friends at Bondi Beach that afternoon. A couple of hours later, climbing the steps towards the footpath, I fainted. The doctor diagnosed '*severe sunburn and sunstroke*' and ordered a week off work. I have never had more than a little too much sun since.

My next main adventure was in February 1964 to Lord Howe Island. On a walk to Watson's Bay, I had passed the Rose Bay '*Airport*' or, as my map called it, '*The Flying Boat Base*'. I always thought that a plane which takes off from the sea was called a seaplane, but I can see no reason why you can't call it a flying boat, even though it certainly looks much more like a plane than a boat. When I discovered where it went to, I decided I would spend my first week of holiday there and experience this flying in a boat transport.

Lord Howe Island is about a 1,000 kilometres east off the coast of New South Wales, straight out into the Pacific Ocean. The experience of taking off and landing on the water in itself was worth it. Lord Howe did not have an airport in those days, hence the flying boat. There was a large lagoon, where the plane landed. Upon landing, the lower part of the plane/boat goes below the waterline from the impact and the window where I was sitting was completely submerged provoking a few seconds of concern but we quickly came back up again. After touchdown, you had to be ferried from the plane to the shore because a coral reef prevented it from going any closer. Lord Howe Island is like a jewel, a small but beautiful little paradise surrounded by the blue-green Pacific Ocean.

The most memorable event of that holiday was the climb up to Mount Gower. It took the fifteen of us, helped by a local guide, nearly four hours to reach the 875 m summit. Small fry as far as mountains go, but big for a relaxing holiday stroll. Some parts were borderline mountaineering rather than a tourist walk. There were slippery rocks, wild mountain goats and very friendly birds with which to contend. Unique to the island, the Providence Petrel is not human shy, or at least was not then, and we could sneak quite close up to it. The panoramic view from the top made it all worthwhile, not to mention the satisfaction of having reached it. You can see the whole of the island from up there, with the blue of the lagoon and the green of the ocean surrounding the long narrow strip of land.

My diary reminds me that a couple of young boys gave me what I called '*my first swimming lesson*' in the shallow warm water of the blue lagoon. I was delighted, and even though it did not lead to me being able to swim, it was a first step towards it. Swimming had not been on the curriculum at my school.

My diary for that week records some of my earliest observations about my way of relating to people at the time. I noticed that I was '*shy and too serious*'. I was also judgmental and probably needed to put other people down to make myself feel better. I was still struggling with English, which didn't help my interpersonal fluency. Shying away from people, for whatever reason, results in being by oneself. Being by oneself means you develop coping skills and you become less dependent on other people. A number of telling diary entries made around the middle of 1964, when I was barely twenty-one years old, show how I was increasingly aware of the issue of becoming independent from the need to be with other people. One entry reads:

'I have worked hard to take care of myself – I have a casino inside me where I can go and play any game I like; I have painting, photography, reading, all of which I can do without needing anybody.' When I took up woodwork at one stage I wrote that I now *'had yet another weapon against loneliness.'*

I struggled with my attitude towards other people during those early years as an adult and the development of my skills in that area was a challenge. I clearly wanted to find emotional warmth and companionship, but my life-experience so far had taught me to be cautious of people because they can, and do, hurt you.

Confiding to my diary became a way of self-reflection. Writing a diary has many benefits, as Anais Nin pointed out when she wrote: '... *people who turn to the diary are seeking themselves, tracing a route towards expansion and awareness, the road to creativity*'.

Ambitions to write also began around that time. According to my diary, on Wednesday 13 May 1964, I gave a copy of a short story I had written to one of my clients called Mrs. Murdoch, whose husband was in publishing. Could it have been *the* Mrs. Murdoch, Rupert's wife? Maybe, but I can't be sure. It didn't get published.

I felt I could not leave Australia (if I would not stay) without visiting the 'Red Centre'. The Alice and Ayers Rock are so much a part of the Australian psyche that to be here without seeing them would have been like visiting Paris without seeing the Eiffel tower. I had seen some indigenous people around Sydney, but I wanted to see them in their natural environment. In the middle of May 1964 I took two weeks holiday.

One of my clients had a friend who was a nurse at the Alice Springs Hospital and I went to see her. She showed me around town and told me many interesting stories about the indigenous Australians. The following day, I took a small fifteen-seater plane to Ayers Rock. I had been looking forward to climbing it and at that time there was no controversy about it being a sacred site. We had been warned some rain was expected, and if it started we should immediately come down as climbing surfaces would become extremely slippery and people had fallen to their death that way. There was nothing to hold on to except small crevices here and there, apart from which there is only steep smooth and hard surfaces. We had been climbing for about twenty minutes when it started to drizzle and the danger became obvious very soon. In the end, we all got down safely though it took twice as long since we took it very slowly, not wanting to tumble and start rolling down.

We did the round-the-base walk and visited the cave paintings and other fascinating sights. We slept in tents that night and visited the Olgas the following day. They were equally impressive and yet seemed to get much less publicity than the Rock. The return journey to Alice was by bus and took a full day, stopping several times on the way to buy artefacts from roadside stalls. I bought several woodcarvings, all '*two bob*' each. I saw Albert Namatjira's work in the Alice and was very much inspired. He certainly captured the magic of the Centre.

The following day I took a tour to Stanley Chasm. In the

afternoon I went off on my own as I usually did. I had become very fond of climbing and as I was halfway up a rather steep incline, the rain came down. Again, the surface became very slippery and dangerous but this time I was on my own and after some attempts to move I froze. I could neither go further up nor go back down. My legs started shaking and I began to wonder what it would be like to be left behind by the bus and die in the Centre all by myself. I had read of new Australians dying in the desert of dehydration. After what felt like a long time, but may have been less than ten minutes, the rain eased. I gradually moved sideways until going further up became possible and I could see a safe way to go down again. As soon as I got to the ground, I ran all the way to where the bus was waiting and just made it in time for its departure. My heart throbbed for at least half an hour after we left, but I was too self-conscious to tell anyone about it.

For the sake of getting off the beaten track, I booked myself on a bus to Tennant Creek for two days. Two minutes would have been enough. The main street had a pub, a general store and a handful of houses. The only natural attraction near Tennant Creek is the Devil's Marbles. They are huge and mysteriously balanced. I recalled the marble games I had played as a child and wondered what size this devil must have been. The return journey by train from Alice to Adelaide took two days and was more of a mobile red shower. Guards would come to sweep up the red dust every few hours. There was little to see except red desert and some bushes here and there. In all, I travelled nearly 8,000 kilometres in those two weeks and I felt I had really seen Australia.

All in all, my first year in Australia was fantastic – the birth of my adult being, an awakening of my independent thinking and a release of my personhood into freedom, at least that's what it felt like then.

There was only one thing missing. I still had no companion. I was twenty-one now and had not yet tasted the '*forbidden fruit*'. Was my Catholic indoctrination still casting its spell on me? Or was I simply extremely inadequate in this field? Was I too shy to talk to the girls? Or was I too critical in selecting possible partners? It certainly was not for lack of desire. My natural pro-creative instinct was in full swing, but my early conditioning and personal shortcomings were standing firmly in its way.

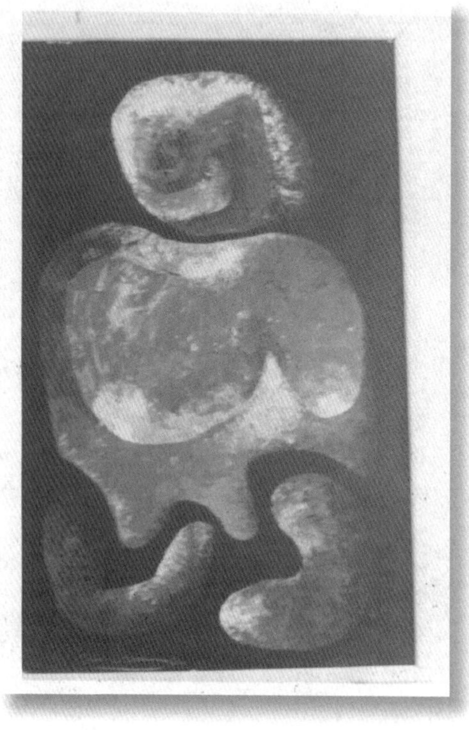

Inspired by central Australia my first experiment with 'knife' painting.

Climbing the 'Rock' (above) and squeezing through Stanley Chasm (right).

13.

Benghazi here I come

Gent to Libya 1967

SHARING these early wanderings in Australia makes them seem tame compared to the Trans-Siberian and Trans-European journeys. The incident in Syria had turned travelling into a dramatic event and had severely restricted my freedom.

Back in Gent, after returning from London, I went to the car dealer from whom I had bought my Opel station wagon and obtained a copy of the invoice and sales papers which would prove the car was mine. All I needed to do now was to go back to the police and tell them to get my car. The local police told me it was an Interpol matter. Belgian Interpol told me it was a matter for French Interpol. Upon asking what to do next, I was told I could go to Marseille and see if they knew anything. By then I was so frustrated by the lack of cooperation and the lack of information that I saw going to Marseille as the only way to find out what had happened there.

It was mid-afternoon on Saturday 5 August when I arrived in Marseille via Paris by train. By the time I found the relevant police department, and by the time they found my file, which took more than an hour, it was time for them to close shop. '*Revient Lundi!*' (come back Monday) was the message.

Marseille is a sprawling port city and I enjoyed exploring it over the weekend. I remembered that the brother of a friend of the family lived there and after some research I found his name and address. During August in France most people are on holiday, and so was he. In my diary I noted that:

'Marseille is full of extremely beautiful women.'

Apart from that observation my mind was preoccupied with what would happen next day. Monday came soon enough – back to bureaucratic nightmares. From the police station to the courthouse. From a court clerk to a court officer and eventually to the judge who presided over the case. Now we would be getting somewhere. His name was Judge Veraille. '*Oh, yes*' he remembered the case all right. It was a case of '*Usurpation d'identite*', the judge explained. To *usurp*, my dictionary tells me, is to seize or assume something wrongfully. Gunther, as he called himself then but which was also an assumed name, had usurped or wrongly assumed my name to try and enter France. As he was already wanted by German, Austrian and Swiss police, he had an Interpol file and once they identified him, he was convicted of '*Usurpation d'identite*'. His real name according to his record was revealed to me but here I will call him *Jan Vandervliet*. He was a Dutch national. I immediately remembered my father often quoting the Flemish saying that '*if a Dutchman hadn't tricked you, it was because he had forgotten*'. How ironic. He obviously hadn't forgotten that day.

'Ah, but what about my car?' I asked the judge. When entering France, '*Gunther*', or more precisely, Jan Vandervliet, did not have my car. According to him he had sold it in Benghazi. '*So my car was in Benghazi after all?*'

'*That is,*' Judge Veraille warned me, '*if he is telling the truth;*

don't forget he is a professional con-man.'

As far as France was concerned, entering the country with a false passport was the only crime for which they could hold him. Stealing my car had not occurred in France and was none of their legal business. The judge also told me that there were a number of items found on him which were mine, for which I could file a '*request for the restitution*'. I assumed, very wrongly as it turned out, that this would involve filling out a form and then picking my belongings up the following day. I was wrong on both counts. The number of forms I had to fill in was more like four or five, rather than one, but close enough. It was the 'tomorrow' bit where I really got it wrong. The first parcel with some of my belongings arrived four months later.

Because '*Gunther*' was now in prison in Marseille and since I was here myself, the thought occurred to me to go and visit him. 'H*ow are you? How was your Easter holiday with your family in Tel Aviv?*' – '*Did you accidentally forget about us and then felt a sudden urge to visit Libya and France?*' – '*And where exactly in Benghazi did you sell my car so I can go and pick it up?*' – '*And by the way, what happened when you met Sylvia?*'

Since I had to wait till the following day for my possessions, or so I thought, I went to visit '*Gunther*' at the prison just outside Marseille. The bus journey was long and very hot. Again there were forms to be filled out and then I had to wait in a sombre, dingy hall, which at least had the virtue of being cool. I was rehearsing the questions I would ask him in my mind and looking forward to meeting '*Gunther*' when I was told by a prison official that, due to the fact the prisoner had appealed against his sentence, it was not possible to allow visits other than by his legal representative. He had filed the papers *yesterday*! Yet another closely missed encounter. After missing Sylvia in London by a week, I now missed seeing '*Gunther*' by a day.

Leaving the prison I tried to understand why a person would

choose a career in deceiving and stealing from other people. This was not a one-off weakness, giving in to the opportunity before him – he was '*a professional con-man*' the judge had said. I recalled reading *The Thief's Journal* by Jean Genet and wondered if '*Gunther*' too had been abandoned as a child, left to find his own way in a brutal world of crime and greed. A touch of empathy tempered my anger towards him and made it easier to walk way from there.

Back to Veraille. The Judge was apologetic saying he had not known about the appeal. The fact that there was an appeal would also temporarily interrupt the restitution of my possessions. So there was no need to wait in Marseille, the Judge recommended, since this would now take some time, as I was to find out.

I asked again about my car, just in case there had been any changes to the story. The issue of my car, the judge repeated, had nothing to do with the French court since that crime was not committed on French soil. Going to Benghazi would be entirely at my own risk, Veraille warned me again. As to what happened to Sylvia, the Judge had no information, and only knew that she had been involved in the process of the arrest but had no other details. All very disappointing, but since I had come this far, I decided I may as well keep going, even if it was against all odds.

I walked straight from the Judge's chambers to the nearest travel agent. I was told there were no boats going from Marseille directly to Benghazi. My options were to go to Algeria, Tunisia or Egypt and then overland to Benghazi. I booked myself on the next available boat to cross the Mediterranean to Tunisia. The boat was crowded, not very nice and took longer than I had anticipated. I arrived in Tunis on Sunday morning 13 August to face a long delay at customs. It was late afternoon by the time I discovered that a bus was leaving for Tripoli the following day. Being Tunisia's national day, there were crowds everywhere. I joined in the celebrations that night and tried Tunisian couscous, generously accompanied by French red wine. The street noise continued all night and sleep was almost impossible.

The bus journey south to Gabes was hot, dusty and crowded. On top of that the effect of the spicy food and the little too much wine of the previous night were beginning to assert themselves on my bowels. I desperately needed to go to the toilet. Holding myself became uncomfortable and caused me to fidget. At the border with Libya, the bus stopped at Rass Ajdir, a very small coastal village, and I scampered behind the customs shed, public toilets not being available, to relieve myself from a serious case of diarrhoea. Luckily there was nothing else there apart from desert sand. I had obviously enjoyed the couscous and the wine too much and was now paying the price. That was, however, only the first instalment. When a bit over two hours later we arrived in Tripoli, Libya's capital, I was in urgent need of another toilet break. I ran all the way from the bus to the nearest cafe. After feeling more comfortable and finishing my orange drink, I went to pay at the counter. My back pocket, where I always carried my wallet, was empty. No wallet, no money. Had I been conned again, by the ghost of '*Gunther*' this time? Had my wallet been stolen or did I lose it?

At least this time I still had my passport. The cafe proprietor was understanding and recommended I go to the police since he seemed certain I had been robbed. After I told the police my story, they agreed with my speculation that my wallet must have fallen out of my pocket in the bus during my uncomfortable journey. They helpfully telephoned the bus company. Unfortunately, the bus had gone into the bus depot which was locked up for the night by now. A smiling police officer offered me a cell for the night at the police station. I was not sure whether he was joking or not but when I said, '*I'll take it*', he showed me the way. Once again I felt like a criminal, even though I was once more the victim of my own doing. Sleeping in a prison cell was not the most comfortable accommodation I had experienced but compared to my inner embarrassment that was the least of my concern.

I thought that the bus I had been on would probably leave early in the morning for its next journey, so when I awoke in my cell about 5 am I asked my hosts if they could take me to the bus depot. They replied, '*Non*.' This simple request turned out to be one too many. They did give me the address of the bus depot, however, and some general directions, so I set out on foot to find it. When eventually I did find it, it was still closed. It was probably 7 am by then, but there was absolutely no one there. The depot was full of buses, all looking the same. Which was my bus and how would I get in there? I considered climbing over the wall, but then what? How would I check all the locked buses? I also did not want to be arrested for trespassing and end up in my cell again, this time as a convicted criminal.

I squatted by the front gate thinking that surely sooner or later someone would come here to drive one of these buses to somewhere. It seemed like ages, but eventually a maintenance mechanic turned up who fortunately spoke good French. I explained my situation and he figured out which was yesterday's bus from Tunis and together we forced the pneumatic doors open. At the back of the bus, exactly where I had been sitting, right there under the seat, was my wallet with all the money still in it. My relief was enormous. I did not need another fiasco in the middle of sorting out the previous one.

The trip from Tripoli to Benghazi was along the Mediterranean coast, right around the Gulf of Sirte, in an old clapped-out Renault taxi I shared with two very big Syrians (and a large Libyan woman in the front) all smoking like chimneys. Many people travelled at night, as it was cooler, especially in the middle of summer. It was impossible to sleep in that car and when we arrived in Benghazi at 7 am after a third consecutive night with no rest, I fell asleep in the first cheap hotel I could find.

At that time Libya, like Afghanistan, was still a kingdom, with King Idris in charge. Little did he know then that a little over two years later he would be deposed in a military coup led by Qaddafi, the man still ruling the country today.

After lunch I set out on my search. In Marseille, a court officer had told me that '*Gunther*' had said he had sold 'his' car at a British garage in Benghazi. British? Like Jaguar or Rover? Who knows? After asking around for the places where one could buy second-hand cars, I found myself in an area where there were at least five or six all nearby. I felt lucky. Some people in Libya speak English: some speak French or Italian, a legacy from Italian colonial occupation at the beginning of the twentieth century; many speak neither. Communication is hard at the best of times when it comes to complicated stories, but when language is an additional barrier, and someone looks like they are snooping around, it's easy to signal '*Do not understand.*' or '*No, I don't know anything.*' I got lots of these messages that day and the following. Was I being conned again by this '*Gunther*' person? The Judge had warned me that it might have been a red herring. I was very close to believing it was and had decided I had better return home rather than waste my time and money on what looked every minute more like a wild goose chase.

I had been walking around in the heat for two days meeting dead end after dead end, so I decided to start looking for a nice little restaurant to have a last supper in Benghazi before the journey back the following day.

There was still a fair-sized Italian population in Benghazi and many restaurants and food shops catered to their tastes. As I was walking somewhat listlessly towards where I had been staying, a small Italian restaurant beckoned me with its colourful tricolour flag and I thought a bowl of pasta would do just fine. I walked up to it and, just before entering, something else beckoned me even more. An Opel stationwagon parked right outside! It was the same colour as mine, pale beige with brown trimmings and seats. The windscreen was clearly not the original and it was the first Opel I had seen in Benghazi. *It had to be my car!* It appeared so unexpectedly that it hit me like a thunderbolt. Although hard to believe, there it was right in front of me, against all odds, here in North Africa. This time he had not lied after all. But now what?

The car had Libyan numberplates which meant someone owned it and was driving it. Suddenly I was no longer hungry, but went into the restaurant and asked one of the waiters if any of the patrons owned the vehicle parked outside. After the owner had asked around, a middle-aged Italian, ready to apologise in case he had parked too close to my car, came towards me gesticulating, ready to move his car.

'No, don't move it. – Il ne faut pas bouger votre voiture!'

'Ou a tu acheter cette voiture? – I want to know where you bought it.'

'Ah, si.'

He introduced himself as Vittorio and vigorously shook my hand. I can only guess that he thought I wanted to buy one just like that, so he obliged. He wrote the address on a piece of paper and added, without me even asking, the name of the person he had dealt with, thinking he would be doing him a favour sending another customer. I thanked him profusely for his assistance and completely forgot about having dinner.

At last I had some specific information to go by. I immediately turned around and went to find the place but by the time I found the dealership it was closed. But I recognised it; having gone there earlier that day, I had been told by one of the sales people that they did not sell second-hand cars. At least I knew where to go back the following day. It was again hard to go to sleep that night.

George, it turned out, was the assistant manager of this dealership and had indulged in a little side business, common enough practice and probably not illegal, at least in Libya. A friend of his had approached him after an Arab-speaking European had wondered where he could sell his car privately for a good deal. That sounded like '*Gunther*' already. George had looked at the car, inspected the papers, and when he saw that all was in good order, bought it privately. He had it cleaned up, took the Belgian plates off and sold it, again privately, to Vittorio. '*Nothing wrong with that, is there?*' he asked.

No, except that this car was stolen from me in Syria. '*But surely that is not my fault?*' George asked.

'*True, but was it not illegal to buy stolen cars in Libya, like in most other countries?*' I replied.

He protested that the papers were in good order and he was not to know that there was anything wrong. In fact, that made him a victim too, he claimed.

Yes, he was right, we had both been duped. He wanted to know from me what had happened before and I wanted to know from him what had happened after. More importantly we both wanted to know what would happen next. We sympathised with each other and decided to work together in our common quest for more information. I was delighted to find him cooperative and taking the matter seriously. We went to the police together that afternoon to find out where we both stood.

I had learned by now that when you make an unusual request of a police officer, and you are being a bit of nuisance, it pays to be patient. Both George and I had to tell our stories in full and they typed it all up, letter by letter. It took over six pages and more than two hours. The one thing that was clear was that there was nothing that could be done today or tomorrow or in the weeks to come. '*This is a case that will have to go before a judge,*' the officer explained '*and a decision will need to be made as to whom this vehicle now really belongs: George, Vittorio the Italian man, or the Belgian man.*'

'But, officer,' I ventured politely, *'I have here the original invoice of the purchase of this car, in my name, plus a passport identifying me clearly as that very same person.'*

'That is just the problem,' he pointed out, *'So did the man who sold the car to George. His name was the same as yours and he too had a passport to prove it.'*

He was right of course. Yet, the fact that that man was now in prison in Marseille and that I very nearly visited him last week was completely lost on the patient Libyan police officer. There was no more to say. He told me that everything possible would be done to make matters right and that the court would inform me of the outcome of the case. He smiled politely as he ushered us out, obviously pleased with himself for having provided excellent service.

George and I went to have dinner together. We certainly had something in common. *'Partners in victim'*, both conned by the same man around the same car, probably equally naïve. I liked George – his fairness, objectivity and good grace in the face of an embarrassing situation made him one of the more mature people I had met in the Middle East. He did not try to brush me away as a foreign nuisance and did everything he could to be helpful. By then he could afford to relax. He knew he couldn't be touched legally, as he had done nothing wrong, the officer virtually telling him so. What's more, he had lost nothing and had possibly made a handsome profit on the deal. George quietly sat back, probably smiling inside himself, waiting for me to go away, knowing he would be safe. He wished me a good trip back and I thanked him for his help. I had been extraordinarily lucky to find the car and there was now some hope that it, or its value, could possibly be returned to me. My trip had not been wasted and I felt positive about the matter. On the way back, I stopped over at the Belgian consulate in Tripoli and the *Charge d'affaire* promised that he would keep an eye out for the case. The boat back to Marseille was fully booked the following day so I flew instead.

Judge Veraille was on holiday but his assistant told me there was nothing we could do until the Appeal had been heard, which could be months he said. They would, however, let me know as soon as it was all over. The Belgian Consul in Marseille would also keep an eye out for the case there. My search had paid off and all systems were in place to take care of the matter. With the thief in prison in France, some of my belongings on the way and the car in Libya, probably to be returned to me later, there was nothing more I could do but go home and wait. I arrived back in Gent late-August. The last of my spare money had gone on the trip to Libya – I needed to get a job. I was still a Belgian citizen, so that was no problem. I started work the second week in September as the manager of a ladies hairdressing salon attached to a brand new shopping centre a little out of town.

Diary entry for October 2, 1967: another reminder of where my mind was going.

'I feel a great desire to write some sort of novel based on my experiences in life so far – I feel inspired by Simone de Beauvoir's book L'Invitee. *What a women, what intelligence and insight.'*

I note two weeks later that I actually bought a typewriter, so I would do it rather than talk about it, and reminded myself in January 1968 that:

'I want to start soon writing an essay based on the events of last year. I now have the time and the typewriter and no one to interfere so what is going to stop me.'

And here we are forty years later, nearly there!

I did not write that novel then but here is what I did for practice:

Clock ticking time
Time clicking tock
All's not well at nine
But don't knock
For I'll let you in, in time
Tick tock, time will rock
The boat that now seems fine
Murky waters hide the hidden rock
That will hole the boat before nine
High in the sky, the stork
Brings her gift, just in time
Out goes the old, in comes the new
No time for time, it's past nine

A small Belgian takes on a big task.

After crossing Siberia from East to West we arrive in Moscow just in time for the 1st of May parade, 1966.

Some of my Papuan friends,
Papua New Guinea, 1965.

Life at Liffey by Rafael Saldaña

Born in Spain, Rafael lived in Liffey, Tasmania. His vibrant and intricately detailed paintings gained him an international reputation.

I met Sylvia in Port Moresby 1965 and we became friends. Still are today.

Climbing Ayers Rock (now Uluru), 1964.

Above: Diann and I in Dangar Street, Armidale, 1977.
Below: Diann in the kitchen.

Above: Joy and I cutting the wedding cake, 1982.
Below: the wedding party.

Above: Me in our home library, 1981.
Below: Johann and I napping, 1985.

Above: Me wearing a dhoti with a friend in Singapore, 1971.
Below: Celebrating Natasha's 20th birthday, 2008.

14.

The Merry Widow

Gent 1967

MY life had changed considerably since I was an apprentice hairdresser here in Gent. I had gained a great deal of professional experience, vastly improved my self-confidence and I now had something to talk about with clients. I even had some opinions of my own. Work took on an entirely different dimension.

One regular client was the rather chatty wife of an American scientist working at the University of Gent, who appreciated being able to chat in English with her hairdresser, telling me all the intimate tales of her family. She found Belgium 'interestingly quaint'. Later she confessed that while many people had been friendly and helpful, some had been openly anti-American. By then I thought of myself more as a world citizen than a Belgian and was beginning to see national pride as narrow-minded tribalism, the same sort that has been dividing Belgium itself for years.

Another regular client was a very sensitive young woman

called Caroline, who confided in me on the eve of her wedding that she did not love the man she was about to marry and would rather elope with me to Australia. We had been practising her recently acquired English, which gave us some privacy in the salon, and we had become friendly, maybe somewhat flirtatious. I was intrigued as to why an intelligent woman would go ahead and marry a man she did not love. She was beautiful and sophisticated and could have had any man she liked.

In my diary I noted:

'She is very inspiring, exciting and sexy – she's intelligent (a teacher at a special school) and asks subtle questions. I will ask her out for dinner to establish a solid friendship. Imagining if instead of playing cards at home I could spend time with her instead. But there is a red light flashing telling me to be careful. There is so much to learn about these things.'

Some time later I made what at the time seemed a discovery:

'I think I am more attracted to intelligent women than any other type. Is this because I like to think of myself as intelligent – but am I really? – Annie, Sylvia, Emma, Caroline – they are all so intelligent and sexy at the same time – is it because they are intelligent that I find them sexy or are they sexy and I see them as intelligent so they are more acceptable to me – I don't think so – I don't know – I want to get to the bottom of this.'

I tried to persuade her, gently of course, that it was still possible to pull out, but she said it wasn't. I asked her why but she wouldn't tell me. I wondered if she knew the reason why she could not get out of this marriage or was it that familial and social expectations were so strong that she could not possibly go against them. It seems that the bars of the prisons which hold us captive are often abstract and non-material, but nonetheless, at times, are impossible to bend or break.

She was interested in art and literature and when I mentioned that I did some writing myself, she asked if she could read some of it. I brought her, among other things, a poem about freedom in an effort to persuade her not to tie herself to a situation in which she would feel trapped. In reply, she wrote a number of short poems to me, screaming with pathos, pain and hopelessness. I cringed reading them and felt sad and sorry for her. One of them said:

I've been away to meet nature
But I saw bullets holding my world
I heard the bomb searching my heart
I thought the pain would never stop

I've been away to meet countries
But I saw a president, he was shot
I heard the hollow whisper of hatred
I thought violence had won on life

I've been away for a long time
I saw the redly burning of jail
I felt the rain crushing my pain
I thought my wounds would never heal

I simply didn't know how to handle this. Then memories of Emma came to my mind, stuck with a man she could not get away from. I was puzzled. What is it about some men that some women cannot leave them? So much I still did not understand. Learning about people is a welcome side effect of being a ladies hairdresser but it often raised more questions than answers.

I had again two staff working for me and they too were a challenge. They were slow, not great with people and not the type of friends I wanted. Fortunately I was aware enough to write:

'I have to get a grip on myself in dealing with the staff and make

sure I don't get grumpy with them – I don't want to spoil my own mood. I must talk to them but not sure what to say, how to put it without creating the situation more tense as it already is. I need to find a way to improve things.'

The following week I note that I started to read a book by Jung.

The most spectacular professional 'side effect' I have ever 'endured' was my encounter with a beautiful young woman about my own age. She was petite and charming and looked very much like the actress Jeanne Seberg. She had come a few times to have her hair cut very short and bleached blond, just like the famous actress she resembled. She had an infectious, friendly smile and sparkling eyes that always made her look impishly happy. She was chatty and funny and there was an easy banter between us.

Her name was also Caroline, although she preferred to be called Carol. In my diary I referred to her as CII, CI being the other Caroline who had since gone to live in Brussels with the newly acquired husband she hadn't wanted.

CII brought the best out in me, both professionally and personally. She often came late in the day or just before closing time, maybe deliberately, so we would be the only people in the salon. I was very happy to stay back just to be with her. I had found her incredibly attractive and very, very sexy. At one time she did not come for a few weeks. Then late one afternoon she turned up, dressed in black. When everybody else had gone she told me that her husband had died the week before. I didn't know she was married so it was a double shock to me. By the time her hair was done, it was nearly seven at night and she asked what I was doing for dinner. She knew I lived by myself in a room above a pub and that I was as free as a bird. So, after she had gone home to change into something less sombre, we went out to dinner together. As she relaxed over a couple of aperitifs, she told me her story.

She had a daughter by a man she loved but who was married

to another woman at the time. He left his wife soon after and came to live with her and together they raised their daughter, who was now about eight. They ran a small intimate little bar along the highway out of town. Then, their 'fairy-tale' life (as she called it) suddenly came to a dramatic end when he was diagnosed with advanced stomach cancer and was given two or three months to live. He had insisted on marrying her during the last week of his life when he knew he would die so she could inherit his wealth and properties. Now he had died and she missed him terribly and had no one she could talk to. All his family hated her for having taken him away from his first wife and her family had forsaken her many years ago for being an unwed mother and living in 'sin'. All she had left now was her eight-year-old daughter and a business she no longer wanted. After a long night of outpouring, Carol took me home to my room in her silver BMW and gave me a goodbye kiss in gratitude for my listening.

My initial sadness had turned to compassion and I now felt good that I had been able to provide a small amount of consolation for her. In hindsight, this was probably the first time I was consciously helping a person in what I would now call 'compassionate counselling'.

Two days later she invited me out again. She took me to a discrete little rustic chalet in the countryside were we dined on '*duck a l'orange*' and drank a lot of French champagne, literally drowning her sorrow. I amused her with some of my travel adventures and we moved closer and closer to each other (both emotionally and physically) as dinner progressed. It was no surprise when Carol suggested we should stay there for the night, using the excuse of having had too much to drink. I agreed and did not care if she had planned it that way all along or not. The expensively decorated room had a huge erotic painting above the enormous double bed, unnecessarily suggesting what we could do there. My compassion led to passion, providing me with the most exquisite sensual experience in my life so far. It was pure bliss. My diary reminds me in underlined red letters that '*CII is a delicious lover – the best! She is passionate but also delicate and sensitive. She is absolutely fantastic. Her gentle smile has rubbed off on me and I can't get it off – good.*'

She was also a grateful and very appreciative companion. Over the next few months, we feasted on each other's company once a week on average. We danced a lot, ate at fabulous restaurants, went to exclusive clubs and shared many very exquisite nights. She recovered her former happy self and the sparkle returned to her eyes. When you are unattached, free from repressive religion and willing to give more than take, anything is possible. Apart from my sharing intimate support with Sylvia in Lebanon, I had never until then considered, let alone experienced, the healing power of physical lovemaking. I would later on another continent explore this further.

I had decided to go back to Australia some time before I met CII. Not going to Australia was an option, but I did not envisage a long-term relationship with CII. She did not want a permanent relationship either and certainly, like me, did not want to get married since she had not even felt the need to marry the father of her child until he insisted before dying. When our passion ran its natural course and as my departure date loomed, we celebrated what we had enjoyed and walked away from each other, not with a heavy heart, but feeling joyous, fulfilled and open to the rest of our lives.

After an account of this beautiful adventure in my diary I concluded:

'What we've had was glorious, just wonderful. I shouldn't be sad not to have what I don't have the right to expect. I am glad that it ended in such a nice way, so smooth and the non-existence of emotional complications was great. I feel more than ever happy, free and an adult and closer to my ideal.'

I was also inspired to write a poem based on my experience with this very beautiful lady, who will always be part of my memory. It is remarkable to me, looking back at it now, how much this emotional experience embodied the philosophy of detachment I was later to adopt intellectually. It had been there, intuitively, all the time, long before I was able to articulate it. Detachment is not only a philosophical but also a psychological concept. Viktor Frankl in his famous book *Man's Search for Meaning* explains the Logotherapy technique called 'Paradoxical Intention' as follows: *'This procedure consists in a reversal of the patient's attitude, inasmuch as his fear is replaced by a paradoxical wish. By this treatment, the wind is taken out of the sails of the anxiety. Such a procedure, however, must make use of the specifically human capacity for self-detachment inherent in a sense of humour. This basic capacity to detach one from oneself… enables the patient to put himself at a distance from his own neurosis.'*

Excessive attachment to another person for the sake of one's own security, as so frequently happens in marriage situations, could well be regarded as a form of neurosis. People who are literally incapable of spending time by themselves could also be regarded as suffering a form of neurosis. Here then is the CII story, inspired by a beautiful angel I once knew.

The CII story

It all begun so unexpectedly
His sudden death from her
She was hurled into emptiness
Gnawed at by an uneven mixture
One of relief and maybe guilt
But which one was the stronger then?
Visibly, it was unbearable to her
Sleepless nights and sleepy days,
No one to talk to but herself.

I unlocked the heavy prison doors
That night I led her to the world
Hesitant only for appearance,
utterly unable to decline.
Life goes on for the surviving
Why should there be a gap?
Once changed to colours,
gone into the noise of night,
seated close nearby me,
she seemed so relieved.
There was warm laughter
and unselfish gentleness.
We drank and danced
till life came back to her.
To me it was as if, well,
as if a fairy dream had just begun.
Only dawn came and parted us.
Not painfully, smooth.
Promising eternity.
Provoked chance arranged the second night.
We ate and drank.
And danced ferociously.
But where does one go next?
Of course we knew it very well, but
did we want to take the risk?
One more fortifying drink.
'Is there anything you want to do?'
'Whatever you decide,' her whisper said.
Responsibility was mine now,
I was given 'carte blanche',
committed by the liberty of choice.
Am I a coward or a man?
She was in pain, in need,
I had the healing remedy required.
By giving I could take,

my generosity assumed a purpose.
Reimbursement assured to be complete.
So, I gave!
It takes little to create happiness.
It takes heaps to keep it.
Yet this was but a start.
And already passion was extreme.
The night flashed for only seconds.
A poetic morning sun was cruel.
Life seemed glorious now.
The future stripped of all importance.
We were not oblivious or in doubt of it:
This is not love but mutual desire.
A purely sensual affair!
Our rhythm often was too swift.
Our thirst almost exasperating.
But we had counter weights to that.
There was a relaxed familiarity.
Discretion and respect as well.
Then again her fresh, inspiring beauty,
her warm and ever ready friendliness
were crushing against weaker points.
It took persuasion and determination
to be close and yet detached.
To keep my thoughts at now.
Torn by pure desire
from an impossible love.
Tempted by speculation,
it took all my strength to shrug my shoulders,
to talk my sentiments away,
to kill attachment with my happiness.
Then at last reason ruled my feelings.
Once resigned to profiteer,
my generosity had no limits any more.
Nothing was to spoil my freedom.

Free to give and take to ones heart's desire.
Then conclusion was to come.
A pre-arranged decision took the blame.
I was to go away!
Perfect coinciding with reality.
Enthusiasm was decreasing.
Passion wearing off.
Why stretch a dream until it hurts?
There was nothing to regret.
It had been magnificent, superb,
meaningfully deep and yet compassionately detached.
Now it was clear cut, not abrupt,
no shreds or nasty feelings.
'Many thanks and wonderful good luck!'
was about our summing up.
I walked away on air.
Kissing every flower woman in the square.
Who could I make happy next?
I promise no pain or bloodshed.
No destructive emotional upsets.
I give what I can,
I gratefully receive.
As long as we are happy,
what is there to lose?

1968.

In January of 1968 I had a dream of going back to Australia. I wrote:

'It is more or less decided now that I'll go back to Australia as soon as possible. But where to go (Sydney or Brisbane?) what to do

when I get there? If it is to work as a hairdresser Sydney is better but do I want to still play this game – but what about financial security – it would be nice to be able forget all about that. There is a struggle between my need for security and my need for freedom. I definitely want to break with my past and only look forward and reorganise my life and my thoughts. The recent past has been good but there has to be a solution to the issue of a way of life that makes freedom and earning a livelihood not working against each other. I think that this could be easier in Australia.'

Metaphoric self-portrait 1961.

PART TWO

THE INWARD JOURNEY

'If one wants to find out what lies beyond the frontier of "self" the only way to do so is to go beyond it and see. On this journey one will do well to obtain both a map and a guide but he will have to travel every step by his own efforts.'

Robert de Ropp

'When the maturation cycles are not followed, adults will find it difficult to be responsible for themselves… and to create successful relationships. Your Inner Child will exhibit aspects of the [Archetypal] Wounded Child which will reflect that somewhere along the line you did not receive the nurturing necessary [and] you may well spend the early years of adulthood trying to heal and compensate for these deficiencies.'

Caroline Myss, Sacred Contracts

15.
Mother and son

REFLECTING on my relationship with Carol raised two questions in my mind. Had the forced letting go of my car and my possessions prepared me for letting go of the most exquisite friendship I had had in my life so far? And why had it taken so long to develop such a wonderful way of relating to women?

The nature of the relationships men have with women is influenced, so Freudian theory goes, by the relationship they have had with their mother. This may be true, but what type of maternal relationship leads to which type of relationship with women is what I wanted to know. Doing what has which effect? The idea that my relationship with CII (which was for me the most uncomplicated relationship up until then and to some extent since) was influenced by the nature of my relationship with my mother did not feel right to me. To start with, my mother was only there for the first six years of my life, and while that would be long enough to do a lot of damage, her complete absence thereafter would have had a severely obliterating effect on the previous impact. The fact that I hardly remembered anything of my early days was more of a concern. Had it been so bad that I needed to blot it out?

When in 1967 I lived in that room above the pub, it was a mere ten minutes walk from where my mother lived. She would have loved me to stay with her, but after so many years without parental restrictions, I could not possibly imagine staying with my mother and being happy there. I couldn't bring myself to enjoy her company. I felt that it would have been even more painful for her when the time came for me to leave to come back to Australia, which I knew I was going to do sooner or later.

So I often wondered why it was so difficult for me to be in her presence given she had never done anything deliberately wrong to me. She had merely made the mistake in thinking that I would be given back to her after she left my father.

I had read some Freud and was fascinated by all these ideas, but couldn't really make much sense of it all. Freud has been massively discredited in the last ten years, but back then, in the late sixties, he was still very much in vogue and I wanted some answers to my questions. I didn't get very far reading Freud, probably because I didn't at that time understand much of what he had to say. The impact of early upbringing is well understood in general terms but it is the specifics that are hard to get. Yet I wanted to know how to fix them in me. I had to wait until 1998 to find at least part of an answer, albeit in a most unexpected way. The method used though had some connection with early Freudian practices.

I first met Graham Moore in 1998 as a fellow student in a course in Counselling and Hypnotherapy, during which we became friends. We regularly helped each other out in various ways and occasionally did some business together as we were both in the Industrial Learning and Development field. Graham practised hypnotherapy professionally and became an occasional lecturer at the college where we had been students.

As the result of all this psychology study (and when looking over my life to write about it), two issues came to my mind pressing for clarification. One was the influence of the relationship I had with my mother on the relationships I had with women in general. While my relationship with Carol had been superb, others before and since have been considerably more complex. Reading Caroline Myss recently, a number of lightbulbs went flashing in my mind, particularly when reading the passage quoted at this part's heading.

The other issue was my need to find out to what extent my mother's treatment of me in the early years of my life influenced my own sexual maturity or lack thereof. While collecting old photos for a pictorial history of my life, I discovered several pictures taken of me around the age of four or five where I was dressed in what can only be described as a 'blouse', with my long blonde curly hair arranged as if I had been a girl. Almost always when showing these photos to people, they immediately comment, '*Noël, you look like a girl!*'. My curiosity was further stimulated when I came upon the intriguing case of David Reimer as fully described in John Colapinto's excellent book *As Nature Made Him: The Boy Who Was Raised As a Girl.*

David had suffered a catastrophic mishap during circumcision and doctors had recommended gender reassignment as a way of 'fixing him up'. The outcome was horrifically disastrous for the boy and was eventually reversed. I knew that nothing anywhere near as tragic as this had happened to me, but what I didn't know was what exactly had happened, as my memory of my early years was particularly vague and mostly blank. Regression under hypnotherapy, we had learned as part of our course, can recover lost memories. So, with the help of a trusted friend, under I went.

'Relax, take some deep breaths and completely let go. I will count to ten and by the time I get to ten you will be very relaxed. One, two, three… four… five…'

'When I count to three you will be twice as relaxed as you are now and feel yourself slightly drowsy. One, two and three…'

This was the first session with Graham – we were exploring events in my early childhood.

'When you are ready let's go somewhere to your early childhood, between about age two and four. Just let yourself be guided by your subconscious. Go anywhere you want, you will be safe there.'

I found myself as a three-year-old, under the dining table in the kitchen of my godmother's house. I was indeed feeling safe there. Then, my mother came into the room and a strange fear came over me. Was I afraid of my mother? I could not remember her ever hurting me physically, although she did speak harshly sometimes. I was running towards my godmother now and I felt safe in her arms. When my mother took me from my godmother, again this strange physical resistance appeared in my body. The same happened on two other encounters in the same session. This session left me intrigued and I wanted to pursue the matter further. The following week Graham and I continued the exploration.

'Now I want you to go back even further than we did last time. See if we can go all the way to when you where born. Is there any reason we should not go there?'

I gently shook my head, thinking this should be interesting. Contrary to popular belief, one is not asleep when under hypnosis, merely very relaxed.

'I want you to go to the time you were born and go to when you were delivered and took your first breath. Then just be there. It will be safe.'

I found myself in the arms of a woman dressed in a starched white uniform with a small cap on her head. I was wrapped in a soft white cloth and she was smiling at me.

'Look Mrs Odou, it's a boy! He's beautiful!'

She turned me, the baby, towards my mother so she could see me. Instead I saw her. Her face was sad and all screwed up and very slowly she turned the other way and pulled a sheet over her head. I had that strange feeling of fear again I had experienced in the earlier session. Being that little boy, but now in my adult body, enabled me, fully conscious this time, to feel as crushed and rejected as I must have felt then as a baby but without realising it. I could feel tears welling up in my eyes.

'*My mother is turning away from me*,' I whispered to Graham letting the tears roll freely now and I felt sad and afraid of what was going to happen to me, the baby.

'All right now, just relax. You, the adult, go there to that room and ask the nurse if you can hold the baby boy. She will let you hold the baby.'

The experience of holding myself as a baby, the opportunity of comforting myself at that early time of need, was an overwhelmingly moving and healing experience.

'Ask the nurse if the baby boy is ready to go home now. Take him to your present home and make him very comfortable. Give him what he needs and take good care of him. He will be safe there.'

Tears were streaming down my face by now. Graham gave me a tissue. I stayed with my baby self for a while and then came out of hypnosis.

I knew my mother already had two sons when I was born, but I had never known she had wanted to have a girl so badly as to reject another boy, at least in gesture, at the birth itself. Now, the question of how much she treated me as a girl, even though I was a boy, became more urgent.

Before the hypnotherapy experience it had often seemed

strange to me that I had very few memories of any experiences before the age of about four, when I started going to kindergarten. Did I suppress most of them and, if so, why? And why did I experience fear and sadness when going back to early childhood under hypnosis?

In the earlier session, when Graham had asked me to go to any early childhood scene, I went directly to my godmother's living room. My godmother was very fond of me and I do remember warm and nourishing times with her. She had no children of her own and had therefore all the time and inclination to lavish her maternal instinct on me. She and her husband lived next door to us. She was my mother's older sister. There were about ten children in my mother's family, mostly girls, and my mother was the youngest of the girls. My godmother had a soft, kind face with smiling eyes, and never raised her voice at me or anyone else. When I saw her twenty-five years later, she had hardly changed and treated me as kindly as she had when I was baby.

Developmental psychology tells us that treating a boy as a girl, and vice versa, can in some cases cause gender confusion. In some cases? Does this mean that one case of treating a boy like a girl may cause gender confusion but another case may not? And if so, what is the variable between the two? One of the most difficult questions for developmental psychology, indeed for all psychology, not to mention physics and philosophy, is: '*What exactly causes what?*' Does Heisenberg's 'indeterminate principle' really mean one cannot determine what causes what? If we knew precisely what to do to our kids to obtain specific results, parenting might not be so much guesswork. But parents do what they think is best, unfortunately, mainly influenced by what has been done to them by their parents.

On the other hand, the question for all adults is, '*Can we change the effect of what has been done to us?*'

Can I overcome the effects of my upbringing and choose the

sort of life I am going to lead? Can I alter my conditioning and re-condition myself with a program of my own choice?

As a parent and a growing person, I have struggled with all of these questions over the course of my life. That **we can** change or minimise our conditioning seems clear to me, not only from my experience, but also confirmed by neurological insights gained in the last twenty years. That we can retrace events to determine what caused what seems much less clear. I organised another session with Graham to focus on the gender question and to find out to what extent I had been treated like a girl.

'*Let's go to a time when you had a particularly enjoyable interaction with your mother.*' There were some vague memories but nothing very clear.

'*Now let's go to some occasion that was not so enjoyable for you.*' Immediately I became aware of my mother brushing my hair in an overly fussy manner and feeling irritated by it, wanting to make her stop. At the same time there was a suffocating sensation of being unable to say anything, let alone being able to tell her to stop fussing with my hair. Another scene flashed into consciousness where, to my painful annoyance, it was my clothes she fiddled with. One further session revealed that there was never any physical abuse of any sort and I was never, as far as we can tell, put into any skirts or dresses. It would seem then that my mother's treatment of me as a girl was relatively superficial and did not have disastrous consequences. What I am sure of, however, is that I suffered from gender confusion and ambivalent sexual identity, at least for some of my teenage years and early adulthood. That this was directly caused by her handling me in a fussy manner is another matter. I have at times in the course of my life been approached by gay people, and later in my fifties at least on two occasions was asked by counsellors whether I was gay. Maybe it is a standard question in today's society?

The question of maternal influence on relationships with

women is much more complex, but the hypnotherapy helped me gain at least one insight which had not occurred to me before. On the whole, I do not enjoy people, and more specifically women, fussing over my clothes, minor matters or me. As I did not always have the assertiveness to ask them to stop doing it, I can remember pretending to be tickled by the fussiness of a particular girlfriend as a way of avoiding it. I certainly did not see it as a major problem in my life and now that I am more assertive, as well as more tolerant, it is not an issue at all. Does it stem from having suffered excessive fussing in early childhood? Who knows? What I am also sure of is that I have changed, and changed in the direction I chose to change.

During my continuing explorations to understand my own behaviour I came upon Dr Havelock Ellis. Ellis lived in England around the turn of the century and died in 1935. He was a trained medical doctor, one of the first people to study sexuality as a discipline, devoting almost his entire life to it. Studying sexuality in those days by itself would have earned him a place in medical history, but it was some of his views, which are still controversial in some quarters today, that made him stand out during his lifetime. He caused quite a stir and is most remembered for his stand on the fact that homosexuals, or 'inverts' as he called them, are neither sick, diseased or criminal people as other theorists claimed in his day, and some still do today. He proposed that they are merely a 'congenital variation' but '*otherwise as variable in personality as normal men*'. Whatever theory of the origin of homosexuality is in favour today, we have certainly come a long way towards acceptance of it, although some may well claim we still have a long way to go.

The other issue Ellis stirred up controversy over was masturbation. Today it is still one of the big taboos in most societies. He declared masturbating 'healthy' and publicly declared he practised it regularly himself. That it is widely practised, if not then but certainly today, is no secret. Kinsey and *The Hite Report on Male Sexuality* gave the impression that nearly all men masturbate. A popular Australian television program survey recently confirmed that nearly half of both the men and women surveyed admitted masturbating at least 'occasionally' and almost one in five 'regularly'. That there is still stigma attached to it is equally clear as we only ever talk about it, even among men, in derogatory tones. I am reminded here of Bill Bryson's matter of fact observation in his 1991 book *Neither Here Nor There: Travels in Europe*. After seeing the vast number of prostitutes in the Amsterdam red light district, he pondered why so many people '*require this sort of assistance just to ejaculate. What happened to personal initiative?*'. (I do not know if the recent cleaning up of that district in Amsterdam is the result of less demand or the return to more resistance against it.)

Imagine the weight that would have been lifted from the shoulders of all of us Catholic boarding school boys if Ellis had been in charge? If our objective is helping children to become balanced human beings, the last thing we should do is to impose sexual repression upon them with all its ugly consequences. The excessive sexualisation of the public domain is of course equally undesirable. The prevailing prejudice against masturbation has also been shown to inhibit the sexual expectations men have of women. As psychiatrist Dr Julian Hafner has pointed out: '*Only if they [men] change their reluctance or refusal to masturbate can they become more flexible about their sexual expectation of women. Accepting masturbation as a pleasurable and acceptable alternative to sexual intercourse is profoundly liberating for many men. But such is the depth of male prejudice against masturbating that a majority of men are unable to accept it as a legitimate option. In such circumstances, pursuit of regular intercourse often remains a central, compulsive aspect of a man's life.*'

An article headed: '*Doing your prostate a favour*' in the Melbourne *Age* July 2003 quotes the head of cancer epidemiology at the Cancer Council of Victoria as not only confirming that '*masturbation is a quite normal human activity*', but that it may also be of benefit to the development and maintenance of a healthy prostate gland. Thomas Laqueur, a history professor at the University of California and author of *Solitary Sex: A Cultural History of Masturbation,* explains that the anti-mastubationists were driven by the idea that '*the activity encourages irresponsible and uncontrollable fantasy, cannot be controlled in any way and makes its practitioners dangerously self-sufficient.*' Well, we can't have people being uncontrollably self-sufficient, now can we?

My own early personal development in this area had been extremely painful and has caused mental anxiety for years. I had by now learned some things about sexuality and was beginning to be able to distinguish mere instinctive sexual lust from being 'in love' without denying either. I knew now that what I had felt for Sylvia was qualitatively enormously different from what had attracted me to Emma and CII. There was no doubt an element of friendship and companionship involved in all these relationships, but the proportions were vastly different. My education generally had been rather silent about sex education and my own experience of growing up had taught me practically nothing of value. I turned once again to Freud, who was regarded as the 'expert' on the topic of sex, but rather than find useful answers there, I was referred to Jung who gave me answers to questions I had not yet asked. As a result of all that, I developed a fascination with therapy and the more complex issues of the mind and human personality.

My attention was caught a couple of years ago, while reading Robin Robertson's *Introducing Jungian Psychology*, by an example he gives of the influence of a mother on her daughter. In the context of explaining the 'mother' archetype he writes, '*If the relationship with her mother has been healthy, she will be able to draw comfort and nourishment when needed from her inner mother. If her relationship with her mother has been unhealthy, she is likely to have difficulty trusting anyone, because she will see any nurturing situation through the lens of her own sad experiences.*' The question is, have I been seeing my relationships with women through the lens of my less than fully nourishing experience with my mother, and, therefore, not allowing myself to trust them as much as I might have otherwise? My intuitive insight tells me that the impact on my early childhood of my parents' marriage break-up and my subsequent incarceration into that dreadful boarding school were the most atrocious events that I have survived. They not only had an impact on my relationships with women, but also, and inevitably, on my feelings about marriage as an institution.

June 1948: The official family studio photo of Andre's 'confirmation'. I wonder if in those days it was the fashion for men to look stern (or were they not feeling too happy about something?) and women to smile, in which case, why am I smiling? Because I am wearing the same blouse as my mother, I guess? Freddy (right) is probably wondering why they didn't take a photo like this for his confirmation.

Me shy? Never!
I'm just embarrassed
about those clothes.

I know these sorts of pants were fashionable in the Spanish court in the 1500s, but what are they doing on me? Mum, I want you to get them off me now!

Now that is a more suitable outfit for a boy! I'm happy now!

16.

Going 'home'

Belgium–Sydney 1967–1968

My interest in the saga of the stolen car had been declining and was now also overshadowed by my blissful relationship with CII, until one day a small parcel arrived from France addressed to me at my brother's house.

It contained about five of my traveller's cheques, unused by our friend '*Gunther*', together with some other personal effects. Some items did not actually belong to me and I assumed they had been found in his possession, but were stolen from someone else. It made little difference. By now I had re-established myself both materially and psychologically and the return of some everyday items was a mere reminder that they had existed in the past, like finding a pair of socks you haven't seen for a year in the bottom of the drawer – '*Ah, that's where they were.*'

The parcel did, however, rekindle my curiosity as to what had happened to Sylvia in Marseille and since I was unable to ask Sylvia herself, as I didn't know where she was, I thought I would ask '*Gunther*'. I knew where he was, so I wrote him a letter, asking all the questions I would have asked if I had been able to see him in prison. Surprisingly, he answered my letter but avoided most of my questions. More surprising still was that he signed his letter to me using my own name. I speculated that he was still in appeal against his conviction and remained in his 'role' of being 'me'. The experience of receiving a letter from 'me' was both comical and baffling. I didn't feel this was going to get me anywhere so I didn't reply to his request for correspondence.

For a short time, letters kept coming from him trying to convince me that he had seen the 'light', had been converted to Catholicism and could now see the wrongness of his ways. He explained how his remorse had set him 'free', even though he was still in prison. It sounded good, but I must have lost some of my naivety by then because I found it impossible to believe him. If he was hoping to elicit sympathy from me on the grounds of his religious conversion, he certainly picked the wrong religion. In one letter he had the gall to ask me for some money because he needed to settle some debts he had incurred. All the letters continued to be signed with my name. I never bothered to reply.

These letters also brought the question of the settlement of the ownership of the car to the fore. The Belgian Consul in Tripoli had promised to keep an eye on the case, so he was the logical person to ask for progress. After three weeks with no reply I wrote again. It took another two months and another two reminders eventually I was informed that the case had finally appeared in court and been thrown out for lack of sufficient evidence and representation from my side. It had therefore been determined that the vehicle should remain the property of Vittorio, the man who had legally bought it from George. It sounded more like '*possession being nine tenths of the law*' and '*seeing that you are not here we'll do what we like*'.

The outcome, while somewhat disappointing to me, was really no surprise. By now I was no longer interested in the car itself and most of the attachment to any particular belongings I had lost had faded. The main benefits of 'letting go', as the essence of what was to be learned here, was becoming clearer to me over that period and the court case merely brought a kind of closure to the outer form of the lesson. Was I now ready to learn the inner form of that lesson? Time would tell. The whole saga could have been closed if it hadn't been for the fact that I still did not know what had happened to Sylvia in Marseille. It strengthened my resolve to go back to Australia and one day find out.

Looking after a small salon, a few staff and some interesting clients kept me sufficiently busy to make the time go by while saving up for the return journey to Australia.

In December 1967 I turned twenty-five. I did some reflecting on my life so far. I had been alive for a quarter of a century and I was asking myself what I had learned.

On January 3, 1968 I wrote:

'1967: one of the most memorable years so far. Buying a new car; long travel with a female companion; a break-through in education on sexuality; reconnecting with Sylvia – until Syria. And then it all changed. Dealing with Emma was hard. Riding in the RR for 16 days, wow. Then the miracle in Benghazi. This job here feels so much easier now – it's fun to deal with all these people. And then CII wow!! I feel more comfortable with myself than ever before. What a big year of growing! What next? Part-time work? Change to more useful work? I really hope so.'

That year I was reading *La Batarde* by Violette Leduc, another member of the Existentialist circle and a close friend of Jean Genet. Her book is a powerfully honest autobiographical account of her struggle to overcome a terrible childhood and a depressive adult life. In the preface, Simone De Beauvoir, who I admired enormously for her intelligence, (another intelligent women) wrote in the preface that: '*It demonstrates with exceptional clarity that a life is the reworking of a destiny by a freedom.*' My childhood had been nowhere as repressive as Violette's and it gave me courage that I, too, could use my freedom to 'rework' my life. The themes of 'freedom from organised religion' and 'how to live' would become major issues in my later life, but it is interesting to see how they, already then, were shining through, and inspired me to write about them, however clumsily. It was a few days after my birthday I wrote what I came to call *The Freedom Poem*.

The Day I Was Born

On the day I was born, twenty-five years later,
A free girl told me she was imprisoned.
A prisoner wrote to me that he had found freedom.

On the day I was born, twenty-five years later,
I realised more than ever
What absolute freedom means to me,
What it is to be free yet in prison
What it is to be imprisoned yet free.

It took the day I was born, but twenty-five years later,
To realise '*I am Free!*'
To decide to enjoy it to its full extent.
Even then there will be too many limits.

It was the day I was born, only twenty-five years later,
I decided that I would go one day,
Just be free and make sure I am.

Then try to break those chains, so hard,
That bound the free ones to themselves
Try to encourage those whose cage is already open
To step outside and be free, like me.

(Dated: *Gent, 29-12-67*)

It provides me an enormous amount of satisfaction to see that finally part of what I do for a living in the last ten years or so, is to help people *rework* their life and conditioning so they too can be free. The dream came true, eventually.

When I had saved up enough to travel to Australia, I applied for a re-entry permit and said goodbye to my brothers and my mother. I didn't bother with my father. His health had deteriorated and apparently he did not recognise people now. I felt neither the need to see him nor any anger or resentment towards him.

Arriving back in Sydney in early August 1968 felt more like coming 'home' than my return to Belgium after my Trans-Siberian journey. On the plane I had been reading Somerset Maughan's *The Razor's Edge*, a tale about a man seeking answers to life's questions in the East, but feeling disappointed on returning to his home country. I don't know what made me choose it. I had never heard of Maughan, but the story made me feel there was some parallel here with my life. I too had been travelling and now I was beginning to search for the real answers and coming back home as well. At that time I didn't know that this story would ring more bells still a few years later.

With my rapidly growing thirst for knowledge driving me on, I enrolled myself in a certificate course in English, even before finding a job. I had managed with 'picked-up' conversational

English, but I knew that if I was going to do any type of serious study or writing I had to improve my English and my literacy skills. While my self-image of 'not being intelligent enough' had faded, it was still nagging me.

About two weeks after arriving back, when looking for a job in the city, I bumped into Annie. She was very surprised to see me. I, on the other hand, had semi-consciously been looking for her. It was nearly five years since Annie and I had first met and we had much to tell each other. We took a cab to her parents' place, where she was now living, and talked for hours.

She had been one of the manicurists at the salon in Double Bay where I worked when I first arrived in Sydney in 1963 and had completely bowled me over. She had the charm and seductive looks of Marilyn Monroe, with an Australian flavour. She would often start doing the clients' nails while we hairdressers were still putting hair rollers in their hair before moving to the dryers. My distraction by her proximity must have been obvious to at least some of my clients. Unfortunately my 'foreignness' and inability at the time to clearly express myself in sufficiently subtle and romantic terms was a barrier to taking it any further. She also had a boyfriend, which didn't help of course. We did become close though, but not close enough.

At one time Annie was studying French and she came to me for help with her translations. I wondered if she was being nice to me only so that I would continue to help her. After my return from my Central Australian trip she actually told me she had missed me while I was away. I thought she was teasing me. A few days later we both stayed back after work for me to do her hair. She became very friendly, even flirty, and our closeness took a big step forward. The kiss she gave me to thank me for the nice hairstyle I had just done for her was very sweet. Ten minutes later her boyfriend picked her up to take her home. The phrase 'mixed emotions' describes well what I felt at the time. A few days later she announced she was getting married to an Austrian man. That certainly helped me get over it.

At that time, I had not yet had a successful relationship with a girl and getting closer to Annie made me reflect already then on my attitude towards relationships with women generally. In an extraordinarily succinct phrase, I summed up my feelings at the end of this whole episode shortly before leaving for New Guinea, by writing in my diary:

'I accept women but refuse to need one.'

Today, I would call this chauvinistic. Then, I think I was merely grappling with independence.

And now, five years later, here we were enthusiastically talking to each other over a cup of tea.

She had married the Austrian man and a few years later the company he worked for had sent him to work in Vienna. By then they had a two-year-old son and the marriage started going from bad to worse. Things became so intolerable to her that she made a dramatic 'escape' and came back to Australia with her son. She was now separated and, guess what, looking for a new husband. I knew that it wasn't going to be me as I had drifted away from the direction she was going.

'Great to see Annie. However friendship and good fellowship is more important to me than being married, just remember it!'

I did hope of course that I might be able to help her in the way I had been to CII, so I was very glad to see her. We saw each other on an irregular basis. I would sometimes baby-sit her son while she was going out with a prospective husband.

Annie's failed marriage gave me welcome reinforcement for my thinking that marriage can do a lot of damage to a person. Of course, it is easy to collect evidence for one's point of view when, as is the case with marriage, there are plenty of examples of failed ones as well as good ones. Hers had been a particularly bad one and I felt ready to do some healing again, as I had with my Belgian 'Merry Widow'. We became close, a few times very close, and at times sentimentality got the better of both of us. One night we actually went 'all the way' and it was absolutely wonderful. After five years, one of my dreams had come true – in bed with Marilyn Monroe! Deep down we knew, of course, that it would never work in the long run but for the 'here and now' at that time it was glorious and healing for both of us.

'I'm having my head in the clouds over Annie, but at least a few toes still on the ground. We certainly do like each other passionately but also realistically. I'll make the best of it, as with CII. Now I can be realistic and romantic at the same time and I will not need to suffer over her as I did before. I decided I will not try to persuade her to move in with me just yet in case it doesn't work out – just wait and see.'

Unfortunately, it seems that in most cases when relationships based on friendship assume a sexual dimension, attachments develop. One wants it again and the future keeps poking its head in. One night when we were having dinner at her place while her parents were out, we had a long discussion about what could possibly lie in the future for us. It's what people need to do, plan for the future, especially when you have a son, are single and are in need of regular legitimate intimacy. When Annie looked at my situation she saw a nice man she liked, but who was not able to provide her with a regular income and was, in fact, thinking of working only part-time. She was being remarkably perceptive and honest when she said that she really liked me a lot but that it wouldn't work out between us because she would want much more than I was able or willing to give. I knew she was talking from a material point of view and she was absolutely right. I agreed with her. My view was that this should not stop us from being friends. From her point of view, our relationship would probably be an interference to her finding a 'real man' with a 'real income' to provide 'real security' for her son. Again I could see her viewpoint and we left it at that. We kept in touch but agreed to abstain from pursuing anything.

I was beginning to learn at last that it is important to accept and recognise our emotions, including our sex drive, but that they need not rule, let alone ruin, our life nor the life of another person. The more we accepted that we were not to be exclusively for each other, the more our friendship took on meaning for me.

A diary entry of the time reminded me of my increasing awareness of my own emotional balance:

'How happily I spent today reading. I sometimes hope for a visit from Annie, but in the deep of my mind I also don't. I didn't want to be disturbed in my pleasure. I thought if Annie came I would be delighted, but I am also happy that she didn't. I like to have her, yet I don't miss her if I don't. Could you hope for a more satisfactory state of mind?'

This describes a state of mind I still perceive today – now I call it 'non-attachment'.

I have often seen her in my mind's eye and fondly recall the warm friendship we had. I don't know where Annie is now, she's another angel flown away. I was getting good now at letting them go, into the freedom they so rightly deserve but often give away in return for illusory security.

In a long rambling diary entry around that time I observed that:

'With Emma long ago disappeared, and now that Sylvia is gone out of the picture because we couldn't make it together, and now I can't even find her, and now that Annie is gone because I can't provide for

her either, I am left without close female friendship. This gives me more freedom and time to do the things I want to do like study and write and paint and read and go to concerts. At the same time I may well find a companion who does understand me and who is not an interruption to my life but a complement to it.'

Indeed, the ideal companion – one who is a 'complement' and not an interruption to one's life! Consciously or not, I was keeping an eye out for this ideal. Later I learned that Jung called it 'projection'.

Ironically, my later study in Esoteric Astrology would reveal that relationships are not what I am good at. At one level I would have to say that this was true then, and to some extent still is. But on another level I have had some very satisfying relationships. The fact that they didn't last is only negative if you believe, like the pro-marriage advocates, that special relationships should last forever. Sequential monogamy, it seems to me, is far more suitable to the human creature than the unreasonable expectation of compulsory marriage because of some weird idea that it is made in heaven. From an evolutionary point of view it makes a lot of sense for the male of the species to generate offspring with as many females as possible, to diversify the gene pool and thereby create better chances of survival. Monogamy, on the other hand, attempts to secure survival of individual offspring and makes sure that the male contributes to the upbringing of his offspring.

'The survival of the species and the survival of the individual are sometimes at odds with each other, but that is a hard message to deliver to young adults powered by a strong sex drive, reinforced by commercially promoted promiscuity and egocentricity.'

It seems from this journal entry in 1969 that I was beginning to dig deep into these questions but not always coming up with answers. Little did I know what was yet to come.

I found a job in a Rose Bay salon owned by a young woman who now wanted to attend to her children rather than work. I was the only male among seven girl employees and I soon settled in. I knew that I would change careers sooner or later, but I had as yet no idea when and to what. In the meantime, hairdressing was easy and would in fact provide me not only with a livelihood, but also with worthwhile contacts and valuable information, as indeed it had done so many times in the past. Not long after, I found a nice flat in a back street of Kings Cross just around the corner from the famous Wayside Chapel where later I would go to see Krishnamurti films organised by a friend of Sylvia's.

I also reconnected with my friends Rafael and Maria Saldaña who were now living in one of the more bohemian suburbs of Sydney. They were thinking of going to live in Tasmania. Rafael was hesitant about it and we often discussed the balance of the potential advantages and disadvantages. There were times I was tempted to go with them and saw it as perhaps my chance to break away from the traditional way of living which was increasingly clashing with what I was beginning to understand about life. Rafael and I both suffered from lack of a creative outlet, although he was painting a lot already then. The problem of finding a balance between the need to give expression to one's creativity on the one hand and the need to earn a living on the other is an old one, and I was struggling with it. I had yet to find a solution to this issue. While there is certainly a good amount of creativity possible in hairdressing, it was no longer meeting my creative needs, if in fact it ever did. The obvious solution is to earn a living doing something which has both personal and career value and at the same time allows for creativity. It is simple when you see it, but I did not know how to put it into practice then.

'Rafael is the most intelligent and wonderful man I ever met. I want to do more constructive things than playing chess or scrabble. Something has to change – I want to be more complete. I feel increasingly confident that I will write – and I will achieve something, I am sure of that now. But I must study first to obtain a general knowledge before attempting to write, it is absolutely essential that I know what I am talking about.'

My need to study and learn was further underscored by the fact that I bought myself a full set of Encyclopaedia Britannica, including the bookcase, and a set of books called *Perspectives*, summing up the latest ideas in various fields of study. It was some of the most stimulating reading I had ever done so far. I was going to the free Sunday afternoon concerts at the Sydney Town Hall, developing a taste for classical music and enjoying the atmosphere. I was feeling good about having come back to Australia. I could sense a promise in the air for something new to happen, but my patience was being challenged. I knew neither what it was nor where it was going to come from, but I knew it was on the way.

It is often said we learn from experience. This is true only if we reflect on that experience and understand what it is teaching us. A diary is a wonderful aid in reflecting on experiences, if not at the time, then certainly later when you can see things with the wisdom of hindsight and, hopefully, some more maturity.

Twenty-five years is a long time to look at everything in one go, but by then, making a specific effort to do so, I was beginning to see some patterns. I was beginning to discover layers of existence I had not known before. I was experiencing states of consciousness and deep emotions I had never felt before.

Humility and detachment continued to be the two guiding principles for my self-development. My natural low self-esteem and my 'wounded child' archetypical background predisposed me well to humility. 'Detachment' and 'letting go' are harder nuts to crack, and while I had had plenty of opportunity to practise them by then, I was still working hard at it but with only a vague sense of direction.

Return to Sydney, Australia on the 19th August 1968.
Where I got a job at Fontanella's in Rose Bay.

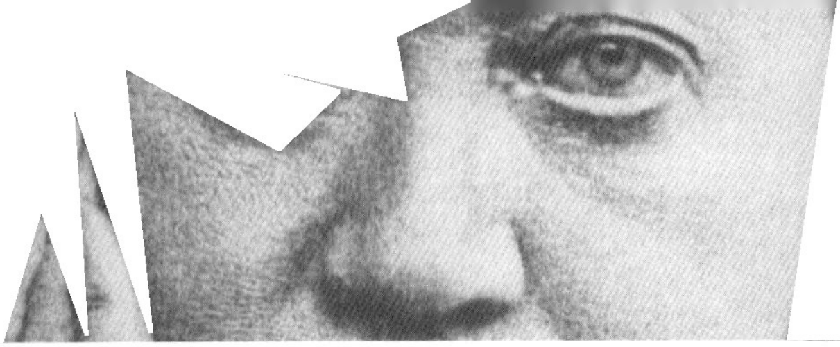

17.

Finding purpose

Sydney 1969

RECONNECTING with Annie was delightful and helped me sort out many things about myself. It also reminded me of my relationship with Sylvia, which also needed sorting out, but of course I had to find her first. I hoped that my chance encounters might continue and that I would bump into Sylvia in the same way that I had met Annie again.

Encountering interesting people is one of the advantages of being a ladies hairdresser as I already pointed out, and it has certainly been true for me. In the Rose Bay salon, one of my clients was Muriel Cohen, a professional pianist studying a work by the French composer and ornithologist Olivier Messiaen called *The Catalogue of the Birds*. She asked me if I could translate some of the score notes for her as they were all in French. I was happy to oblige and was later invited to attend her recording of the work, an exciting experience for me since I was continuing to discover and explore classical music.

Messiaen and his style of music were new to me. The following year I attended a performance of *Messiaen's Vingt regards sur l'Enfant-Jesus*, performed by the prodigious British pianist John Ogdon, a musical meditation on the Mystery of the Nativity of Christ, written at the time of the liberation of Paris in 1945. Ogdon is said to have preferred to tackle large scores and certainly had his hands full with this work, which lasted over two hours. I made a note in my diary at the time wondering whether the fact that my concentration did not waiver for the entire work was due to its mystical power of drawing attention or to the fact that I had recently started to meditate.

Another one of my clients who contributed to my personal development was Mrs Stranner. She was a soft-spoken, very friendly lady in her fifties. Though she was always reading books, she never failed to ask about my personal life and how things were going with me. She had a warm smile and deep blue eyes. One day at the salon she was reading *The Power of the Subconscious Mind* by Paul Brunton. She said it was a very interesting book and thought I would like it. She gave me the address where I could get it. It was the Adyar Bookshop in the city.

I had been a keen reader of interesting books, but I had never been in a bookshop like the Adyar. It was like walking into a different world. No, not 'like' – it was a different world. Every shelf had books on it about topics and people I had never heard of before. It had sections labelled with words whose meaning I didn't comprehend. I discovered that it was run by the Theosophical Society, an organisation I had never heard of before. In the note in my diary for that day, I called it the 'theological society' – I hadn't even read the word properly let alone understood what it meant. The shop was full of people browsing intently and there were rooms off the bookshop where people were gathering for, at least to me, some unknown purpose. When the shop closed, I left with my book and several leaflets about the Society, including an application form for membership as there seemed to be an apparent inevitability that I would join.

On the bus home, one of the leaflets told me that the three objectives of this society were, first: *to form a nucleus of the universal brotherhood of humanity without distinction of race, creed, sex, caste or colour; second: to encourage the study of comparative religion, philosophy and science; and finally: to investigate unexplained laws of nature and the powers latent in the human being.* I could understand what that meant, even though I did not know the implications of these objectives, and they sounded eminently worthwhile to me. I felt strongly that this was just the sort of 'club' for me. My thirst for knowledge seemed to have found a generous fountain from which to drink copiously.

I applied for membership before investigating any further. There is a probationary period during which you go to introductory sessions and I eagerly read books about Theosophy in the meantime. I think it would be no exaggeration to say that my relationship with the TS, as we affectionately called the 'Theosophical Society', was love at first sight. Not only did I fall in love with it, it also nurtured me like no mother ever had. It quenched my thirst for knowledge and fed my hunger for wisdom. The intensity of its influence on me, at least in those early days, is well illustrated by my diary entry for 10 May 1969:

'Congratulations on becoming a full member of the Theosophical Society! It is astonishingly incredible, to say the least, the effect my contact with Theosophy has had on my life... The importance of it is almost undiscribable... I feel a strong desire to abandon the entire of my worldly possessions and go to India or Japan to become a monk... I feel like a child who has found a new toy. I am looking forward very much to get to know much more about Theosophy and I feel strongly I want to work and do something constructive in the world. I shall strive not to judge people by what they have but by what they are and even more so by what they do and why they do it.'

I did go to India two years later, something most 'seekers' did in those days, but I didn't become a monk. My 'd-grade' Catholic upbringing had effectively inoculated me against it.

Around that time I contracted an inflammation of the iris in one of my eyes. I had to put drops into it which made my vision blurred so that I couldn't read just when I was so keen to spend every minute of my free time absorbing all this wonderful wisdom I was discovering. Sitting quietly at home one afternoon, it occurred to me that my condition (of not being able to see clearly) forced me to look more deeply into my own state of being and to discover what was happening to me.

I began to meditate, do relaxation exercises and become a vegetarian. There were lodge meetings on Wednesdays, public lectures on Sunday evenings, discussion groups for young people one evening a week and a study group on Sunday afternoons. I went to all of them. I could not stop telling all my friends and work colleagues about it and I am sure some of them must have thought I had gone off the deep end. My friend Rafael remained sceptical, although his wife Maria seemed a bit more open. Annie thought I had become a religious nut. Sylvia, who had introduced me to Krishnamurti in New Guinea, would have known better and would have understood what I was going through. Alas, she was not there – I still had not found her.

The salon where I was working then had about six staff, all young women, but no one was in charge when the owner was not there. Following a series of arguments, misunderstandings and outright sulking, which was having a negative effect on customer service, the owner asked if I would be the salon manager. I had run my own business in New Guinea and managed salons in London and Gent, so I knew that I could do it. Technically, the job of managing made no difference; the main challenge was to handle the girls and to get them to work together. One evening there was a talk at the Theosophical Society about 'responsibility' that made me think about what I was doing at work. The following day I put a large sign up in the small staff room saying '*Only when you have done your work first, then helped others with theirs, can you come here to rest.*' In my diary I asked:

'*Is this manager business a test sent to me to help me find out if I can be responsible for other people as well as for myself? It certainly helps having the TS behind me. I feel more confident already.*'

I became an active member of the Young Theosophist Group. This group attracted sons and daughters of long-established Theosophists and genuine seekers of spiritual insights, but also a collection of outcasts and misfits, as well as some borderline mental cases. They had guest speakers on every fringe or alternative topic you could think of, often leading to vigorous debates, sometimes continued in nearby coffee lounges or while walking home late at night. A group of us went to see the stage production of *Hair*, the famous rock musical, to the embarrassment of some of the more traditional members. I also became the treasurer of the Theosophical Order of Service, the philanthropic arm of the Society, which raises money for needy causes both in Australia and overseas.

The Sunday afternoon group, called the Isis Lodge, studied the *Secret Doctrine*, a massive work by Helena Petrova Blavatsky, one of the founding mothers of the Theosophical Society. It is supposed to have been 'transmitted' to her by the Masters from other planes of existence and is both a cosmology and psychology of esoteric wisdom. The process was to literally read passage by passage and discuss it to share understanding and try to figure out what was meant by it. The national lecturer for the Society, Leonard Wade, led this group at the time. He and his wife Kathleen were very personable and took a close interest in me. They were down-to-earth, no-nonsense students of esoteric wisdom, with their feet firmly on the ground, as opposed to some other members of the Society who had their heads permanently and inextricably in the clouds. When Leonard and Kathleen Wade became more familiar with my circumstances and discovered that I was looking for a cheaper way to live, they invited me into their house. It turned into a sort of adoption, as they had no children of their own, and they effectively became my surrogate spiritual parents. I moved into a room in their house in October that year.

The connection between the TS and Krishnamurti now became clear to me and I continued going to the film showings and to study his books. I discovered the work of Rudolph Steiner, formerly of the German TS, and the Anthroposophical Society he had formed. I also became a member of Amnesty International, the worldwide organisation that tries to free political prisoners who have expressed political or religious opinions against the prevailing regime, but who have not committed any crime. They apply pressure to the offending governments by writing letters to them until the prisoners are either released or properly charged and tried. I also discovered, to my surprise, that the Theosophical Society had a loose association with the Liberal Catholic Church, a Dutch offshoot of the Catholic Church steeped in Theosophical lore. Its rituals and dress-ups reminded me too much of my earlier experiences of the Roman Catholic Church to be of interest to me. I once attended a wedding in an LCC chapel and to me it felt more like a bad dream than a celebration. Naturally, given my feelings about both the Catholic Church and weddings in general, this was only to be expected and does not reflect on the LCC or the people getting married on that day.

During the remainder of 1969 and most of 1970 I became increasingly involved in Theosophical activities, studying and changing my lifestyle. The initial 'romantic aura' of the TS had subdued by now, but the seriousness of my involvement and the sustenance and direction it was giving me did not diminish –

on the contrary. In fact, as all this was taking up an increasing amount of my time and energy, I had been speculating how I could change things in my life so that I could devote more time to what I wanted to do rather than merely earning money. So it was both a surprise and a delight when the owner of the salon where I was working asked one day if I knew someone who would work part-time in addition to the people we already had. I promptly said '*Yes, me.*' She agreed to hire a new full time person and have me as the part-timer. Now that I was living more cheaply at the Wades, it was financially possible, if I lived modestly, to work Thursdays, Fridays and Saturday mornings, and have three days off doing other things. The year ended with renewed promise of further change, but I still didn't know in what direction it would go. I felt very happy and my life was settling down. Being less tossed by impulsive desires, I was now more and more in control of my emotions. My focus was on spiritual development. A telling entry in my diary for June 1970 is typical:

'I have a feeling I must become a lot more unselfish, I must also get rid of a lot of unnecessary possessions and become freer in movement. I must concentrate on one thing at a time in order to get somewhere – I want a close friend and some good company, but patience and detachment are the key notes.'

My diary entry for Tuesday 3 February 1970 reminds me that Bertrand Russell died that day. Russell had been a hero of mine and I had been reading him lately, especially his experiments with education, an issue that was to gain limelight in my life soon.

In the same month I went to visit my friends Rafael and Maria Saldaña who had finally moved to Launceston. Rafael was painting more than ever. He was now inspired by the natural beauty of Tasmania, which is reflected in many of his paintings. I was inspired by their exit from city life and them putting into practice a simple way of living, of which I could but dream. Working on simplicity in my own life and achieving some measure of success, I was attracted by the peacefulness of the country and toyed with the idea of joining them.

I met with some Theosophists in Launceston and one of the members took me on a tour to Hobart, which was followed by more meetings with Theosophists. One visit I clearly remember and often think about was to a lady who was going blind. Her house was a complete shambles and poorly maintained. But, she explained, '*I don't have time or energy for this physical stuff, relationships with people are far more important.*' She proceeded to ask me all about my life and my journey and we had a great afternoon. I didn't mind the chaos around me in the least. I was taken to a Quaker meeting in Hobart and was most impressed. When you think of how many people blabber on only to hear the sound of their own voice, to only speak when one has something important to say that would be inspiring to others, which is how Quakers worship, should be a rule for most social situations. It reminded me of a quotation I saw later which read: '*Most conversations are monologues in the presence of another person.*' I have also discovered recently that I may well have an intellectual allergy to meaningless chatter, to which only patient compassion may be the occasional antidote.

I left Tasmania and my friends, wondering when I would return there and, if I did, what I could do there to sustain myself while nurturing my development. I did not know then that it would be twenty years before my next visit.

Over the Easter weekend that year I attended my first Annual Australian Theosophical Convention in the Blue Mountains near Sydney. Being the 75th anniversary celebrations, the convention was graced with a foursome of eminent international guests: the International President of the Theosophical Society, Sri Ram, a quiet but spiritually inspiring Indian man; Jeffrey Hodson, a prolific author from New Zealand; John Coates, an Englishman, who was vice president and looked like a giant panda, cuddly, friendly and full of good humour; and, finally, and to me most inspiring, Will Ross from the United States, representing the more contemporary view of Theosophy.

I had never been to a convention of any sort, let alone one as important as this. The format, it seems to me now, was conventional. Plenary lectures, small group discussion, some free time, and some decision-making and official business sessions. One of the issues concerning the TS members that year was what to do with the YTs, the Young Theosophists. By then, I had been around long enough to form an opinion about what they were doing and what they could be doing instead. I was also naïve enough to say what I thought and discovered that I had sufficient conviction to stand up in public and say what I felt, even though I suspected it to go against the general trend at that time.

It was an extraordinarily meaningful experience for me. On the one hand I felt safe, given the spirit of brotherliness of the whole meeting, yet on the other hand I had no experience of publicly convincing other people. On the contrary, I had always been painfully shy and embarrassingly awkward when it came to talking to more than one person at a time. (An interesting contrast to my standing up in front of groups all day, and sometimes for several days on end, as part of my current work life as a Learning and Development practitioner.) But there I was, expressing my view with what must have been sufficient conviction, since several of the younger people came to talk to me later on, all wanting to hear more of what I thought and share with me what they thought. It made a very healthy change to my self-image, one that was overdue and most welcome. I began to believe that I did have worthwhile opinions of my own and could make sense to others.

After I mustered up the courage to approach Will Ross and discuss some of my opinions with him it was even more remarkable to me that he completely agreed with most of what I shared with him. I was over the moon. I had ideas that were out of sync with tradition but in sync with what I thought to be a progressive view. My inner fire was aglow. I had found other people with similar ideas to my own and I felt less alone or odd.

Another event that was significant for me personally was my response to the presence of a delegation from Vietnam. One of the ten-member-strong delegation publicly thanked the Australian Theosophical Order of Service for their contribution to an orphanage in Vietnam. I was the treasurer of the TOS at that time and I had argued their case during the funds allocation meeting. More importantly, Australia had done some terrible things to Vietnamese people and I felt the collective guilt on my shoulders. Tears were streaming down my face when the young girl who spoke on their behalf had the good grace to thank us for our modest help. I was overwhelmed and inspired by my own sense of outrage about crimes against humanity. I could not remember ever before having felt a universal human connection as strongly as then.

On the evening of the second last day, I was chatting with one of the delegates, a shy-looking but bright-eyed young man by the name of Doug Peterson. We were sharing our impressions of the conference and we got talking about Krishnamurti. Doug was a great fan and told me that Krishnamurti had written a book called *Education and the Significance of Life*. He also told me that he knew of a small school near Sydney where a group of parents were trying to implement these educational ideas. We talked enthusiastically about many aspects of Theosophy, but mainly about education, till late into the night.

I was tired enough to go to sleep quickly, but my subconscious mind was hard at work that night. It was connecting Krishnamurti, a high value in my thinking, with the issue of education as a potential direction in my life, and came up with a very clear dream. The dream, the most extraordinarily clear and explicit I have ever had, simply showed me to myself as **an educator: a person helping other people to learn and grow to be better humans.**

'*That is what you are, should be, and will be,*' the dream said. That's it, very clear and simple. Education, it was shown to me in my dream, was the most useful and important thing I should do with my life. As I had wanted to do more interesting work than being a hairdresser, it was now clear what the alternative was. The following morning I searched for Doug to share my dream with him but he had already left to go back to Sydney. I wondered for a second or two if he had been part of the dream, but he was on the participant list, so he must have been there and wasn't an apparition after all.

I was dizzy with excitement, buzzing with plans and fired up with enthusiasm, ready to act. If I had been a more sentimentally inclined person and devoutly religious one at the same time, I would have said that I had received a calling from God and now knew my vocation. Fortunately for me, I was somewhat more practically inclined and I wrote in my diary that evening:

'*... the importance of this event [referring to the dream] will be measured by my actions upon returning from the conference.*'

This convention had a great impact on me and I revelled in it for a very long time after it.

Years later, I was delighted to discover that according to Logotherapy, and in the words of Frankl himself, '*One should not search for an abstract meaning of life... for the meaning of life differs from man to man, from hour to hour [but] everyone has his own specific vocation or mission in life to carry out a concrete assign-*

ment which demands fulfilment. What matters, therefore, is not the meaning of life in general but rather the specific meaning of a person's life at a given moment. According to Logotherapy the striving to find meaning in one's life is the primary motivational force in man'.

A few days after returning from the convention, I went to visit Summerfarm, the school Doug had mentioned to me. Summerfarm was a small, private, progressive primary school, hidden away behind a large architect-designed family home in an outer suburb north of Sydney. It was primarily guided by the educational philosophies of famous Italian educator Maria Montessori, with some of Rudolph Steiner's ideas thrown in for good measure. The impetus to start the school had come from Krishnamurti and the name was inspired by Summerhill, a progressive school near London, started by AS Neill.

Marcus Rossi, an Italian architect, and his English wife Margaret had started home schooling mainly to educate their own children. After reading Krishnamurti, who in his book *Education and the Significance of Life* exhorts parents to start their own school if they are not satisfied with the school system, they had done just that, together with some friends.

Marcus and I talked about the TS conference and our common friend Doug for a while and then he took me to the one-room school on the farm behind the house. Before I had a chance to articulate why I had come, he explained that last night he and John, the only teacher working at the school, had been talking and had agreed that what they really needed was another person to help. There were about a dozen kids and only the one teacher and they wanted a better ratio than that. Unfortunately, Marcus said they could not afford the salary for another qualified teacher as they wanted to keep fees as low as possible and still pay the teacher a decent wage.

The Swiss psychologist Carl Jung defined 'synchronicity' as an event that is bound to happen against statistical probability. Within less than twenty-four hours of their expressed need, here I was, a person offering to help them for two days a week at no cost at all. Of course, I explained that I was not a trained teacher and that I had come to learn as much as, if not more than, to help. I stayed for the rest of that afternoon learning about pottery from one of the children. On the train home I could hardly believe what had happened. It felt more like a dream than a reality. It was in fact my dream, my purpose beginning to fulfil itself already. I was twenty-eight years old and going back to primary school to learn the most important lesson in my life: learning how to fulfil the 'purpose' of my life. In a sense I had just started an apprenticeship or on-the-job training and there was much to learn. At the time I may have been tempted to explain what was happening to me in mystical or magical terms as certainly some of my TS brothers and sisters were. Today I would use this as an example of one's own thinking and anticipation leading to actualisation because this is how our absolutely incredible brain works. When in my current coaching practice, I explain the importance of having clear goals and the right kind of thinking in relation to it, I point out the neurology of it, but often add that it works just like magic.

Being a teacher's aide at Summerfarm, ideal and fantastic as it was, was not without its difficulties. Some of the kids were there because they were no longer wanted at their previous school for a variety of colourful reasons. My patience and my very limited understanding of developmental psychology were severely challenged. My sense of logical order, practical organisation and basic hygiene were all tested to their limits. My few crisis management skills were on red alert. As a new world opened up before me, I was frantically looking for a map and some direction.

All my spare time was now devoted to reading up on education according to Montessori, Krishnamurti and Steiner, as well as anything that would help me survive. At times I was reading something one day and putting it into practice the next. A few weeks later I wrote in my diary:

'*... it is getting more and more interesting at school but at the same time I am becoming increasingly aware how difficult this is.*'

I kept going to Summerfarm for two days a week for the rest of that year. In retrospect, I think I learned more about the practical side of education during my time at Summerfarm than at any other time in my life, including university.

A few months later I attended an information evening at the Rudolph Steiner School in Middle Cove and proceeded to enrol in a short course on Steiner education. While it took me some more years to become a professional educator, the direction of my life had been set and today, thirty-five years later, I am still **an educator and a facilitator of learning.**

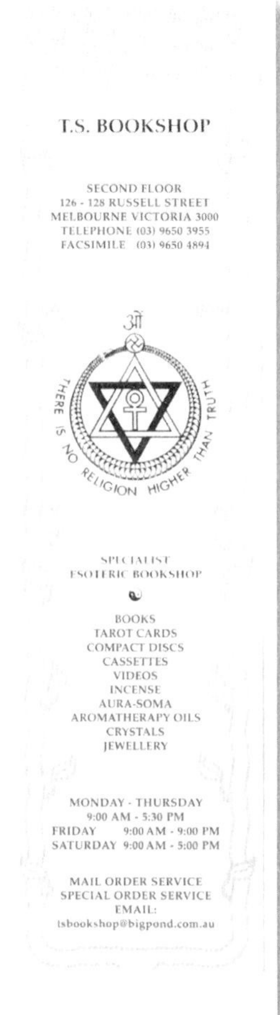

Helena Petrovna Blavatsky, one of the founders of the Theosophical Society.

THEOSOPHICAL SOCIETY OBJECTS

To form a nucleus of the Universal Brotherhood of Humanity without distinction of race, creed, sex, caste or colour.

To encourage the Study of Comparative Religion, Philosophy and Science.

To investigate unexplained laws of Nature and the powers latent in the human being.

18.

The Zen of paying attention

Sydney 1970

STUDYING education reminded me again and again that this was exactly what Sylvia had done at teachers college in Port Moresby and that she was probably teaching in a kindergarten somewhere at that very moment in this country or maybe even this city. I was still looking for her, but without any success. I was aware that her mother's first husband lived in Sydney, but I neither knew his name nor his address and I had no contact for Sylvia in New Guinea.

The year 1970 was one of transition. I had found the ideal of eduction as a new focus and direction in my life, but despite the fact that this was clear and overwhelmingly enthusing, other things didn't necessarily fall into place because of it. No matter how clear our goals are we have no control over the outside world, only how we respond to it. Going to Summerfarm was certainly the most practical application of anything I had ever strongly believed in, but I wanted to get better at it faster than that. The more I learned at Summerfarm the more I realised that I needed more knowledge, study and experience. Then, as if to thwart me, the New South Wales State Department of Education rejected our formal application for registration and we were no longer able to legally operate as a school. Marcus's determination was not weakened and he immediately investigated how to appeal against this decision. In the meantime the school had to close.

It was now clear to me that if I were going to be an educator or a teacher in the formal and professional sense of the word, I would have to go to teachers college or university to get qualifications. Given my educational background, which did not even include high school, that prospect seemed telescopically out of reach. I had made a great start to my new found 'vocation' but it seemed that it had come to a rather suddenly disappointing halt.

The salon where I was working had been sold to an Englishman, recently arrived from London. He wanted to renovate the place and generally raise the standard of professional service and quality. He certainly wanted me to be part of his 'new' team, but by then I had lost any enthusiasm for hairdressing. I spent a lot of time looking for alternative employment. I still needed to work for a living and not being qualified for anything else made it difficult. One day I saw an advertisement in the paper for instructors at the Sydney Hairdressing College and thought that this would be an ideal compromise. I didn't get the job, like the many others I applied for. On eventually leaving hairdressing, I wrote the following poem which could have served as a blueprint for a first year ladies hairdressing curriculum.

The Essence

I am a favourite of Lady Drucker
And fondly thought of by Mrs. Pucker.
There is Mrs.Brash, Mrs. Flash and Baroness van Loetcher
Rita from the bar and Nelly from the butcher.
And of course the impossible Mrs Teak,
Yet I played her calmly every week.
Until I once left her nearly naked just around the brain
And never had to attend to her again.

The more intelligent of you, I'm sure, have guessed by now
In my early youth I took scissors and a vow:
'Whatever country, town or city,
I would make all the world's maidens pretty.'
It delights and pleases me so much
To lavishly enchant them with my gentle touch.
I play and frolic and fiddle with their hair
A large curl here, a small one there.
'Good afternoon milady, Oh I like your hat.'
Never mind if it makes her look twice as fat.
You see it takes diplomacy and charm
No matter how ugly they look, to never sound alarm.

I love to snip and snap and cut away
Add some colours, yellow, red or grey,
I can make it lighter, darker, with stripes or streaks,
French classic, Neo-Italian or ancient Greek.
I do pirouettes and somersaults and give them all the fuss
Even if she's eighty and looks like a hippopotamus.
She may have hair aplenty, none at all or very few
I'll sell her a wig to make her look like new.

No matter what her misery or problem is,
Whether she's old, a lady or a miss,

Whether she resembles a boxer-dog, a puffed-up frog or even a horse,
I'll make her beautiful, of course.

And so you want to be in business too I guess?
And you want to know the secret of my success?
Theorists call it service, romantics call it sex appeal.
Call it what you will, its very essence I shall now to you reveal.
As long as you flatter, titivate and charm the woman in that chair,
Little will it matter what you're doing to her hair.

(Dedicated to all hairdressing apprentices)

Both the Theosophical Society and Summerfarm had firmly established a study mode in my life, and even though education as a topic of study was not any less important, my focus shifted towards psychology as I realised that education is not merely about teaching kids to read and write but also helps them learn to become balanced human beings. I also realised that if I was going to help other people become more balanced human beings, I would at the same time need to do some more work on myself. The changes to my inner balance over the last two years had been enormous and because of it I knew I could go further. Study and self-observation, without being morbidly introspective, was the answer I decided.

My continuing study at the Theosophical Society of both Eastern and Western Wisdom traditions was now blending with a need to understand 'the person' as a psychological concept. The notion of how to live, not just in theory but in the actuality of everyday life, was grabbing my attention.

To my enormous surprise and gratification, I found this very blend that I had been looking for in the Eastern and Western wisdom on the one hand, and theory and practical application on the other hand, in the work of French psychiatrist Hubert Benoit. Both his *Let Go! Theory and Practice of Detachment According to Zen* and his earlier book *The Supreme Doctrine, Psychological Studies in Zen Thought*, with an introduction by Aldous Huxley (which was republished in 1990 under the title *Zen and the Psychology of Transformation*), kept me spellbound for months.

'Brilliantly sharp – what an excellent expose – very clear and elegantly clever – it continues to fascinate me. Benoit is so deep and complex yet clear and well-presented – I continue reading parts of it again – its importance and its impact on me cannot be overemphasised. I feel like a light has been switched on somewhere inside me which was in the dark before.'

Here was an explanation of how to live and work on the inner plane by a practising psychiatrist who had an understanding of both Western psychology and Eastern Wisdom. These works appealed enormously to my search at that time and I found them both extremely helpful intellectually and emotionally, as well as practically, and they have remained so till today. Detachment, as one of the keys to a balanced emotional life, had already emerged into my consciousness from my own experience and now here it was confirmed in such eloquent terms that I could hardly contain my excitement. Zen, and how to live it, was now my focus. Here was something you could not only understand but do something with to help yourself.

Belgian author Robert Linssen's book *Living Zen* also contributed generously to my understanding. While the Australian branch of the Theosophical Society had put me in the right frame of mind and prepared me for it, these Europeans dragged me into the heart of what I have come to regard as pure Wisdom. Their approach, while based on pure Zen thought, is articulated in a way the Western mind can understand. Linssen drew Zen and Krishnamurti, the two main influences on my thinking at the time, together for me. In a nutshell, Benoit and Linssen helped me understand the illusion of the egocentric self. It could be said that all our problems stem from excessive attachment to the idea of 'self'. We make such a big fuss of this 'self' that, in our efforts to validate, promote and enhance it, all else gets spoiled in the process.

My all-time favourite cartoon is of a psychiatrist talking to a sophisticated business man after a consultation saying; '*The good news is that your large ego is perfectly healthy and strong. The bad news is that it has no basis in reality.*'

Understanding this concept is difficult enough – actually living it is yet another matter. As I learned to observe the activity of my own egocentricity, it became increasingly important to me to work on minimising it. As Linssen put it in *Living Zen*: '*By adhering to a particular system of thought, beliefs or dogmas, we are conditioning our minds. The great strength of Zen on the one hand, and of the Krishnamurtian stand-point on the other, lies in the fact that they are not systems of thought, but statements of a way of living freed of all ideation.*' It was that 'way of living' that I was aiming for.

To be free from conditioning, to be free from egocentricity,
to live simply and psychologically uncluttered,
is what I was looking for.

But how to get there was another matter.

Jiddu Krishnamurti, the person I had been studying and admiring for his absolute strength and clarity of purpose, came to visit

Australia in November that year. I attended all three talks he gave at the beautiful Sydney Town Hall, where each was so full it was standing room only, such was the demand to see him. I was surprised at his popularity. Some twenty years earlier he had been billed as the Second Coming of Christ, who would walk into Sydney over the water into an amphitheatre. More sober Theosophists who had organised the event thought better of it and cancelled that show.

It was a very moving experience to actually see him live and hear his words. I had by now worked hard to forge some degree of coherence inside my own head as to how Theosophy, Krishnamurti and Zen Buddhism, all of which impressed and inspired me, fitted together. Absolute consistency may be an unreasonable expectation of most human beings but logical consistency has something to recommend itself. Hearing Krishnamurti live reinforced in me the belief that he was way ahead in terms of making sense, at least to my mind. Reading Benoit's explanation of Zen also further gave credence to what Krishnamurti was saying. I was feeling increasingly comfortable with this world view.

One of the great mysteries for humans is what happens to them after they die. Almost all religions have invented some story about the soul, of it being your essential Self with a capital 'S', and how, not being material, it survives your corporal existence. For most Christians, this soul goes to heaven if you have been a 'good' boy or girl; and according to Oriental religions, you reincarnate again and again until there is no 'bad' Karma left to work out. Theosophists are generally more enamoured with the Oriental view and the topic of reincarnation appears regularly on their lecture schedule. Popular Buddhism and Hinduism seem to go along with the general theory of reincarnation. It made a lot of sense to me, so for a long time I went along with it, even though in scientific terms it is certainly an open question.

One of the turning points for me was during Krishnamurti's

visit to Sydney when one of the post-talk questions asked was whether he believed in reincarnation. His answer must have been a shock to many. He responded: '*Does it matter? Should you not live rightly because it is right, rather than because it will earn you a seat in heaven or a better caste when you come back next time?*'

From an ethics point of view, that was perfectly logical. Even the moral development theorists tell us that doing something because the rules tell you to do it, or because you will derive personal benefit from it, is not the most developed moral way to behave. It was not until reading Benoit and some of the Transpersonalists that I fully grasped the implication of the fact that our self-concept is a construct of our mind. Being driven by survival, it is only reasonable that the thought of no longer 'being' after death leads us to invent some other way of existing so that we think we can continue to 'be' in some other form. It was ultimately the pure essence of atheistic Zen which drove home to me that assigning a permanent and eternal 'self', to one's ego, even if you spell it with a capital 'S', is the most egocentric act of all. Such psychological trickery flies in the face of the essence of Buddhist selflessness. That the actions we take in our present life have some repercussions in another time may well be the case, but to project the illusory selfhood we now use to deal with each other, upon such consequences, is a fantasy of that very selfhood in order to sustain its apparent existence.

In October that year I wrote:

'A couple of incidents at work made me fume inside myself. That women wanted a different colour after her hairdo already finished!! I definitely must give up playing that comedy of being a hairdresser. If I go there I have to play that game – and playing that game is being

untrue to myself. Going to the salon is becoming intolerable, its so contrary to my nature! So I must quit since I must be true to myself.'

I had to play that game another two months but that would be it.

My summing up for that year was:

'Obviously again a much better year than the last one – that seems to be the usual conclusion the last few years. I have gone through a tremendous amount of moods and phases which each have taught me something and each of these put together has made for a very definite and marked progress in my general understanding. Going to that school was perhaps the single most important step this year together with discovering Hubert Benoit and hearing Krishnamurti. All of this has firmly contributed to my firm decision to definitely change my occupation and switch to teaching. I am consciously feeling myself grow and develop both emotionally and intellectually and in practical application terms.'

'Zen demonstrates the nullity of all belief in a personal God, and the deplorable constraints that necessarily flow from this belief. It says: 'Do not put any head above your own'; it also says: 'Search not for the truth; only cease to cherish opinions.' Zen says: 'There is nothing complicated that man has to do; it is enough that he sees directly into his own nature.' [But] '… no one on Earth can do this work for us.'

The Supreme Doctrine: Psychological Studies in Zen Thought, Hubert Benoit.

Several years later in my 1973 diary I noted, mixing insights with playfulness:

'Just finished the Supreme Doctrine once again and I am more and more of the point of view that Advaita Vedanta, or Absolutism, is a useful background intellectually (but) psychologically I feel more and more that ZEN according to Benoit is the way to live by. If we can see their complementarity without letting them interfere with each other – what a superb supreme sublime surprise surpassing suppositions sofar seen!!'

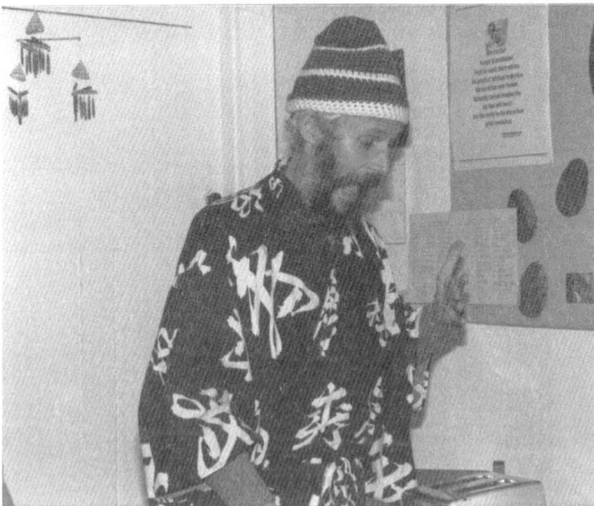

Zen and the art of making toast
without burning your hand.

Instructions:
don't touch the toaster!

19.

My 'Passage to India'

Sydney and India 1971

A young man called Norbert moved in at the Wades, in the spare room opposite mine. He was very seriously enthusiastic about many things, but mostly the mystical and parapsychological. He entertained me with his theories on UFOs and Tarot cards, and white and black magic. He also practised meditation and I went to watch him do Aikido on a number of occasions. He came with me to TS meetings and we discussed our views over thick raisin-dotted pancakes he used to make in our shared little kitchen. (I would meet him and his mother in Port Douglas the following year for an 'authentic' psychic experience.) Four days before my twenty-eighth birthday, Norbert took me to a Hare Krishna feast in the city. He liked to go there because they served free food and played Indian music. I had never been there and I had no attraction to the Hare Krishnas, but the food was excellent. It would soon become evident that I was there for more than the food.

Milling among the distinctly hippy-looking crowd, I met

Jenny, who on the face of it was there for the free food also. We were both mistaken. Jenny was one of those enigmatic people who had an aura of the mysterious about her. She was like an apparition. Was she a sign from one of the many Hindu '*Gods*' telling me something? Or was I merely falling in love again? Zen was teaching me to pay attention, but something has to be happening before you can pay attention to it. It was happening all right. *Attention! Attention!* a voice was crying out in my mind, but the noise of the flutter in my emotional heart was so loud that I didn't hear it. There is destiny and there is freedom. *I freely chose to go with destiny on this occasion.* It turned out that we were there to meet each other so that we could go on an interesting journey together covering most of the following two years, not that I knew it then of course. So, you tell me why I would not freely go with that destiny!

My encounter with Jenny at the Hare Krishna temple in December 1970 had ended without exchange of addresses or phone numbers. We had merely expressed our hope to meet again. I guess we must have known intuitively that such was inevitable. (Great source of insight, intuition, if you know how to use it well.)

One night in mid-January, due to a cancelled Theosophical meeting, I found myself in the city with a spare evening in front of me. I decided to go and see a musical play popular at the time called *The Legend of King O'Malley*, by Michael Boddy and Bob Ellis (no relation to Havelock, I assume). It's a musical extravaganza, passing commentary about Australian culture and politics. There was just enough time to go for a meal in my favourite vegetarian restaurant near the TS before the show. Who should be there, munching away at her salad? Yes. Jenny! We simply smiled as though this was a surprise to neither of us. We ate together, went to the show together, and then walked and talked together till the early hours of the morning, which I wrote of in my journal:

'Is this proof of the power of the mind to attract what you want? I do not doubt that there was an attempt on both our sides. All I can say is that there is a very strong attraction for a closer and deeper understanding of each other without having much to say.'

Jenny, who had come over from New Zealand only a few months before, was on her way to India. Many young people were doing it in those days. An Indian Swami who had visited her Yoga class back in New Zealand had made a blanket invitation to anyone who wanted to study in India to visit the ashram to which he belonged. Jenny had taken him up and was earning some money from a part-time job in Sydney en route. To meet someone with similar interests and aspirations is not so unusual, but there was clearly much more to our encounter than that.

On 14 January, practically in one sitting, I wrote *An Old Friendship?*, clearly reflecting the state of mind I was in. The dynamic balance between my philosophical and spiritual ideas at that time and my emotional and instinctive needs is blatantly bared. I was now rationalising my innate reproductive desires not with romantic love this time, but with 'spiritual soul-mateship'.

An Old Friendship?

Our meeting, I think you will agree,
Was certainly not very accidental,
Nor did our friendship, it is clear to see,
Begin only that Sunday at the temple.

How can we logically explain,
the strong attraction and the two-way flow,
the certainty we would meet again,
and the sparkle in your eyes when they met mine?

You recognise incurable romanticism?

Why, I shall unashamedly confess,
Small a poet but with great idealism,
I have no interest in disguising who I am.
Yet a realist who dislikes sentimentality,
I am puzzled, bewildered and at a loss of what to do.
The chances for such a rediscovery
Are probably as rare as a one-eyed kangaroo.

Is this the language of exaggeration?
Could I be seeing things that are not really there?
Or am I raving on in desperation.
On some path which is not leading anywhere?

How many times have we gone through this before?
Are we waking up and becoming sober?
Can we analyse this to its very core?
Or is there anything at all for us to wonder over?

No! I do not doubt that all is right!
It may, of course, be hard for us to see,
Yet there are stars in the deep dark night
And even prisoners are a little free.

Remember that 'speaker' old and wise?
He said: 'Be very quiet and look,
Bring calm and peace into the heart and mind,
The answer is within you, not in any book.'

It seems we have not much will or power,
Yet even a little choice and freedom is divine.
If each cause has its effect, and each effect its cause,
Maybe I am yours and perhaps you are mine?

Sydney, 14 January, 1971 (Dedicated to Jenny)

One morning the following week, while swimming at Balmoral beach, a thought struck me like an ocean wave – I wanted to get out of hairdressing, and my plans at Summerfarm had fallen down around my ears and I was un-attached, so why not go to India with Jenny? It would be safer for her that way. I had heard that women should not travel in India by themselves. Who knows, it could be interesting? I could visit Adyar, the Theosophical Society's International headquarters, and have a break from the drudgery of work and possibly never to return to hairdressing.

On 20 January I wrote in my diary:

'Jenny is now a permanent backdrop in my mind blending with what's in it. And I am not even trying to get her out of it. She seems to fit in quite comfortably.'

Just two days later I recorded a vivid dream where:

'I was in a far away place looking after small children but it was safe because Jenny was there to help me. The children all had dark skin and black hair. Does that mean they are Indian?'

What other signs did I need?

I went to visit Marcus at the school and we talked about my possibly going to India. Looking at it from his point of view, he immediately suggested that this would be a great opportunity for me to attend the Montessori teacher training college in Karachi. A famous Theosophist by the name of Goal Minwalla, who I had met during her visit to Australia, was running the program there. Then when I came back I could be the teacher at his Montessori school.

I thought that if I needed a practical reason to go to India and Pakistan, as well as an emotional one to be with Jenny, I might as well use this one. It certainly fitted in with my vision of myself as an educator. I could no longer contain myself and went to see

Jenny the following day. Cautiously, in case I was intruding into her plans, I suggested that I could come with her to India if she would like me to. I need not have worried. It was exactly what she had been hoping for. We were both very excited, but mature enough not to go overboard. We did what it takes to get practicalities organised, resigned from our jobs and acquired what we thought we needed. We left Sydney by train for Wauchope about three hundred kilometres north on Tuesday 23 February 1971 and did not return to until 1 November that same year.

Before we even left Australia, during the month we took to get ready, we solemnly committed, blessed by a short meditation, to what we called a 'treaty'. It stated that *'the need for solitude and the need for companionship are equally important and ought to be equally respected'*. This was clearly to be a mature, wise and insightful relationship.

From Wauchope we got a lift with a professional hairdressing salon product salesperson to Southport where we visited friends. In Brisbane we stayed with Jennie's aunt for the night and in Rockhampton we slept outdoors, being summer and up north.

Our first planned stay was Magnetic Island, just off the coast of Townsville. It took six days of hitch hiking to get there, including short visits on the way. We arrived in Townsville late in the day and slept under a picnic table in the park as there were no more ferries to go across to Magnetic Island. The niece of my sister-in-law, Jacqui, who had sparked my interest in coming to Australia in the first place, had moved there and I was to visit her at last.

Jacqui explained during a drive around the Island the following day that she and her husband had fallen in love with the place and found themselves unable to leave. We later experienced what she meant. It took us more than a month to extricate ourselves from this paradise even though it was intended only to be a short stopover visit.

One afternoon, a friend of Jacqui's who was the manager of a nearby motel called to see if she knew anyone interested in looking after her place while she went to Brisbane for business. We thought that maybe we could stay for a short time and that this casual job would add to our meagre funds. There were no guests, it being in-between seasons, and all we would have to do was clean the pool, sweep the garden paths and answer the phone in return for free accommodation and food from the freezer. We took the job – even if it didn't pay any money, the offer was too good to refuse.

Looking back now, it sounds like the setting for a Hollywood movie called *Lovers in Paradise*. There were times that I could hardly believe my luck. We had a moke to drive around in. We were a two-minute walk from the beach and there was a pool at hand. We had a big double room with ensuite and full privacy. The bud of spiritual-sexuality was about to bloom into its full splendour. What else do lovers need? It felt more like a honeymoon than a spiritual pilgrimage.

In spite of the idyllic environment, we were thrown onto each other within a psychologically confined space (confined by us) and it soon became too much for Jenny's fragile core, which I had not met until then. I was, no doubt, eager and bursting to give full expression to my then newly fashioned idea of spiritually-based sexuality. When it was the right time it was fantastic, but when it was just a little off being 'right', being together caused more harm than good. Jenny had periods of perfect calm, yet there were other times when a casual incident or an innocent remark would send her into black and deep depression. Jenny's background was riddled with traumatic experiences causing havoc with her inner balance. She wondered whether she was possessed by some evil entity and I quickly learned an elementary form of exorcism just to keep things from getting out of hand. It worked most of the time, but I wanted to change the whole of her inner set-up so that the very idea of possession would disappear from her mind. That was not so easy. I wrote:

'Jenny is back to normal. Lovemaking also back to normal. She called it "the biggest thing in the world". Last night was full moon, full tide, full-on love. But tides regress!'

The fine pleasures we feasted on were interspersed by morose entanglements of guilt and fear of pregnancy. We were on an emotional trampoline – up and down, up and down – and the ups turned into downs so quickly that occasionally it made me dizzy and scared. My on-the-job training as a psychological support person was a steep learning curve and served me well when becoming a counsellor many years later.

After about a week, Susan rang to say that one of her children was sick and needed medical attention. She asked if we could stay for a little longer, offering to pay us to be there. We were keen to get going but the need for money, not to mention the sheer attraction of the place, swayed us to stay on.

'We went to visit the local TS yesterday, interesting people. We are getting to know each other better every single day. I have been reading Krishnamurti to Jenny – good for both of us. We will proceed cautiously.'

Soon after that, several local people came to visit looking for Susan, wanting to be paid for services provided weeks ago. Was she in financial trouble? It certainly appeared so when the phone got cut off. People were thinking she had skipped town and abandoned the place. Another week went by with no word from Susan. Then, a young couple arrived who were booked to be at the motel for their honeymoon. So we looked after them as best we could, playing chefs, waiters, and chambermaids, as well as pool cleaners and gardeners. We hardly saw them, and when we did they were looking at each other, not concerned in the least about our lack of professional hospitality.

It was also on this Magnetic Island that I had what I thought to be an out-of-body experience. Those things are very hard to describe. Could it all have been a dream? Yes, but if it was a dream it was the most psychedelically vivid and extraordinarily realistic dream I ever had, and we were not even taking drugs. We had been having an emotionally pleasant day or two and Jenny and I had meditated and done some inspirational readings before going to bed. Jenny had gone straight to sleep and I was just lying there enjoying the peace and quiet, listening to the sounds of the sea.

'Extraordinary experience last night – I was seeing the serene and peaceful face of a woman with the features of both Jenny and an Oriental Buddha-like face. The face was growing bigger and bigger, coming towards me, and I felt like I was being absorbed into it. Eventually, I was floating inside the face yet I could see myself lying on the bed, smiling and glowing slightly. I was awake yet dazed by the experience. The blending of Jenny with Eastern flavours seemed very realistic. Then Jenny half woke up: lovemaking just occurred, smooth, and beautiful in a semi-dreamlike state and we promptly went back to sleep. Waking up with lots of questions this morning.'

It would take me some years before I would study non-ordinary states of consciousness, but at that time I thought of it as both strange and exciting. While the fine details have faded, the essence of the experience has always stayed with me.

When we eventually heard from Susan, she told us she wanted us to stay longer, but we replied that we really had to be going, and that we would be leaving the following Sunday, which we did.

Easily getting a lift to Cairns, we stayed a day or two with local Theosophists. One of the advantages of belonging to an

International Society is that they are everywhere and almost always very hospitable. From there we went up to Port Douglas, where we visited Norbert. I knew about his interests in UFOs and other such unusual matters from our time as neighbours at the Wades in Sydney, but that was not to prepare me for what was to occur there.

His mother, a softly spoken woman of Italian origin, took to us immediately. Her husband, Norbert's stepfather, equally immediately didn't take to us and, for reasons of spiritual purity, made us sleep on the veranda that night. (Good thing Port Douglas is far up North and night is always warm.) He was a self-proclaimed 'psychic medium' and told us that he had to be very careful who he let into the house, lest the visitors pollute the purity of the house we assumed. We must have passed his very stringent quarantine test the following day since we were allowed not only inside the house, but also inside his inner sanctum, the first visitors in four years. I didn't work out whether that meant that all the other visitors didn't pass the test or that nobody had called during all that time.

This inner sanctum, a room filled with candles and an altar covered with sacred images, Eastern and Western, had a rather spooky feel to it. Jenny, who was much more sensitive to such matters than I, refused to go in and went for a walk with Norbert instead. So the 'psychic' did a reading on me and told me that there was a likelihood that a pulmonary disease would strike me, but that he would be able to cure me of it if I was willing to let him have a go. I had no idea if there was any risk involved, so I let him do his thing. Norbert's mother was there. She smiled at me benignly and held my hand during the 'operation'. I didn't feel anything, but the medium went through all sorts of grunting spasms and shrill incantations. When it was over (my guess, in less than twenty minutes), he was dripping with sweat and had to lie down for a rest.

Norbert's mother gave me a drink of weak tea and again smiled gently. She explained that '*he gets a bit carried away with this game but that he doesn't mean any harm*'. I was certainly glad to hear that. Then she added that it was, in fact, she who was the medium – that there was absolutely nothing wrong with me and that from her point of view I was more spiritually pure than her husband. If he was a charlatan then she wasn't saying anything flattering about me either. Still, I felt quietly confident that I was on the right 'path' in my so-called spiritual development and humbly thanked the medium for his assistance. Since I never developed that pulmonary disease, the medium must have 'cured' me of it before it happened.

We had to go south again before moving west, recommencing our journey to Darwin from Townsville, which took us just over a week. The weather was wet and we spent a lot of time beside the road, waiting and waiting and waiting. Often local drivers would pick us up but they wouldn't go very far on this stretch we must have been in at least a dozen vehicles, ranging from big cattle-trucks to small utes and an assortment of family cars. Hitchhiking is good practice for building patience, especially on roads where there is hardly any traffic. We finally arrived in Darwin on Anzac Day, Sunday 25 April 1971.

After exploring our options for the next stage of the journey, we realised that if we wanted to fly, rather than row, to Singapore, more money was needed than we had, so it was back to work.

Within a few days, I found a job in a hairdressing salon run by a young Singaporean woman who was married to an Australian. Jenny did a number of casual jobs. We lived in a small flat just out of town and got to know some of the local Theosophists and other young people.

I remember Darwin as a difficult time for our relationship. Anzac day diary entry was typical:

'In the morning we had to straighten out a misunderstanding and the results from it on the emotional level. With the help of the 'Divine Light' we got Jenny to see what previously she couldn't. Big lesson for me in patience and humility.'

Jenny suffered severe emotional ups and downs. She also experienced what we came to call 'blackouts'. She would sink into deep black depression, or sometimes fly into angry outbursts. Again, I would use all my untrained counselling and soothing skills available to perform some sort of homespun, prayer-like incantation that would usually bring her back to some degree of equilibrium. These blackouts could last from a few hours to a whole day and were demanding on both of us. Sometimes it would be small incidents that would spark them off. A letter to me from a friend in Sydney that did not mention her; somebody at work saying something critical of her; me having my hair cut too short for her liking. We consulted various alternative healing people, practised meditation, did yoga and Jenny even fasted at one stage. When she was well, she was embarrassed about these episodes and wanted them to go away as much as I did. Amongst all this, Jenny's period was several days late that month, bringing with it all the emotionally-charged issues of what we would do if she were pregnant.

One of the naturopaths we consulted took a special interest in us both when he discovered that we were interested in spiritual development. He became even more interested when we told him that we were on our way to India. He casually inquired whether we were going there to study Tantra. We coyly admitted that we wanted to increase our enjoyment of safe sex, although this was not our main reason for going to India. He then asked if we were really serious about spiritual development because, if we were, he said he could help us. My initial internal response was, '*Here comes another psychic operation for my pulmonary condition*'. We must have looked sufficiently convincing to him because he gave us a small booklet called *The Karezza Method or Magnetisation: The Art of Connubial Love* privately published by William Lloyd in 1931. Lloyd was a student of Dr Alice Bunker Stockham, who devised this system of '*non-religious sexual metaphysics*' in the mid-1800s.

Based no doubt on the original Hindu Tantric approach, she had stripped all the religious paraphernalia away and gone straight for the spiritual effect of the practice. Answering its own rhetorical question, '*What is Karezza?*' the booklet states that it is '*controlled non-seminal intercourse*'. In plain language this means having sex where prolonged heavenly spiritual pleasure is the objective, not orgasm. After very detailed and explicit instructions, and warnings of possible early failures (no kidding!), the author extols the rewards: '*When the full magnetic rapport of Karezza has been realised, in which the two souls and bodies seem as one, supported and floating on some divine stream in Paradise, all sense of restraint and difficulty gone, and succeeded by heavenly ease, power, exaltation, pure and perfect bliss diffused throughout the entire being, it is then that the eyes and faces shine as though transfigured, every bone becomes music, every motion poetry. And this continues for a long time, perhaps hours, gently subsiding, finally, into a sweet child-like slumber.*' (My emphasis added.)

If ever one needed a perfectly good, spiritually-valid sounding excuse for having lots of sex, that was it. Either we didn't do it right or we didn't practise long enough because we neither found the paradisaical stream (even though most of it was pretty good) nor did all our difficulties disappear. As we were on our way to India, we thought that maybe our education there might include a comprehensive study of the Kama Sutra or any of the other Tantric practices to help us out.

In Darwin we met quite a few kind and interesting people. One of the local Theosophists introduced us to the work of Russian artist and explorer Nicholas Roerich, whose expeditions in the early 1900s throughout Asia contributed to the theory that the so-called 'lost years' of Jesus were spent in India and Tibet, a view taken quite seriously by some historians. The Sunday before we left (Trinity Sunday) I felt in a particularly loving mood and thought that the step we were about to take could be very significant for us both. As was often the case I experienced a strong need to write about it and I dedicated *Flowers* to Jenny.

Flowers in my head
Flowers in my bed
Flowers from the sun
Flowers when it's wet
Flowers when we meet
Flowers as we greet
Flowers when we're walking
Flowers covering the street
Flowers crowning your hair
Flowers bubbling everywhere
Flowers in your eyes
Flowers filling up the air
Flowers in the sky
Flowers floating high
Flowers is a way of life
Flowers never die
Flowers of infinity
Flowers for divinity
Flowers blooming with love
Flowers for all eternity

We finally flew out of Darwin late afternoon on 10 June landing in Singapore four hours later.

Nataraja Guru teaching children.

20.

'All right then, we'll go to Malaysia.'

Singapore and Malaysia 1971

JENNY and I were about to enter a world where spiritual life dominates ordinary, everyday life, rather than the other way around as is the case in most Western so-called 'civilised' countries. It was therefore perhaps just as well that we started this stage of our journey with a very down-to-earth reminder of how brutal everyday life can be in any part of the world.

The day after arriving in Singapore, we visited a young man who had spent six years in prison for his political stance. He had only recently been released with the help of Amnesty International and was one of the adoptees of the Sydney AI group to which I belonged and for whom I had personally written to the Singaporean Government on his behalf. It was a sobering experience to be talking to a man who had a conviction the size of Mount Everest and the humility of a Buddhist monk. Humility, a prerequisite to selflessness, is a high-value concept in my world view and to me he was a champion. He was also living proof of the power of peer pressure, both positive and negative. Was it Socrates who urged us to stand up for what we believe, even if it means walking in the opposite direction from the flock of sheep to which we belong? To stand out or walk in the opposite direction from your family, your tribe or your religion of birth, for the sake of what you think is right, is one of the more difficult things to do in life for most people. It is the classic dichotomy between our need for individualism and our need to belong. I had by now had some practice coping with this dichotomy but compared to the person we just visited I felt like a child learning to walk when he was already an Olympian. However, as with most other difficult things, with some practice and reflection we can get better at it.

We had two main contacts in Singapore. One was the Theosophical Society, which was rather big there. The other, the Gurukula, was the regional branch of the organisation the Swami who Jenny was looking for belonged to.

Having the address and phone numbers of the Theosophical Society, it was easier to start there. One phone call opened a dozen doors. Most members of the TS in Singapore are Indian and Hindu, though there were quite a few Chinese people also, who were mostly Buddhists. All of them were very hospitable and liked having us to visit their lodge and their homes. One of the office holders of the lodge, Mr Chen, a very charming Chinese man in his sixties, took on a pastoral role towards us. When we explained what and for whom we were actually looking, he personally took us to the ashram in an outer suburb called Sambawar. An ashram is part residence, part Hindu temple and part educational institution where you go to learn about the spiritual side of life.

On the outside, the small building had all the appearance of your everyday Hindu religious temple, but as we walked in we had no idea what was to come.

Completely unexpectedly, Swami Nitya Chaitanya Yati, or *Swamiji* as Swamis are referred to, was simply sitting there, a few people around him – some Indian people and a few Westerners. He had long curly black oiled hair and a considerable girth. Dressed in a faded pale orange cloth and wearing thongs, he looked very comfortable and self-satisfied. He smiled, welcomed us, directed us to sit on the floor and continued his discussion with the people around him.

My initial reaction was one of severe discomfort. I think that by association I felt I was back in church. The sense of religious reverence, institutionalisation and 'followership' that pervaded the room was not what *I* was looking for. My reaction was more than mere culture shock. It was fear and repulsion of being taken in by something I didn't know. Despite all my reading on spiritual matters, I was not prepared to just give myself over to a particular flavour of it.

Jenny, on the other hand, looked like she had just been given a blood transfusion. She was shining like a star, glowing happiness through every pore of her face and smiling as if she were high on something. She had just reached the reason for her originally leaving New Zealand more than a year ago. It was this man she had been looking for and here he was at last, in the flesh, within reach, just sitting there. Her contentment must have been as intense to her as my annoyed confusion was disturbing to me. What was I doing there? I was unable to take much notice of the discourse and I am sure I had no idea what they were talking about, not because I could not understand it, but because my mind was preoccupied with wondering why I was there.

The discussion with Swamiji dissolved into '*puja*', a Hindu religious service, the equivalent of Catholic mass I supposed, and then afterwards a traditional Indian meal was served. Sitting cross-legged on the floor, eating with our hands from banana leaves was a lesser challenge than making sense of the situation. After the meal, we were told we could stay there and the Swami and his entourage took off, where to I had no idea. Later there was a pre-bedtime meditation led by the resident Swami. During this meditation it was my turn for a psychological blood transfusion. The weight of my discomfort and resistance, due to mistaken associations and assumptions, slipped from my shoulders like a silk scarf in the breeze. I had the sensation that I had been wandering in a dark alley and suddenly found a brightly-lit avenue that was familiar to me. There was nothing to fear – I was safe. The speed of this transformation was puzzling enough, but the memory of the initial reaction faded like it had been a bad dream of no particular significance. There was a lot of rain and a heavy storm during that night and it was refreshing and cleansing to my state of mind. I felt back to normal.

The following morning, Jenny, coming out of her trance of the night before but infinitely happier than she had been for weeks, and I, in a calmer and more 'open to what comes' state of mind, went to pick up our things from the hotel where we had been staying. Jenny bought some culturally appropriate dresses in the city and we returned to our new 'home'. After settling in, the resident Swami explained that tomorrow we would join Nitya's party and travel to Malaysia. *'All right then, we'll go to Malaysia.'* My resistance had miraculously slipped away overnight and I was willing to go with whatever was offering.

A short convoy of four cars was enough to accommodate the small party of a few local supporters and about six Westerners. One of them, François, a Frenchman of my own age, I got to know quite well. We would have side chats in French and talk about art and music and the difficulties with the English language. There was an American, a Canadian and a sweet girl from

Switzerland who Jenny took to. Some of them we would meet again later in India and upon our return to Singapore.

At Johore Bahru, just across the bridge, we checked in at private residences of the Narayana Gurukula Movement followers and were treated as special guests by virtue of being part of the entourage of this 'holy' man. For the next two weeks, we travelled up and down the east coast of Malaysia to Kota Bharu near the Thai border and back. That side of Malaysia was still very traditional with very lush vegetation everywhere. We had stopovers of two or three days in Kuantan, Dungun, and Kuala Terengganu, always staying with devotees and looked after extremely well.

As my head cleared completely from the initial resistance, I discovered from talking with some of the other Westerners (François in particular) that this unassuming Swami had a Masters Degree in Philosophy. He had also been Head of the Psychology and Philosophy Departments in several Indian Universities and Director of the Institute of Psychic and Spiritual Research in New Delhi. What was more, he was not teaching mere Hinduism but Advaita Vedanta, one of the most sophisticated of the Indian philosophies. Given my personal biases, my respect and admiration for him shot up through the ceiling.

Apart from the time spent travelling, our daily routine consisted of early morning meditation, followed by Hatha Yoga classes, breakfast and then discourse and study or visiting local places and people of interest. There was often a siesta in the afternoon and a talk at somebody's house or a small hall by Swamiji in the evening, then service, to satisfy the needs of the devout Hindus, followed by a feast of mostly Indian curry, prepared with love and devotion to the gods of taste. Most of the people with whom we stayed were Indians living in Malaysia and the curries they prepared for us were among the best I have ever tasted. The hosts would lavish us, the 'entourage', with almost the same royal treatment as Swamiji received. By the second day, Jenny and I were both feeling much more at ease.

When we were getting to know some of the other people, it turned out that none of them were 'holy' yet and were just people like us, looking for something, experimenting and appreciating what we were given, both physically and spiritually. It took a couple of days also for me to hear what Nitya was actually saying. I had to see past the outer form of what looked like mere Hindu religion, and actually hear what was being said. Once I did hear at least some of it, I could not escape the comparison with some of the things Krishnamurti had been saying and some of what I had been reading about Zen. I was now ready to relax and give myself over to the process of spiritual growth in action.

One evening, Nitya gathered the Westerners around him and talked with us about our own personal journeys and how we related to each other. To my embarrassment, he singled me out for exemplary behaviour and attitude. Considering this later, I thought that it might have been a test to see if my humility was only skin deep or went to the core. A couple of days after that, Nitya invited Jenny and me for a private 'audience'. He wanted to know how we were getting on and what our plans were. When we told him that we were on our way to India to see him, he urged us to go anyway and be with his Guru and stay for as long as we could. He then took us into a deep meditative state and touched us at several places along the spine, which later we learned to be the chakras. He did not tell us what he was doing or what it was for, but there is no doubt in my mind that it had some positive effect on my inner state of being, at least for the following few days, and who knows if the imperceptible effects could be still there today. I felt more peaceful in the core of my being than I had ever before in my life. Two days later, I learned that Nataraja Guru, Nitya's Guru or Teacher, had obtained a Doctorate in Philosophy of Education from the Sorbonne University in Paris.

I could hardly wait to get to India.

One night, Nitya talked about beauty. He had a great appreciation of art and loved Western classical music. Somewhere during his talk he said that the quest for physical beauty should not stand in the way of spiritual beauty. That seemed inoffensive enough to me. To Jenny, and a couple of the other young girls around us, it appeared a personal rebuff to their natural attention to their appearance, as girls would at any age. This, of course, sent their mood into a downward slide, which it turned out to be my challenge to resurrect. I had hoped that all this would be behind us now, but unfortunately it wasn't yet. It was just one of the many challenges Jenny and I would have to cope with on our inner journey to the heart of Advaita Vedanta.

Another was to come a few days later when again Nitya singled me out for complimentary remarks. He had delegated a short talk on education at a local school to me and praised me not only for how I had handled it but also for my attitude generally. I am sure that in some way Jenny was pleased for me, yet at the same time, she explained to me later, the more I became comfortable in this environment and the more I seemed to give myself over to it, the more she had the impression of losing me. She said we were more like brother and sister now, no longer lovers. Of course the situation we found ourselves in was not conducive to wild sexual activity. We would often be housed in different quarters and since we were not married, we were treated as just a boy and a girl who came from the same country. Premarital sex is also not part of the Hindu culture and we had to be sensitive to that. Tantric experimentation was strictly not part of the regimen here.

By the time we got back to Singapore, it was time for Nitya to move on to the next part of his journey and for Jenny and me to proceed to India. Nitya gave me a personal introduction to Nataraja Guru, the head of the Narayana Gurukula Movement.

Narayana Guru was the founder of the movement and had been Nataraja's Guru.

In Singapore, while waiting for our visas to stay in India for six months, we spent some time with the Theosophists who were all delighted at our good fortune of the last two weeks. When we went to pick up our visas from the Indian High Commission, we were told they had been refused, but we were granted a twenty-one day tourist entry. The reason given was inadequate funds at hand. This did not deter us, of course, and we booked a passage on the SS Rajula from Penang to Madras. We had a week to get from Singapore to Penang. (However my new Atlas spells it 'Pinang'.)

We had been given Gurukula ashram addresses to add to our Theosophy contacts and we stopped over at Melaka, Seremban and Kuala Lumpur, ending up in Penang. In Seremban I was invited to speak on education and Australia at a TS lodge. We met a young Indian woman who was on her way to be trained as a Montessori teacher and was very excited to talk with me when I told her that I too was contemplating this. Everybody was very hospitable and interested in what we were doing and from where we came. In Penang, we stayed with a theosophical family with young children. John, the husband, was a very active person in the community and was planning to open a school for teenagers with special needs. On the way to take us to the boat, he invited us to come and work with him at the school after coming back from India. I was most impressed with the way he dealt with his own children and I had a very strong, positive feeling towards him. He also took us to the famous snake temple, a Buddhist temple where there were hundreds of snakes freely and peacefully sliding around. They are said to be safe because they have nothing to fear from the humans there, so tourists are allowed to handle them, which I did. It is a fantastic experience to feel the cool silky skin of a snake slowly slithering over your arms, hands and neck. I enjoyed it enormously.

The five days on the *Rajula* were uneventful and gave us some time to reconnect with each other. The events of the last few weeks had pulled us each into our own inner selves and in different directions. I had been pulled into the limelight on some occasions while Jenny had been feeling a trifle neglected. I had ended up connecting well with Nitya while she was now not so sure if he was the one that would 'set her free'. Apart from a little seasickness, I enjoyed the peacefulness on the ship. While it was crowded, there was enough space for us to feel by ourselves. We met some enthusiastic young Australians – most of them seeking something, others running away from something – all of them widening the 'hippy trail' to India. The five-day journey was relatively uneventful:

'Relaxing, lots of sleeping – some reading (Psycho Cybernetics) – played some table tennis – movies at night mostly Indian – a little sea sick… Jenny mostly good, met some nice people.'

Upon arrival in Madras, which is now referred to as Chennai, we went straight to Adyar, a suburb south of the city and also the name of the International Theosophical Headquarters. Adyar is not a building full of administrators – it is more like a small village, with European and Indian style living quarters, offices and a publishing house, a very large dining room serving both Indian and European cuisine, and a huge fabulous library. The whole complex is nestled in beautiful gardens, meticulously maintained without being rigid.

The buildings, of various sizes and styles, are spread out among the bushes and the trees. There are temples and churches of all religions dotted amongst the more functional buildings.

The whole place is much more like a monastery or spiritual retreat centre than the headquarters of an international organisation.

'Absolutely spiritual place here, every tree looks like the hair of a God.'

The most interesting aspect of all is that the people who live and work there, as well as the visitors, come from all over the world. During the week we stayed we met two Belgian Yoga teachers who I was able to help with their English; a New Zealand couple who had just had a baby; two young Dutch girls who laughed at my Flemish; and several Americans.

One of the reasons we stayed for a few days was that a friend of mine had asked me to do some research at the Adyar archives for his Doctoral thesis. The archival section of the Adyar library is said to hold ancient religious documents and other material not to be found anywhere else in the world. It was my privilege to be allowed to go in there and look for information under the watchful eye of the archival assistant librarian of course.

Apart from being a superbly serene place, full of extremely well-meaning and good people, Adyar exerted a certain amount of pressure on us. Because of its very spiritual nature, it is hard to be less than perfectly well-behaved there and we felt we had to do '*the right thing*' at all times. At the time of arrival we had been taken to our room. The following day, when we did the formal registration, they discovered that Jenny and I were not married and asked us to take separate rooms. They were not unpleasant about it but expressed the view that we should have told them. It was small matters of this sort that tripped Jenny up a couple of times and made us both feel somewhat relieved when we left. We did not know then that we were jumping from the frying pan straight into the fire.

'Bought some white Indian shirts – feels great to wear them. Jenny has matured two years in the last few months. I feel my love for her as solid as a rock. After meditation love occurred in a very beautiful way.'

Next day:

'Had a very animated conversation in Dutch with a lovely Dutch women over lunch. Then Jenny wanted to know every word we said as if I was hiding something. Darkness came over in seconds – what a contrast to yesterday.'

The Theosophical Society-Adyar, International Headquarters, India.

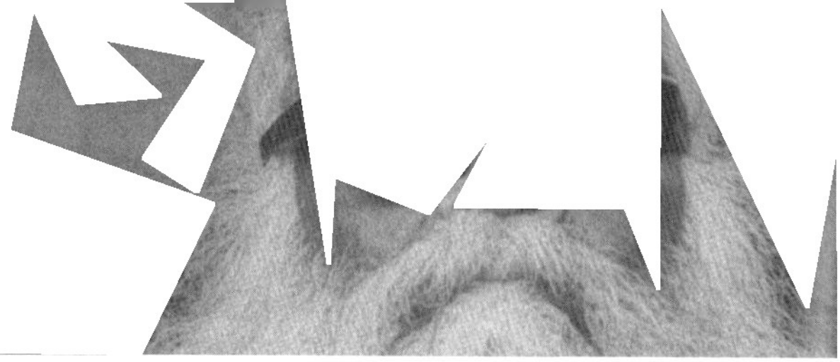

21.

‘Christmas’ at Shervatur

Kerala 1971

ONE of the Indian gardeners working at the Adyar estate had what could be described as a backyard travel business and, for a very small fee, arranged a ride for us in the back of a truck to Vellore, about a hundred kilometres straight east of Madras. Later that day, we took a train to Coimbatore, arriving there early the following morning, taking most of the night to travel less than 400 km. A bus took us north and up to Kotageri and another from there further up still to Ootacamund, which they now call Udagamandalam, in the Nilgiri Hills.

Travelling in India is an experience in itself. Standards of personal space, comfort and hygiene are very different to those in Australia, at least then, things may have change with their recent economic boom. But the beauty of the people and the magnificence of the scenery amply made up for it. Thinking of India now makes me see bright colours, smiling people and liveliness. India is also poverty and misery and having to cope with beggars. You cannot go there, even as a tourist, without being challenged and changed to some extent. I was soon to find out how much challenge and change I personally could take in the following months.

In Kotageri we visited Mrs Gladys Taylor, an English Theosophist who had spent much of her life working with Indian women and who told us about the local cooperative set-up and its struggle for survival. She was still as English as if she had never left England, but she had taken the Indian people into her heart. She took us to the TS cottage for the overnight stay.

The bus ride from Kotageri to Ooticamund, or '*Ooti*' as the locals call it, wound around steep turns and twists, making all the passengers lurch from side to side, an experience reminiscent of the big dipper at a fair. The higher you climb, the more breath-taking the views but, like on the dipper, some people do not have the stomach for it. However, as many buses did not have window glass, all you needed to do if you felt queasy was put your head outside and let nature take its course. Ooti, being in the hills, provides a cooler climate and was therefore a favourite summer retreat for the British colonials from all over South India. The English flavour is still very much present in many of its cottages and mansions around the town.

It was only a short walk from the town of Ooti to the Narayana Gurukula Movement headquarters. A very modest English-style single storey dwelling was nestled in between some lovely trees and it looked like a retired English couple could be living there. It was quiet and felt peaceful when we arrived and soon we were greeted by Bill, a young American in his mid-twenties, wearing an ochre 'dhoti', or loin cloth. He introduced us to the resident Swami, who spoke little English. For the next two days, apart from lengthy gossip sessions with Bill, who had been deprived of European company for some weeks, we took the opportunity to rest and dip into some of the many interesting-looking books that were available in the small library. That evening we were introduced to 'cungy', a rice, water and curry mixture, standing in for dinner. The following day we went shopping at the colourful Ooti market, returning with bags of vegetables and fruit. Ooti was an enormous contrast to Adyar in many ways and yet contributed equally to our experience and development.

Then, on the fourth day, Nataraja Guru, the current head of the movement, arrived with an entourage of a half dozen Westerners and a couple of Indians. He was probably over sixty, balding, short and very round. His face was friendly and he smiled and joked a lot. He had a long flowing white beard and was wearing a plain Indian shirt and a dhoti. After some tea was served he called us to him for an introductory chat. He explained some of the basic rules of the place. Westerners were welcome to stay, but they had to contribute both money and work for everyday necessities and to keep themselves. He did not want money for himself. '*If you want toilet paper you will have to buy it yourself*', he laughed, '*or adopt the Indian way.*' '*If you are married you can sleep together, if not the boys sleep in the boys' quarters and the girls sleep in the girls' quarters.*' There would be meditation at six in the morning and six in the evening and during the day there would be study and domestic work. Tantric practices did not seem to be on the menu here either. When the semi-formal part was over he addressed me in French, asking me why I was there and what I wanted to do. I was both delighted and a little intimidated by his casual straightforwardness. He certainly did not live up to the stereotypical picture of the saintly Guru or of the strict spiritual teacher. He was both approachable and friendly, and very unassuming. I liked him immediately and he remains to this day one of the kindest and most interesting and inspiring people I have met.

When I explained that we had trouble with visas and would have to go to Ceylon to obtain new ones, he said he would fix it. We were to go to Cannanore on the Malabar Coast where he knew the director of the Foreign Registry Office who would help us. We would then go to another Gurukula near there in Elimali and wait there. We left the following day on a bus, taking most of the day to get to Cannanore.

'Jenny and I discussed the changing nature of our relationship in the context of the Gurukula. She wants us to be 'normal' – I want her to be happy – but I also want to get the most from being with Guru. Are we having different agendas now? Our idea was doing this together and doing the same thing.'

In Cannanore we found Mr Nanda Gopal, owner of a shoe store, who said he would take us to the Foreign Registry Office the following day. He also happened to know the people from the local TS lodge and, since they were having a meeting that night, I was promptly asked to speak on the work of the TS in Australia. During our stay in India, as in Malaysia, the Theosophical Society and the Narayana Gurukula Movement kept on intertwining like the strands of hair in a braid, in this case an Indian braid, naturally.

At the Foreign Registry Office we had to explain why we did not have proper visas and why we had not applied for them before coming to India; why we had not applied before today instead of travelling around; and so on, and so on. They made it seem like a big drama. It was, in fact, just normal Indian bureaucracy at work. All interactions with officialdom seem to get entangled with finicky little rules and as a result take much more time than we are used to. We asked when our visas would be ready and for how long they would be valid. The official sternly said, '*You must wait,*' and that was that. My situation was not unlike that of Lebanon, Syria and Afghanistan a few years earlier, so I was neither surprised nor upset, and off we went to our Gurukula in Elimali.

If Ooti was the Gurukula Movement's headquarters, Elimali was definitely an outpost of minor significance. It consisted of one partially finished two-storey brick structure and a couple of traditional huts in the surrounding bushes. The physical surroundings were absolutely idyllic. A short walk through lush green vegetation would take you to the beach for a cooling swim in the Arabian Sea. Many parts of India are very crowded but this place was completely away from any social life, except the inmates of the Gurukula.

There were about a dozen people camping in this small settlement, many of them from European countries, including a couple from Gent. They had been there for some years and considered themselves somewhat senior in rank. Our common origin did not make for a close relationship, although we did enjoy reminiscing. I did not see anybody that would have been over twenty-five, and most looked like hippies, took drugs and seemed to have no money. A few were genuinely interested in studying the work of Nataraja Guru and followed some sort of routine. There was also a lot of coming and going, and I never quite knew who was in charge. The complexity of this situation manifested itself in a number of different ways.

In the first instance, there were the everyday practicalities of obtaining and preparing food. The nearest market was over an hour's walk away. Cooking facilities were primitive, to say the least. Indian vegetarianism was the rule, but many of these people could no longer handle curry and had suffered serious gastric upsets. Conversely, the few Indians there would eat nothing but curry, so for every meal both Indian and European cuisines had to be catered for.

Privacy was non-existent and the toilets were a series of holes in the ground. Laundry was done in the nearby ocean. The shower was under the leaking guttering of the partially completed building when it rained, which it thankfully often did. Work consisted of trying to finish the building, the laying of a brick path so we wouldn't bring in the mud from outside in the rainy season, which had just started, and establishing some sort of vegetable garden. There was no particular system to work out who would do what and so it was not surprising that some things often did not get done at all. Cleaning the place was one of them.

Apart from the practicalities, there were the people themselves. A student of group dynamics would have had a field day observing us. When there is no established leadership in a group there are always some who will take it, for whatever reason. The resulting challenge to those self-styled 'leaders', from those who do not want to be told what to do, is a foolproof recipe for interpersonal conflict and tension. Communal living is difficult at the best of times, but when there are differing personal agendas and blatant disregard for the overall purpose, the situation can easily turn to anarchy and become very tense. Open physical hostility was very rare, although there was a scuffle or two during the short time we were there. However, the moral condemnation and disapproval of your behaviour from your 'room-mates' can be as crushing as a blow to the chin. We were there, after all, supposedly to learn about a spiritual practice and philosophy and we all knew, at least vaguely, what we should be doing. If the atmosphere at Adyar created some pressure because of its convent-like flavour, the tension here was more like that inside a psychiatric ward. Our philosophical discussions often slipped into something much more akin to group therapy and there were at least one or two members of our group who would have been given medication if they had gone to see a psychiatrist. For the most part these were essentially good and friendly people, but in a pressure-cooker setting like this, even within glorious natural surroundings and despite the context of spiritual development (or perhaps because of it), it was enough to raise the hackles and break the patience of even the most devout student.

'Did some heavy work today. It is unfortunate that there is some tension between people here; such a perfect place ought to lead to a

perfect atmosphere. I have a suspicion I would not be able to fully abandon myself to this life as it is here. Did my washing on the beach – it's good to get out of the house.'

Against this background, there was Jenny and me with our own very sensitively-balanced relationship and my increasing difficulty in handling it. Jenny's disappointment with the whole set-up was only the start. This was not the spiritual community of which she had been dreaming. Then there was her disappointment with me for not being able to be her lover in the way she wanted me to be. The blackouts became increasingly frequent and the mood swings were as regular as a pendulum. Jenny had also had some bad experiences with drugs in the past and their presence around her now was having a frightening effect on her.

Jenny sought refuge in looking to the future, wanting me to commit to a life together and having children. She not only wanted to be with me, she naturally wanted me to want to be with her as well. She needed me to get her out of her black holes but I needed not to be needed by anybody. In contrast, I was seeking refuge in my practice of living in the present without specific choices or looking to the future – to be free rather than committed and bound by social conventions.

'Plunged into a spiritual soul-digging. Jenny wants to sort out the future. But what can speculation about the future bring but disappointment?'

I was trying to understand the writings of Nataraja Guru. I could sense wisdom there, but it was hard to get hold of it amid all this chaos and emotional turmoil. I was struggling to establish some rational connection between what I was studying on the one hand, and what I was experiencing on the other, and it eluded my grasp. There were also moments of joy when Jenny and I went on a walk along the beach to take a breather from Gurukula life, and one time we went to the dentist together, which I labelled in my diary as 'psychologically refreshing'.

After about two weeks, Nataraja Guru turned up unexpectedly, somewhat like a parent coming home early to find the teenagers are having a party instead of doing their homework. He was calm but not his jovial self, and although he had a touch of the flu, continued his work as usual. The following day while we were all gathered for morning meditation, Nataraja Guru expressed his displeasure in no uncertain terms. He did not raise his voice or display any anger: he simply said he was disturbed by what was going on here and that it was entirely contrary to the intention of Gurukula life. He explained that '*kula*' means '*family*' in Sanskrit and that people living in the Gurukula are family of the Guru and should behave like it. He spoke most harshly of all about the prevalence of drugs and likened those who use the Gurukula as a cover for their habit to leeches living off his family. The story was told by one of the older hippies that one time someone had put LSD in Guru's tea, but the absence of any effect whatever rather spoiled their fun.

He then addressed the girls, expressing his disappointment with the standard of cooking. Preparing food, he explained, is like a spiritual ritual and should be undertaken with a reverence and care you would give to your family. Several of the girls, Jenny included, saw this as a sexist remark and rejected being singled out to be responsible for cooking. They did not express this verbally but their looks were not lost on the Guru. Such feelings may have been reinforced a day later if they had been present at a private conversation the Guru and I had about my relationship with Jenny. After a short discourse on the complementarity between men and women in general, he simply asked if I had some money left. I said I had. He replied: '*Take her to town and buy her something.'*

I was to have several private conversations with Nataraja Guru during the next few days, some peppered with French expressions. On one occasion when I expressed my desire to serve through education, he said he had just the project for me. Another Gurukula near the town of Shervatur was in a village where they did not have a school. We could build one and I could be the teacher. Krishnamurti's words '*Start your own school*' flashed through my mind, but how long would it take to build a school? This Gurukula here seemed to have taken years. Guru explained to me that I didn't need a building to start a school – all that is needed is children and a teacher willing to teach. Was he throwing me a challenge, testing my willingness to act on my conviction? I smiled and asked him when we would start, thinking this could be one of those future plans that may never come off. He looked up for a moment, as if to consult his inner diary and simply said '*We'll go there the day after tomorrow.*' There was no doubting he was serious and I nearly dissolved with excitement.

My joy was short-lived. It wasn't me remembering the spectre of failure at Summerfarm that brought me down, but rather Jenny. When I told her about this new development, she saw it as my abandoning her for this sexist old man who did not seem to care for her. Down we went into the emotional black pits once again. I assured her that she could come too and that there would be plenty for her to do at a school. It was not what she wanted to hear.

'More speculation about the future. More tensions. Then she cried – what to do? I said I don't want to live in the future. Now I am torn between an opportunity to fulfil my purpose as an educator here in this beautiful country and what seems to have become my responsibility to look after Jenny.'

After the morning study group on Saturday 28 August,

Guru, Jenny and I left Elimali Gurukula in a little black car driven by a local supporter of the movement, and late the same day stopped on the edge of a paddock not far from a small town called Shervatur. Nataraja Guru had a few words with the resident Swami and, after introducing us, continued his journey to Ooti, saying he would be back soon.

Elimali, compared to Ooti, was an outpost, but compared to Elimali, Shervatur Gurukula was no more than a guard shelter. It consisted of a two room dilapidated stone cottage. One room served as sleeping quarters, the other was the kitchen and everything else. Twenty metres behind the cottage stood a shoddy one-room wooden hut the size of a family camping tent. It looked as if it would fall over if you sneezed too hard. The immediate surroundings were a large grassy undulating paddock, some bushes here and there and then forest all around. If Elimali Gurukula was crowded and chaotic, this one was simple and had only two residents. There was the usual Swami caretaker, this one called Krishna, and his assistant, a twelve-year-old boy called Raja. Krishna needed the assistant because he was old, walking with a stick and speaking absolutely no English. Since Krishna and Raja lived in the main cottage, this left the hut for Jenny and me. Seeing there was no choice, we were allowed to occupy the 'married persons' accommodation. This pleased both of us enormously.

The Swami performed a special '*puja*' evening service to welcome us and the '*cungy*' had an extra pinch of curry in it to celebrate our arrival. We were a special event in the life of this Gurukula.

Our first day there started with a bout of diarrhoea. For me it was the first and only digestive upset during our entire stay in India. Most people travelling in India, including Jenny, suffer a bug of one sort or another. Living in the conditions we did, it was surprising we didn't suffer from all sorts of other things as well. That morning Raja took us to the village market and we bought some barley and green vegetables. Raja's English was poor, to put it generously, but he was very keen to learn. That morning during our walk to the village, lesson number one in this newly-opened school took place. Raja was delighted; school had come to him. What was equally exciting for him was that he was able to teach us words in his native tongue so that he was now both a student and a teacher. Raja had one of those photogenic faces that smiles with simple happiness. He was not only very handsome, but clever and always helpful. I would have loved to be his older brother.

Due to our condition we thought we should stay off curry for a while and Jenny decided she would cook a more Western-style meal seeing there was only the four of us. First we had to explain to Krishna, via Raja of course, what we wanted to do and why and the advantage to him of not having to cook that day. Then it took the rest of the day to rearrange Krishna's way of doing things, compromising on what could and could not be done, what could be used for what and what couldn't be touched for what reasons. Lesson two for Raja was about negotiating and compromising between cultures. His English and his maturity were stretched beyond his age. Krishna's cultural flexibility and patience was tested to the limit and Jenny's frustration rose by the minute. After that we decided that we would buy the food and let them do the cooking. It worked much better that way.

Despite the fact that we had the naturally curious Raja hanging around us whenever he had nothing to do for Krishna, our surroundings were infinitely more peaceful than in the previous Gurukula. One of the most delightful memories of Shervatur is my barefoot walks on the dew-soaked grass at sunrise before the heat of the day. I came to look forward to my peripatetic meditations, and the solitude was a balm to my inner being. There was also time for Jenny and me to reflect more calmly on our relationship and where it was going, or rather where it wasn't. By now I was beginning to feel that I was getting better at handling the blackouts and the mood swings and that my practice of non-judgement and compassion were paying off. Seated in the shade under one of the few trees around, I remember discussing with Jenny the nature of her state of mind. She articulated more clearly than I had ever heard before that she experienced more or less permanently states of tension, doubt, hesitation, mistrust and fear. In my diary I noted,

'I wonder if there is a touch of "paranoia" here – maybe professional help is needed? What am I going to do? I am well out of my depth here.'

My sincere desire to help, my limited skills and knowledge of counselling and my so-called 'love' for her were unfortunately not adequate to the task. We often meditated together under that tree and at the end Jenny would glow with peace. We had a couple of days of almost complete rest and emotional stability before our world flipped upside down again.

Nataraja Guru, accompanied by a handful of Westerners (some of whom we had met before) arrived to prepare for the celebrations of the birthday of Narayana Guru, the founder of the Movement. The Guru stayed in a house in the nearby village and came every day for services, discourse and work. The Westerners camped in makeshift tents on the grounds of the Gurukula. Every year the Guru chooses a different Gurukula to be present at the celebrations and we seemed to be at the right place at the right time this year. I was given the task of writing an article about the event for publication in the Movement's journal. I was also enjoying Nataraja's company and getting to appreciate his intelligence, wisdom and above all his humility. Here was a man who had achieved the highest academic level (PhD) in a notoriously difficult discipline (Philosophy) and in a foreign language (French); who was a published author and scholar in both Eastern and Western philosophical traditions; and who was also head of a religious and philanthropic movement... walking around in a loincloth and a T-shirt. He had no personal possessions or money and lived from day to day, teaching and helping those in need of advice and guidance. The so-called spiritual world is littered with self-proclaimed 'god-men', preaching selflessness while living in palaces, lapping up blind adulation and being chauffeured in cars only successful capitalists can afford. With Nataraja Guru, humility was not a hollow concept worthy only of lip service for public consumption; it was an integral part of his everyday life. No hypocrisy here.

Sunday 5 September was the big day. It was all hands on deck at 5 am. The Gurukula building was decorated in bright colours and wood was brought for the massive amount of cooking required to get the food ready. By mid-morning the formal part of the celebrations could begin. I don't know where they all came from, but I estimated there were over two hundred people present – we had catered for one hundred. Manipulating the physical elements to impress the crowd, as some Indian Swamis do, was not on the menu here. There was a lot of chanting, music, prayers and all sorts of rituals, which were later explained to us. The children were the first to be treated to something they called '*prasadum*', a mixture of rice, sweet coconut and spices. They would not have been happier if it had been Christmas. Then came the fire sacrifice ceremony, a ritual designed to cleanse the spirit. And finally, what most people had come for, the big feast. The contents of large cauldrons of rice, curry, dhal and vegetables were served on banana leaves and greedily gobbled up by what seemed to be a hungry crowd. There was some sort of 'thank-you' prayer and by mid-afternoon they had all gone, leaving us with some volunteer helpers to tidy up the mess. 'Christmas' was over.

During our discussion the following day, Guru was asked why he performed religious rituals with the local people while in our studies we were taken well beyond popular religion into universal spiritual wisdom. He said that the people would go to some other Guru, if he didn't perform those rituals because that's what they wanted. He preferred them to come to him so he could eventually show them that there was more to their religion than they thought and maybe even wean them off their religion to a more spiritual path. Then followed a lengthy discussion on the help one can provide to other people in their quest for 'enlightenment' and to what extent one had to do all the work for oneself. This spilled over into the question of whether one can walk the path together with a so-called 'soul-mate' and together reach the 'Absolute', Guru's word for 'enlightenment', or 'Nirvana' as the Buddhists call it. Guru's opinion on this was very clear. '*No, you cannot.*' In my understanding this is also what Krishnamurti and Zen would say.

I am sure that to some people there this was all academic and of no real consequence to their everyday life or practice. To my surprise, for Jenny this became a matter of '*all or nothing*'. She took me aside as soon as it was practicable and in a very angry tone confronted me with her opinion that '*it has to be possible to walk together into the Absolute with another person because if it isn't, what were we doing together?*' And if I believed that he, Guru, was right then '*We're through*,' after which she burst out crying and stomped off into the forest. Now metaphysical differences were being mixed into emotional entanglements. 'Oh what a tangled web we weave' indeed. Still, if you want to live by your convictions as I believe we should, you need to clarify what they mean, especially if you want to do it together with another person.

The following morning Jenny decided to go away for the day. I walked with her to the village where she was to take a bus, hoping I could straighten things out on the way. Instead her anger and frustration got worse. I was shaken, saddened, and at my wits' end. Upon my return I talked with Guru. He was very understanding and compassionate and made some helpful suggestions, but nothing concrete.

The following day Guru and the Westerners left and it was back to us four residents. The mood was tense but Jenny and I made a supreme effort to reconcile. The most baffling aspect of the whole situation to me was that when Jenny was in a stable emotional frame of mind, we got on well and there was a great deal of affection between us. But as soon as the wind changed, the black clouds that seemed to have been following her for years would zap her. In one of our more harmonious moments together I tried to explain to Jenny that if my very presence next to her and the beliefs I held made it impossible for us to be happy together, then we should perhaps not be together. I pointed out that to stay or to leave was her choice, not mine. Instantly the wind changed again and off we went into the deep black depths of emotional turmoil. I was now accused of abandoning her and conspiring with Guru, all for our male chauvinist selfish ends, not caring at all for her needs. The next day Jenny developed a fever and severe diarrhoea. Over the next two days she got gradually worse and we decided to seek medical help in Cannanore, the nearest big town. She was given some Ayurvedic medicine and treatment and felt a little better.

While in Cannanore, we contacted Mr Nanda Gopal who had helped us previously with the applications for our visa. He was delighted to see us because he had been trying to contact us for some time, not knowing where we were. Gurukulas did not have telephones then. He had received news from the Foreign Registry Office. Our visas had been denied and we were to leave India immediately. We had to sign a document accepting the verdict and apply for temporary permits to be in India till we could actually get out. Jenny's case was somewhat different because travelling on a Commonwealth Passport she could have reapplied for a tourist visa. Again, the choice was hers to stay or leave. My only choice if I wanted to stay was to go underground and live as an illegal migrant a situation that one or two people in the Gurukula were actually in.

In the moments of peaceful meditation back at Shervatur, it became clear that the best thing for me to do was to go back to Australia. Jenny decided to come with me. On our way through Ooti, we stopped to tell Nataraja Guru what had happened. In a non-judgemental tone he commented that '*it is for the better, disharmonious couples cause disturbance which is not good for the Gurukula.*' I had to humbly agree. To call our relationship 'disharmonious' was to be kind and generous. I thanked him for his kindness and hospitality. I told him I had learned many lessons while in his presence. He looked me straight in the eyes and without smiling simply said '*Au revoir*'. No fuss, just '*letting go*'.

'My turn to speculate about the future now. Many questions were answered during meditation before asking Guru. Yes I do derive benefit from pure awareness and meditation. Peace!'

We arrived back in Madras on Sunday 19 September and went straight to Adyar. At the travel agency we were told that the next boat to Malaysia was the Rajula leaving on the fifth of October. During those two weeks, in the peaceful surroundings of that superb sanctuary, there was much time to relax and also to reflect on our time in India – the lessons we had learned, or failed to learn, and the pain we had endured. A diary entry of that time reads:

'I feel rather different… my ego has been knocked around seriously and humility has grown… there is more steady awareness and a more mature understanding of the nature of spirituality. It will take some time to really process all this learning, but I am convinced that it will be worth it in the end.'

The dozen or so lessons with Guru and the reading I had done had given me some understanding of Advaita Vedanta, but only enough to realise that intellectually, I knew very little. My increased 'understanding of spirituality' had come much more from the behaviour of all the people we encountered. Literally understanding what Nataraja Guru's commentary on the Bhagavad Gita means when he is dealing with verse nine on page 662 ('*When necessary action is done, O Arjuna, recognising its imperative character, relinquishing attachment and benefit, such relinquishment is considered pure.*') is one thing; seeing 'relinquishment of attachment' in action and then trying to do it yourself is quite another.

I am not sure what Guru meant when he wrote about '*Bergson's structural prognosis of Einstein's two theories of relativity*' in his *Integrated Science of the Absolute*, but intuitively I am sure of the purity of his actions. Some of those around him served well as contrast and I would like to think that the example was not wasted on me. Nataraja Guru and Swami Nitya were certainly not the only people adding to my learning. Apart from Jenny providing me with daily opportunities for practice, the countless people we had to deal with on our journeys were living in a culture that is based on spiritual wisdom and yet riddled with corruption. The contrast between its physical and inner beauty on the one hand and poverty and misery on the other is what makes many people either absolutely hate or love India. Any serious student of Eastern philosophy would do well to see it in action if he or she wishes to understand its roots.

During our last two weeks in India, there were two more specific contributions to my education. Within cycling distance from the Adyar compound, a modern but modest building houses the Madras Krishnamurti Centre. To my pleasant surprise its schedule of events was posted on the notice board near the dining room in Adyar. Since Krishnamurti's break with the Theosophical Society, some Theosophists were not exactly sympathetic with his cause, while others continued to be great devotees. On Sunday afternoon there was a film showing one of Krishnamurti's talks, so I went. My diary note reminds me that for me it was '… *one of the most stimulating talks ever.*'

I had heard many talks and read a considerable number of pages on Krishnamurti and thought I had a good idea what he was about. Having had my mind stretched by the very culture Krishnamurti grew up in allowed me to see even more of what he was saying. Several pieces of the puzzle fell into place and it reached deep into my heart. It was a profound experience and a valuable complement to the growth of the last two months, somewhat like icing on a cake.

The Adyar library, where I had spent some time researching information for a friend, attracted me like the proverbial moth to the flame. One of the great things about well-stocked libraries is that you can browse and always find something interesting. With the concept of synchronicity firmly at work, I found a book by my old friend and Zen master, Hubert Benoit, called of all things *The Many Faces of Love*, first published in France in 1952 as *De L'Amour*.

This book is neither about Zen nor about romantic love, as the French title might suggest. Rather, it is a map, a cartography, an aid to find one's way among the many instances, or faces, of 'love', that little word we so glibly use in so many different ways. Benoit drew my attention to the differences between physical desire and appetitive or possessive love; between positive self-love and negative narcissism. He raised many important questions, which I had not considered seriously before. How many forms of 'adoration' are there? When does erotic love become pornography? Is there such a thing as aesthetic love or do you just 'like' this painting or that face? What about the love of truth and justice, or the love of your country and your parents? And is it possible to love purely benevolently and unconditionally? What happens when you love God, and how does he/she/it love you? When a woman (or a man) asks you '*Do you love me?*' how do you know what sort of love she means and in what way you do love her if you think you do?

Benoit, the psychiatrist turned philosopher, student of Zen and observer of human relationships, brought all his wisdom to bear in the service of helping us see what happens when we think we 'love'. This work was so appropriate for me at that time that, more than anything else, it guided me to work on dealing with the relationship I was having with Jenny. Some years later when asked to give a talk at the Melbourne lodge of the Theosophical Society, I chose this book as my topic. To understand the '*many faces of love*' I believe is one of the most useful insights we can gather if we are serious about learning how to live harmoniously with other people.

These few days in Adyar brought together into my consciousness Advaita Vedanta, which I had just been studying with Nataraja Guru; Krishnamurti who I had just revisited via film, and Benoit with his 'faces of love' and the psychology of Zen. A great deal of academic debate could be devoted to the differences between Zen, Advaita Vedanta and Krishnamurti. It occurred to me then that it is much more important to see their commonality than to quibble over the differences between these points of view. To me, they have all helped in my trying to come to grips with the big questions in life and they were all pointing me in the same direction. *Awareness, detachment, non-judgement and compassion* are all key elements in all of them. Of course, understanding something intellectually is not the same as being able to put it into practice, but it is a start. Krishnamurti certainly told us that if you see something clearly, completely and totally, not only with your brain but also with your whole being, then you would act upon it in the right way without hesitation.

Adyar provided room for both Jenny and me to do our own thing, while coming together from time to time. It worked well for me but not for Jenny. Despite our pact to respect solitude as well as companionship, it was not always easy to match our time of wanting to be by ourselves. I think my need for solitude had become greater than hers.

During one of our peaceful moments together, Jenny again brought up the idea that she wanted to have children. It is, of course, a natural and instinctive desire and Jenny was at a point in her life where it must have felt the right time, but I certainly was not ready. When her period finally arrived at least a week late that month, my diary recorded that:

'There was a note of disappointment in her voice when she told me she wasn't pregnant after all. She still wants to be with me and still wants me to want to be with her as well. But if Jenny and I could keep sufficiently apart we could maybe be successfully together.'

On 1 October, Adyar was ablaze with celebrations for the birthday of Annie Besant, one of the great figures in the early days of the Theosophical Society. The following day it was Ghandi's birthday, with more celebrations. These were welcome distractions from our self-reflection.

For me, a mixture of laryngitis, seasickness and extreme tiredness dominated the return journey on the *Rajula*. We met a young Australian couple who claimed to be Buddhists. As we got to know them better, it turned out that they had similar problems to Jenny and me in reconciling their spiritual beliefs on the one hand with their normal man-woman relations as prescribed by society on the other. It made me feel a lot better and helped Jenny and I make a resolution:

'Jenny and I came to the conclusion that when we get back to Sydney we might as well give living together a go. Of course there are many

factors that will come into play once we get there.'

We revisited John in Penang and he was as helpful and inspiring as before, even though he was disappointed we didn't stay to work with him. Here was a man who acted on his beliefs *and* had a family and children at the same time. I was waiting for Jenny to point that out to me and ask me why I couldn't do that, but she didn't. I would not have known what to say.

In Singapore we stayed in the Gurukula for a day or two and met up with François again. He, too, was struggling with applying the wisdom he had gained to his everyday life. We were able to provide some much-needed support to each other. Jenny and I flew out of Singapore by the end of October and Sydney was a welcome sight. It was good to be back home again.

22.

Double resolution

Sydney 1971

First resolution

Once again, coming back to Australia felt like coming 'home'. Exciting as travel and going away is, coming back home has a pleasure all of its own. Just as change and the exotic 'foreign' are stimulating, the familiarity of home is comforting and reassuring.

Kathleen Wade came to pick us up from the airport and we stayed at her place that night. The following day we got a small flat near the city for $16 a week. The day after, Jenny got a job at a health food shop. We were on our way. Would more stable circumstances enable us to live less 'disharmoniously'?

The following week, among my many unsuccessful attempts to find work other than hairdressing, I went to see Marcus at Summerfarm and he promptly engaged me to organise the rebirth of the school. I was to plan a curriculum, organise a marketing campaign, be the Public Relations Officer and even take part in the physical erection of a new prefabricated building four times as large as the previous one. We would also engage qualified teachers. In short we would do everything to become a certified school and beat the system. For me all those tasks were new and I had absolutely no expertise to bring to this adventure except my goodwill and blindness to its likely failure.

Still, I was enthusiastic and did the best I could. In the blurb of the pamphlet promoting the school I wrote:

'People of all walks of life, the trades, artists, business and the labour force, MUST realise that the education of our children comes about not in the school only, nor only in the presence of the parents, but occurs at every moment of contact with the world all around them. Each of us then, through our own personal and professional skills, must actually participate, directly or indirectly, in assuring the best education is provided for the children we meet. We must do this not only because we are part of the social chain in our community but for the continuation and improvement of human existence.'

In another document titled '*Information and Advice*' addressed to prospective parents we suggested:

'Regular and punctual attendance is naturally expected. Punishment is never resorted to, but when serious difficulties arise contact with parents is made. Children are free to learn at our school but NOT to disturb or prevent others from doing their work; NOT to be destructive or to be aggressive to others; obedience to the rules for safety and general order is in the interest of each and all.

'NO one of the organised religions or practices is preached, preferred or opposed. We study the religions of the world from the point of view that the underlying truth is more important than the way in which they differ, and we take the attitude of basic Unity, not only in mankind but throughout the known universe.

'We recommend lunches of nourishing and fresh food and fruit. Please DO NOT include sweets or other distractions in your child's lunch box.'

Amongst the papers I still have about that ambitious project, I found what must have been an early draft of a daily sequence of activities:

9:00 – Group exercises (while individual health is observed)

9:20 – 1st Main lesson (conversational and according to interest but roughly following curriculum, and not necessarily in the classroom)

10:00 – Discussing, planning and distributing PROJECTS. (Either in relation to the main lesson or individually chosen)

12:00 – Lunch break (optional)

1:00 – 2nd Main lesson (continuing from the 1st if required)

Reflection: Summarising or commenting in writing on the project or main lesson.

2:00 – Reading – Study or private lessons

3:00 – Group conversations – reading to the group – quiet moment before going home.

Remember this was the early 1970s and I had not yet studied education formally.

I re-established my connections with the TS and the Youth Group and I became a member of the TS Youth Group Committee. We changed the format from having guest speakers and discussions to one of self-discovery and called it the '*Discovery Group*'. The idea was to put into practice what Krishnamurti was telling us to do – '*Look and see for yourself*'. It attracted a different sort of person and I learned a lot about both running groups and facilitating personal development.

I intended my life to be as before and, given some increased understanding, better if possible. However, it now felt like I had a dependant – a person who needed me to do certain things and be in certain places at certain times and feel in certain ways in order for her to be happy. The more the school took up my time, energy and focus, and the more I gave to the Theosophical Society and other causes, the more Jenny asked of me. Her mood swings returned and it wasn't just the insecurity of travel or the pressures of a disappointing India this time. I steadfastly refused to see us as a 'couple' in the conventional sense (like a marriage), and wanted no more for us than being two people living together who had great regard for each other, but who are completely independent.

I did not see then that my view of the concept of a marriage-like conventional relationship was based on my rejection of my social conditioning. My anti-marriage stance had its origins in my emotional experience as a child. I did not understand that my very quest for freedom had been the cause of the breakdown of every relationship I had embarked upon so far. My explorations of spiritual development and the psychology of love had not yet sufficiently explained to me that the instinctive drive to procreate operates very differently in men to the way it does in women. For men it is easy to procreate – all it takes is to '*sow one's wild oats*'. The burden of childbirth and the care of offspring, much more difficult tasks, rest traditionally with women and therefore require a stable and secure support system from the mate with whom she has offspring. Not that marriage provides this security any more, as divorce rates testify, but at least it was designed to provide it, or so one theory amongst others tells us. Security comes from a commitment to provide and protect the children as well as the mother. In my case, I had a strong commitment to the education of children in general, being a form of sublimation, and thus reducing my instinctive need for children of my own, something for which I did not feel ready. Jenny, on the other hand, was ready and did not want to wait any longer. Powerful drivers those instincts!

In November I wrote an affirmation that I have used often since and use still today:

> ***'May there be health in this body, compassion in this heart and peace in this mind.'***

By the end of December of that year, I had created a progressive, integrated curriculum spanning a five-year period and was very proud of it. Too bad it never got used. Even though we got articles in a number of publications and newspapers, we failed to enrol enough people to become a commercially viable school, let alone meet departmental regulations. It was disappointing but not surprising. In the meantime Jenny and I had moved to Pennant Hills on the other side of the city to be closer to the school. We were sharing with two other Theosophists, trying to create our own little communal group. It worked, more or less, for a very short time. December 5 entry:

'Jenny has black clouds again – long drawn-out conversations about what to do. It must change for it cannot remain like that, it cannot go on like this. There must be a way out of this.'

This rather desperate sounding statement turned out to be the last entry about Jenny in my 1971 diary. It was to be also the last diary note-book I kept. These nine small diaries have been of great assistance in the recalling of those years' events.

Jenny had taken a part-time job at a local alternative Steiner school and met a young man there who taught guitar. She took up lessons with him, though she had not expressed interest in playing music before. I thought nothing of it. One day I came home early from work and found them in the shower together. When they were done, we sat cross-legged on the grass in the garden, the three of us, smiling. They were smiling because they were 'in love', the romantic sort that is, and could now be released from the burden of hiding it and share their 'secret'. I was smiling because I had just been relieved from taking care of my 'dependant', however unsatisfactory it had been for her. I sincerely wished them well. We had a short meditation and off they went into the sunshine and their future together. My 'letting go' skills served me well, again.

After the failure to resurrect the school and wanting to break with hairdressing altogether, I worked as a storeman in a dried flower wholesaler's warehouse. It was a family business and the people were very supportive of their workers. It was physically hard labour but I enjoyed it. I worked there for most of 1972. I bought my first motorbike, a Yamaha 120, to go to work and learned to enjoy the breeze and freedom of motorcycling.

By the end of the year, my back was giving me trouble and I had to give up my heavy-lifting job at the flower sellers. A friend who worked in a factory referred me to her superintendent to see if they had a job as a storeman. After talking for a while he said he had another job which he claimed would suit me better. He was right. The job he had in mind was that of timekeeper. I was part of the personnel division and my task was to calculate, on the basis of timesheets filled in by operators, how long specific jobs took to complete. It was easy work, not too much of it and the pay was very reasonable. I stayed for two years.

Second resolution

Sydney 1972

My vision of education had not gone off the rails. I may not have been teaching but I was certainly learning a lot, both theoretically and practically. At last my means of earning a living had changed, at least for the time being. The TS '*Discovery Group*' was also an excellent training ground for tutorial work, counselling and public speaking, all of which I would need later on. My interests in psychology and philosophy did not diminish during that time either. As well as all that, I had also begun studying for my mature-age Higher School Certificate by correspondence, taking the compulsory English and General Studies, with French as my elective. I passed the exam and was now more eligible to enter university than without it, for that was my goal. It seemed clear that if I was to be serious about education, I had to study it and get proper qualifications. I turned thirty in December 1972, but it is never too late to learn and when Whitlam, the then Labour Prime Minister, abolished university fees I was ready to apply.

The lessons from India were beginning to sink in. Jenny was gone. I had a job and a place to live, and a direction to move towards. Life seemed to be going well. Yet there was one issue hanging over me. Where was Sylvia and what had happened to her? Sydney is a big city and I no longer expected to bump into her the way I had reconnected with Annie. Instead, completely unexpectedly, I ran into Sylvia's father, who I had met during a brief visit to Sydney years ago before leaving Port Moresby on my Trans-Siberian trip. He was waiting for a bus and as I walked past I recognised him, though it took a few moments to remember where I had seen him before and to identify who he was. Luckily he was not in a hurry and we went for a coffee. He gave me some of Sylvia's recent story, but more importantly he was able to give me her address in Darwin on the other side of this vast continent. That explained why I had not accidentally met her in Sydney. To top the list of the unexpected, he said she was coming to Sydney for a holiday in two weeks time. I wrote immediately, inviting her to visit and stay with me if she wanted to.

I was now living in a small one-bedroom flat overlooking Centennial Park and when Sylvia came to visit we decided to enjoy the open space and the warm sun and tell our stories while walking in the park. She had changed her hair and looked older, but we were both happy to meet again. I asked her to tell me absolutely everything that had happened in Marseille, but first things first, I had to ask '*Why Darwin and since when have you been there?*' She simply wanted to be somewhere entirely different and make a completely fresh start away from anybody she had known before. She had been there now for the last two years, working in a kindergarten, and had met a very nice man with whom she now lived, and marriage was definitely on the cards. Well, that settled that. A little calculation revealed that she must have come to Darwin some time after Jenny and I spent two months there in 1971 on our way to Singapore. Another close miss.

'So, what happened in Marseille?' I wanted to know.

'The first two days on the ship from Beirut I got sick with a stomach virus. You may remember that I was already feeling tired before leaving, so by the time we got to Marseille I was exhausted. As the liner prepared to dock at Marseille, I had overheard an Englishman tell another passenger that he planned to travel by train to Dover. I approached him and asked if I could accompany him on the train, as I did not speak French. He said 'Yes, as long as you are not jinxed.' which was a rather funny thing to say, but I just laughed. He said that he had just had the worst month of his life and that he did not want anything else to go wrong. His name was Henry.'

Sylvia did not seem upset having to retell the story, so I encouraged her to go on.

'That was assertive of you to invite a stranger to be your guide, after the "*Gunther*" experience.'

'He looked a nice person and at least we could speak English. So we disembarked together. While Henry was going through customs I was waiting my turn in the line casually looking around. Then suddenly to my amazement I saw my red crocodile-skin suitcase that I had bought in New Guinea, do you remember it?'

'I sure do, it was an incredibly unique piece of luggage, and it would have stood out anywhere. But how did it get to be there?'

'It was just sitting there next to a pile of other bags. I excitedly told Henry a short version of what had happened to us in Syria and explained that it was unmistakably my case, which was in the car when it was taken. As I completed my story I saw a man wearing a white uniform complete with epaulettes and cap, pushing through the crowd and he picked up my suitcase and walked to the exit. And you know what, I recognised him immediately, it was that "*Gunther*" guy.'

'But how could you be sure it was him, it could have been someone that looked like him?'

'I ran after him to the door, I saw him clearly as he was talking to the customs officer at the bottom of the gangplank and moments later walk up it to the ship I had just come off. I only saw his face once but I recognised that scar he had on his cheek. I remember looking at it when we were having lunch at that place by the seaside.'

'I don't remember a scar; you must have been looking at him more closely than I did. So then what happened, did you go after him?'

'I felt light-headed and physically ill and so helpless I was shaking. Henry offered to help. He obtained temporary boarding passes to go back on board the ship.'

'That was good of him to do this.'

'The customs officer told us that this man was a UNESCO doctor.'

'This was his newly usurped persona then?'

'Yes, but wait, it gets more complicated. We boarded the ship and after some enquiries found "*Gunther*" in the salon having drinks with two other people. I felt emotionally mixed-up and almost speechless but finally managed to ask, "What have you done with the car?" And he said: "Who is this woman? She must be crazy!" and called a ship's officer. So he told the officer in his capacity as a doctor that I was obviously mentally unstable and should be removed from the liner. Immediately two men we took to be plain-clothes gendarmes escorted Henry and me from the ship.'

'So he not only pretended to be a doctor but they believed his instant diagnosis and you ended up the guilty party. Unbelievable!'

'Yes, that's right. I was furious, but what could I do? Luckily Henry was still willing to help but he needed some convincing that I was telling the truth. After I told him a few more details about what had happened to us, Henry was convinced and we went back to the French gendarmes and they took us to a police station in Marseille.'

'At least you were being listened to now.'

'Yes, but things progressed very slowly and I felt increasingly frustrated and agitated thinking that they were stalling us till the ship left the port. One of the police officers had a note in his hand, written in French. I asked Henry to find out what it said.'

'Did Henry speak any French at all?'

'No, but the police officer volunteered that it was from the UN doctor who claimed that if we continued to pester him he would have to lay charges against us. Then the note was placed in front of me and when I saw that it was signed "*Noël Odou*" I felt we finally had some proof.'

'You mean he was still using my name even though he now pretended to be someone else again? It doesn't make any sense.'

'Yes, he was, and no, it doesn't, but when I explained that the said "*Noël Odou*" was my travelling companion and had been robbed by this character in Syria a few weeks ago, the police acted. They drove us back to the wharf. They had, in fact, delayed the departure of the ship pending their investigations. After we were back on board they got him to come to a meeting in a private room. So there I was, seated at a table with two police officers and "*Gunther*" and Henry. As the interview was entirely held in French I didn't understand what they said but their body language and facial expressions showed soon enough that the police were getting somewhere. They escorted "*Gunther*" to his cabin and Henry and I were taken off the ship.'

'How long did you have to wait?'

'Not long, about half an hour, and then a police wagon arrived and "*Gunther*", now in handcuffs, his white uniform spattered with blood, was put into it. The police told us that he had gone berserk when he realised he had been caught and was about to be arrested. One policeman showed me teeth marks on his leg and another showed me bruises from what had obviously been a violent arrest.'

'I am so sorry you had to go through all this Sylvia, all because I was silly enough to give him the keys to the car.'

'Well that's all in the past now, and it doesn't matter now what you did then.'

'I am still very glad you are not holding it against me. Thank you. So they caught him thanks to you, and you went off to London with Henry?'

'No, not straight away. Henry and I were booked into a hotel in separate accommodation and I was ordered to report to the police station the following morning at nine. After a mostly sleepless night my statement was taken. In the meantime, "*Gunther*" had made counter charges against me, claiming I was a jilted lover seeking revenge.'

'And were you?' We both laughed.

'I can tell you it wasn't funny then. For the next two days I had to attend the police interviews with "*Gunther*". The police would badger him and he would often react violently, the commotion spilling on to me.

During that time Henry stayed in Marseille at his own expense and accompanied me to the police station each day. Henry was not permitted to attend the interviews and had to wait in the common charge room.'

'That must have been very unpleasant for you, why did you have to be there?'

'I don't know, they didn't explain that to me.'

'Is that when you sent me the telegram to Kabul?'

'Yes, and by the way, why didn't you reply? I wanted you to come and help out.'

'I did reply, asking if it was necessary to come. I sent it care of the French police in Marseille. Didn't you get it?'

'No, and that doesn't surprise me, they didn't seem to care much. Anyway, it was on the morning of the third day when I reported as requested that to my amazement I saw the police display a relaxed and friendly attitude towards "*Gunther*". I was shown official documents from Interpol stating that "*Gunther*" was wanted in seven countries for a large number of similar offences. "*Gunther*", whose real name was Vandervliet, or something like that, was an internationally known confidence trickster.'

'That much I also discovered when I went to Marseille myself trying to find out what happened to the car. I will tell you more about that in a minute. What happened to you next?'

'In a very off-hand casual manner the police told me I was free to go. That was that. After all the events of the preceding weeks and the drama of the last few days, I found myself emotionally drained and physically exhausted. Leaving that police station I felt as if I was walking in a fog, my legs shaking, walking a foot off the ground. Henry decided that we should fly to London as he had business commitments which he could no longer delay.'

'I bet you were very glad you asked Henry for his help on the boat, he was obviously a great support to you. Did you see him again after you were in London?'

'No, and let me tell you why. While on the aircraft Henry told me that although we had not had a physical relationship, even though he had wanted to, he had fallen in love with me and wanted to marry me.'

'What, just like that, like in the movies?'

'He claimed he had seen every possible aspect of my personality, from innocent child to forceful woman who, when pushed to the limit, had shown enormous courage and fortitude, and so on, blah blah. I could hardly believe what he was saying. That in itself was bad enough, but I was even more amazed when he insisted that I should give him an answer there and then, before the plane landed in London. This was the last straw. I was literally speechless. I had my fists clenched at the time and later was unable to unclench them. I was locked in tension and frustration and fear of what would happen next.'

'Why was he so insistent? It's one thing to fall in love, it's another to force the issue at a time like that.'

'I don't know why, I didn't psychoanalyse him. I was too scared as to what he might do. Anyway I didn't talk to him at all after that and I never saw him again. When the plane touched down at Heathrow I was physically unable to move and had to be taken off the aircraft in a wheelchair. An ambulance took me to a hospital.'

'Poor Sylvia, you had to go through all that on your own and I didn't know what was happening.'

'Yes, it was terrible. When a doctor asked what had happened to cause all this all I could say was "Nothing." Eventually it all came out and the doctor ordered complete rest for at least a week. After a day or two I felt strong enough to go to a hotel and had a few quiet weeks by myself. Later I moved in with a friend I had known in New Guinea. After teaching at an English school for a few months, I returned to Australia.'

'That was the week before I got to London looking for you. And now, have you got over it all completely?'

'Yes, but it took a long time. Talking to you now without feeling bad about it means that I must have gone past it completely and I'm glad about that. Thanks for inviting me.'

'Sylvia, it's the very least I can do, and it's me who should thank you for filling in the blanks that I had to live with for a long time too. I've been hoping to see you for so long, I've so often thought I saw you in a crowd but it was never you. And now here you are safe and sound. I'm very glad! '

After telling her what had happened to me there was a lull in the conversation. I felt some hesitation about how to proceed. Our friendship in New Guinea and our journey together to the Middle East had given us a lot in common historically, but that was obviously not enough to reconnect in a serious way. Sylvia's situation was clear for her and there was no hesitation on her part that going back to Darwin was the best thing for her to do. Another angel flew away that day, strengthening my 'detachment' and 'letting go' capacity.

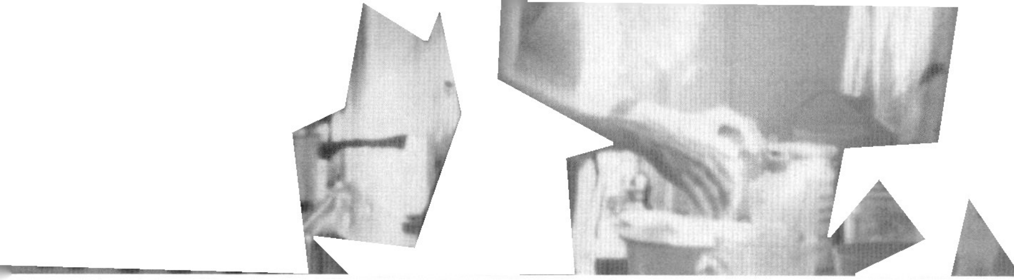

23.

Blackberry jam and Transpersonal Psychology

Sydney–Armidale 1975

IN Sydney there was a small group of supporters of the Narayana Gurukula Movement, and Swami Nitya in particular, run by one of the ladies who was also a Theosophist. One day I was invited to one of their gatherings at her house. One of the guests was a very shy young American woman with masses of long, wavy, golden-red hair, and an unusual bone structure. My own non-demonstrative nature is more likely to be attracted to quiet people and since the other guests were mainly chatty busybodies, I was naturally drawn to talk to her. She had met Nitya in the States on one of his visits there when she lived in Portland. She had only recently come to Australia and was just finding her feet. She was a fully trained Yoga teacher and wanted to be a serious student of Advaita Vedanta. She smiled coyly at me during our conversation, her clear blue eyes shining brightly. She was also a full head taller than me and seemed perfectly self-contained. She called herself Daya. Was it the goddess of the hunt or an Easternised form of Diann? 'Diann' became the currency.

The romantic part of my mind said, '*Wow, what a girl, so beautiful and so pure!*' The more realistic part said, '*Take it easy mate; you have fallen for angels before!*' The under-confident part said, '*You are not good enough for her.*' I had been reading Huxley's *Island* and the mynah bird on my shoulder was howling '*Attention! Attention!*' So, I stepped back and looked at me instead of at her. What I saw was perfectly simple. A young man meeting a young woman with similar interests, with compatible temperaments as far as one could tell at this stage, wanting to get to know each other better, with absolutely no intentions to possess, own or reserve for exclusive use. (I knew about the many faces of 'love'.) We had the potential to become friends at the very least, so why run away?

We met again, and then again, and then some more. I took her on a ride on my small motorbike. Some of my friends at the Discovery Group were getting a house in South Dowling Street overlooking Moore Park to share and I was invited to join. I knew she was looking for a place to live so I invited Diann to join us as well and she accepted. We shared a room upstairs, having become close enough to share the bed as well. It was handy for me to go to work from there by motorcycle as the factory where I still worked was only two suburbs away.

There were five of us in that little house and most of the time things worked very well. We all studied Eastern Philosophy and were all interested in spiritual development. We had no TV, too many interesting books to read and too many fascinating meetings and lectures to go to.

We organised for Diann to teach Yoga at the Theosophical Society and I, of course, joined the class. We practised regularly at home and the benefits soon became evident. It was great to have one's own personal live-in Yoga teacher. As we became more involved, we naturally discussed the nature of our relationship. Further 'attention' made me aware that I had just come out of a situation where my need for personal development and freedom was largely responsible for the relationship not working the way Jenny wanted it to. This time, Diann was also more interested in personal development and freedom than merely being with me, so we made an agreement that our individual personal development and growth and freedom would take precedence over our relationship together. As long as our being together contributed to our own personal development, it would be enjoyed and valued, but if it stood in the way or became a distraction to it, the relationship would have to give in. *We also agreed that you could only have a relationship when both people want it.* When one wants out, the other has to stop wanting it too. So another pact was entered into, but I liked that one much better.

This gradual becoming friends and getting to know each other openly and cleanly allowed me to see that Diann was neither the angel she appeared nor was I falling for an image. Studying the '*many faces of love*' seemed to have had some effect. We were two people who got on well on many levels and enjoyed each other's company. It transpired that Diann wanted to do more than teach Yoga for the rest of her life. She, too, wanted to study formally or '*go back to school*' as the Americans call it. She had already done one semester of uni study in the States before dropping out, so when the time came for me to make a decision to go to university, we decided to do it together. Even though Sydney University was within easy reach from where we lived, we decided to go to the University of New England, in Armidale, northern New South Wales. We wanted the clean air of the country and less crowded uni classes. We bought a small second-hand van, loaded up all our belongings and set off north. Another new relationship coinciding with yet another travel adventure albeit in somewhat more familiar surroundings.

We leisurely explored some of southern Queensland as well as northern New South Wales, camping in forests and paddocks.

We meditated, fasted and explored spiritual sexuality. We studied the writings of Nataraja Guru and Swami Nitya, amongst others. We visited theosophical lodges and generally had a great holiday before settling down to study.

By the time we got to Armidale, we had missed the final enrolment date for the following academic year. Oh well! We were mature enough to wait. We got ourselves part-time jobs, found a small cottage half an hour outside of Armidale, in Black Mountain, and 'deferred' till the following year. We grew vegetables, made blackberry jam, chopped firewood and enjoyed the peace and tranquillity of the country. Some of our Sydney friends came to stay for periods of time and Black Mountain became a sort of unofficial Australian Gurukula cum TS lodge. Looking back, it was one of the most enjoyable periods of my life – a nourishing period after some disappointments and before a sharp turning point in the direction of my purpose. Being in a very positive, emotionally well-balanced relationship, living in simple facilities with the future ready organised and simply biding time was just what I needed. It may sound idealistic but that is what it was.

I felt that many pieces of life's puzzle had fallen into place for me and that I had reached a certain level of inner comfort and peace. The years of focus, attention and study had delivered some results and I was appreciating it now.

I did Philosophy, Psychology, Sociology and Social Science in my first year at uni. A few years earlier I had been concerned about my intellectual ability to undertake university level studies, and even though I had read and studied a lot privately, I was still unsure how it would work out. I had no experience and didn't know quite what to expect.

I need not have worried. Almost everything in all my first-year subjects, apart from the statistics in Social Science with which I struggled since I had not done high school maths, was disappointingly simplistic. Philosophy was a superficial historical review of ideas – starting in Athens, of course, ignoring anything that had gone before. Psychology talked more about rats in mazes and the language of chimps than about people. The psychology professor, who was about to retire, delivered lectures he must have written when he was first appointed. There was plenty of work to be done, but I discovered that once you got the hang of how they wanted you to dish up what they were looking for, it was easy enough. Apart from the work, I enjoyed meeting new people and made some very good friends. But above all, I enjoyed our simple, uncomplicated rural life at the cottage.

Diann and I shared enough interest in each other's studies to be sounding boards, and sharing the domestic duties never seemed to be a problem. Amongst our busy studies there was enough time for us to be with each other, and I do not think that I am exaggerating when I say that we never quarrelled. We may not have always agreed on issues, but we always seemed to come up with acceptable compromises. The contrast to my previous relationship was staggering. There was a lightness and easy flow between us. I liked it.

The second year, 1977, was considerably more intellectually interesting. I did two units in education, one in developmental psychology and one which was an overview of educational philosophy. In my third year I studied five units, all in education. I was now a well-known student at the Centre for Educational Studies and I became good friends with at least two of the staff: Max Lawson, who I had briefly known in Sydney and who was a champion of alternative education, now a senior lecturer; and Tom Moore, one of the most creative and sensitive people I have met.

While I was a student in Max's course, 'Boats Against the Current', Max invited me to give the lecture on Krishnamurti's idea of education as he considered that I knew more about it than he did. I gave the lecture in the Krishnamurti style, without any notes, inviting the students to explore with me what education really is. I had a great response and was very pleased with myself. I was now not only studying education, I was actually applying it and at tertiary level, not just primary school. My humility had to have a word with my pride, stopping it from going to my head.

During the third year, Diann felt the urge to devote herself more directly to the work of the Narayana Gurukula Movement and went to India to work for them, deferring uni. True to our 'pact', if this is what she needed to do for her personal development, then that was to take precedence over our being together, but not at the expense of friendship, which continues to this very day. I would need more time and energy to devote to my studies and thus, in a practical sense, it suited me too. We wrote occasionally and stayed in touch.

When friendship is not dependent on physical presence one is free to move around and be oneself. Relationships that are exclusively based on the need for sex, on the other hand, are dependent on physical presence and therefore restrict movement and freedom.

During that time Yvonne Malykke, a friend I knew from my time with the Young Theosophists, started a New Age publication called Cosmos. She knew my areas of interest and current study and asked if I would review some of the books she was being sent by publishers in return for keeping the books. Some of the more interesting ones included *Consciousness: Brain, States of Awareness and Mysticism* by D. Goleman and R.J. Davidson; *R.D. Laing: His Work and Its Relevance for Sociology* by Martin Howard-Williams; *Mysticism and the New Physics* by Michael Talbot, and two by the well known Ken Wilber, *No Boundaries* and *The Atman Project: A Transpersonal View of Human Development*. Other topics ranged from animal liberation, super-learning and psychic massage to pendulum power and Jewish mysticism.

This activity not only sharpened my analytical skills, which would increasingly be needed, but also informed me more widely about what was to become the topic for my Honours thesis, and my interest in psychology and counselling.

I was now becoming very much absorbed in my intellectual development and, despite a slow start, university life was so fulfilling that I did not want it to stop at the end of the third year. I became strongly attracted to Philosophy of Education, the discipline Nataraja Guru had studied for his PhD. There was also a full-time tutoring job available the following year at the Centre and I had a good chance of getting it. I enrolled as a part-time Philosophy of Education Honours student and got the job as a tutor. I had become an educator in the formal sense of the word and I was thriving. My new career was at last fully launched. I was completely living my purpose.

During the previous year, my friend and colleague Tom went on a study tour of the US. His interest was in alternative psychology and counselling practices and their relevance to education. He came back, having discovered *Transpersonal Psychology*, an as yet obscure but fascinating new theory.

While Stanislav Grof used the term before him, it was Abraham Maslow who, in the late '60s, popularised what he called '*fourth force*' psychology under the new label of Transpersonal Psychology. Maslow is also credited with being the founder of humanistic psychology. However, in his later years he came across so many new issues in both science and philosophy that he revised his views about the ultimate goal of human development and added 'self-transcendence' to his hierarchy of needs, which formerly had stopped with 'self-actualisation'. While this was the newest insight in contemporary academic psychology in America, Advaita Vedanta, Zen and Krishnamurti had been telling me that self-transcendence was the ultimate of human achievement for years. Buddhists and Hindus and Taoists have seen transcending the self, or ego boundaries, as the goal of life for centuries.

For my Honours thesis I had wanted to do something that combined Philosophy of Education with something that was personally important to me. For some time I had hoped to write on the educational importance of the work of Krishnamurti. However, when I learned in one of Tom's courses that educational developments usually follow developments in psychology, and when I understood more about what Transpersonal Psychology was about, I thought I would speculate on the implications of Transpersonal Psychology for education. Since Transpersonal Psychology was only a more organised and somewhat academically respectable way of looking at ancient wisdom, both Eastern and Western, with modern research principles thrown, in I felt well qualified. To show the relevance to modern education of this 'newest' psychology was not so difficult for someone who had been studying it for many years. Both Tom and Max encouraged and supported me and Peter Hobson, another colleague at the Centre, was an excellent supervisor. My thesis, titled *The Transpersonal Paradigm and its Relevance for Education*, obtained First Class Honours. I was delighted. I am not sure, but from what people tell me, it could well have been the first academic work on Transpersonal Psychology in Australia. More than twenty years later, today Transpersonal Psychology is still not taught in universities in Australia.

Tom and I shared an interest in this new psychology and together we ran experimental group sessions in what we understood Transpersonal Psychotherapy to be. We met weekly with a small group of people and did more or less what I had done in the TS Discovery Group but with Transpersonal insights added to it. I don't know whoever else benefited, but it helped prepare me for later studies and practice of Transpersonal Psychotherapy.

During my last year in Armidale, after Diann had gone to India, I had a short relationship with a single mother. She was a philosophy student and needed some coaching. She also needed a mate, and I was free. We went camping during the school holidays together with her daughter. I got to know the seven-year-old charmer well and enjoyed her company much more than I thought I would. Were paternal instincts rumbling in my genes at last? Probably. After four or five months, during an embrace and on the verge of crying, the mother said she wanted 'out'. Absolutely nothing had gone wrong. She simply realised that the relationship was getting closer than she wanted it to be at that time. She wanted to remain free and so did I. I had yet another opportunity to practise detachment and put into practice my belief that you should not impose your so-called 'love' on someone who does not want it. I had walked away from my 'merry widow' in Belgium – I could walk away from a single mother in Armidale. Incidentally, they had very similar physical features, and both their daughters were of the same age and had the same name. The world is full of angels, and human life is full of patterns.

Des and Robbie come to visit and stay for some time.

PART THREE

THE DOMESTIC JOURNEY

Gestalt Prayer:

‘I do my thing, and you do your thing.
I am not in this world to live up to your expectations
And you are not in this world to live up to mine.
You are you and I am I,
And if by chance we find each other, it’s beautiful,
If not it can’t be helped.’

Fritz Perls

24.

North or South

Armidale–Melbourne 1980

THE tutor's job I had held for two years was no longer available the year following me finishing my Honours work, so I was completely free – free from the job, finished with my studies, at least for now, and with no attachments to any person in Armidale. Naturally my thoughts turned to what to do next. The world was an open invitation and I could go wherever I wanted. India was one option. There were other 'aid' organisations I wanted to explore. I had also heard that there were some interesting communes up in northern New South Wales, and one in particular, inspired by Krishnamurtian thinking, interested me. Where people live together, there are children. Where there are children you need educators. Where better to practise what you teach than in an environment and life style supporting your ideas? Now that I was a formally qualified educator, no longer an amateur as I was at Summerfarm, contributing professionally to the education of children in the way Krishnamurti proposes was a very exciting thought. I had bought another van, trading in my motorcycle, in readiness for a completely aimless wander towards the north and into an open-ended future.

I had moved into Armidale town during my years of tutoring to be closer to the students. Then, one afternoon in September 1980 when my thesis was already submitted and tutoring was winding down, Alf and Muriel Foote turned up at my front door. I did not know who they were, what they were doing there or how they had come to be there. It was simple really, Alf explained. They were the conveners of the Sixth International Transpersonal Conference to be held at Phillip Island, Victoria, from the 26 – 30 November that year. There were to be many international guests and they were looking for Australians who had anything to do with Transpersonalism so that we could at least show the international community that we too had some people who knew something about it. They had heard I had done my thesis on Transpersonal Education and no one else at the conference was listed to talk about it, could I do a workshop or a lecture? They had no money to pay me, but would waive the conference fees and allow me to attend the whole thing if I could get there under my own steam. My ego was very flattered, but a little daunted at the same time. Me talking to an International conference, really? Memories of the Theosophical Society Conference flashed in front of my eyes and I thought that it could actually be quite interesting to see what goes on at such a gathering. When I talked it over with Tom he said he wanted to go too and we could share accommodation, plus it would be good for my CV, he reminded me. I was convinced, so off we went.

After settling in at our hotel and on seeing the program of the conference, I was blown away with excitement. It read like the '*Who's who?*' in the Transpersonal movement. Stanislav and Christina Grof, June Singer, Ralph Metzner and many others, presenting sessions with titles like *Metaphors for Self Transformation*, *Transpersonal Frameworks for Western Magic*,

Consciousness, Awareness and Mysticism, *Awakening Intuition* and among them was one labelled *Transpersonal Education in Practice*, since that is what I wanted to do.

I got even more excited when, during drinks for the presenters before dinner the first night, right next to me, just standing there, were James Fadiman and Frances Vaughan, live and in person. They were both authors on Transpersonal topics and both on the teaching staff at the Californian Institute for Transpersonal Psychology. They had also both held the position of president of the Association for Transpersonal Psychology. I could not resist walking up to them. After apologising for my intrusion, I thanked them for their inspiration during the writing of my thesis, throughout which they were quoted profusely, and wished them an enjoyable stay in Australia. I had occasion to talk a little more to each of them later on in the conference and found them as inspiring live as they were in their writings.

While all of this was going on, another event occurred which would leave its mark on my life far more than the influence of all of these people put together.

My workshop was in the afternoon of day two. I talked briefly about what I saw as Transpersonal Education and then took the twenty or so participants on a guided fantasy into their own world of ideal education. They then shared their visions and it became a very inspiring gathering. It went well and I was pleased with the response. Several people wanted to talk more afterwards, as happens in those situations. Among them was a very attractive twenty-ish young woman with a charming smile. Her near-black hair was starkly drawn back into a ponytail, revealing a high and intelligent-looking forehead. She asked all sorts of questions, including if she would be able to read my thesis on Transpersonal Education. She was particularly impressed with the fact that I had applied philosophy to something practical like education, because she too had a First Class Honours degree in Philosophy, but had generally found philosophy often dry and academic. She stayed talking when all the other interested participants had left and we talked some more after dinner that evening. We covered all the topics we were both interested in, which were wide ranging, but importantly about education. It was then that I discovered that Joy (what a name for a friend) was currently studying to be a kindergarten teacher. I distinctly remember recalling that Emma, my first significant relationship, was a kindergarten teacher and so was Sylvia, another significant relationship in my life so far. *Maybe third time lucky.* I think it was 2 am when the need for sleep asserted itself very strongly, and I was reminded of that other late-night discussion about education at that other significant conference many years ago. What would I dream of this night?

We talked more the following day and the day after that. After dinner one night we went for a walk along the beachfront just across from the conference venue. The moon was full and the wind was cool. I put my arm around her to make her feel warmer and without words we melted into each other, yet another face of love smiling upon us. By the last day of the conference it was overwhelmingly obvious that this was not going to be the end of it, and we agreed to stay in touch.

The following January we spent a short holiday together. I met her at the airport in Sydney and together in my little car we travelled to Armidale where I showed her off to my friends and colleagues. We meandered along the beautiful New South Wales coast on the way back to Melbourne and by the end of the holiday, it was settled that instead of heading north to look for a commune, I would come down south to Melbourne to be with Joy.

Having ended my connection with the university, with no other job in sight, I was as free as a bird, whereas Joy was still studying. By the time I returned from Armidale, having gone back to collect my books and a few other things, we were ready to look for a place to move in together. We both felt strongly that this was 'it' and became fully committed to a life together.

We rented a small house in Box Hill South, which had the toilet outside the back door and a huge bathtub, big enough for both of us at the same time. My qualifications in education and my interest in philanthropy landed me a job as education officer with Austcare, an organisation devoted to raising awareness of the causes and needs of refugees as well as collecting funds to meet those needs. One of my duties was to give talks, sometimes in churches, schools or community groups.

By the end of that year, Joy completed her studies and graduated, earning a prize for overall excellence. I had never bothered attending graduation ceremonies at the end of my own academic achievements, finding them pompous, boring and meaningless rituals. But when I saw Joy receive her Diploma and her prize, I felt moved to tears, not of course by the ceremony itself, but by the intimate connection to the person who had done such a good job.

After Joy got her first job as a kindergarten teacher and was drawing a professional salary, one night in the bath, she suggested that, since my job had sustained her during her studies, and by now my job was not really fulfilling me as I thought it might, she would sustain me if I wanted to go back to university to do a Diploma of Education. I had been tutoring and lecturing to Diploma of Education students in Armidale and spread my passion for alternative education all around me, but I had no qualification to actually teach at a school. It would only take one year and it should be easy enough for me to do this, so I accepted her gracious offer.

I was accepted at the University of Melbourne and given credit for the philosophy of education portion of the course, due to already having a First Class Honours degree in Philosophy of Education. I had hoped they would just have given me the Diploma but in retrospect I am glad they made me do the course, as it turned out that I needed it.

My teaching subjects were English and History. My English group was led by Dr Ian Hansen, a most interesting and sensitive educator. (During a pause from writing this work I was introduced by a friend to Dr Hansen's own autobiography *The Naked Fish*, the account of his journey from Baptist 'fundamentalism' to 'critical liberalism', in which he also shares his passion for education.) Ian personally supervised my teaching practice rounds and in his 'Professional Readiness Report' on me wrote that my '*teaching practice performances have ranged from merely adequate (initially) to very good to outstanding. At the beginning of the year, his classroom management strategies were less than effective but, as he later was able to adjust to secondary students, he showed firmness and flexibility in gaining and maintaining attention.*'

Yes, I was flexible enough to show firmness when I needed to, like when you are being observed and want to pass the course, but when it came to real secondary teaching in an outer suburb of Melbourne, it was another story. I obtained a job teaching at a Catholic school, of all places, given my background, and one of my duties was to teach comparative religion, which suited me well, and I thought it was generous of them to include this in the curriculum.

However, from the students in Year Nine and Ten, I found little interest in the subject no matter how much I tried to make it interesting. I often wondered what response students encountered at home from their predominantly Catholic parents to my homework assignments on Buddhism and Taoism. My Year Eleven and Twelve students responded well to my philosophical and psychological approach to the novels they were studying and I enjoyed our tangled discussions. It was a particularly difficult Year Nine English class that was the thorn in my side. I simply could not manage them and one morning I was so frustrated that I lost control of myself and yelled at them that if they didn't want to be there they should go outside and walk around in the schoolyard. To my surprise and relief, nearly half of them actually did.

By lunchtime I was asked to see the vice-principal, and the principal the following day. They were very empathic and counselled me to the realisation and admission that I neither wanted to be a policeman nor a bully of a teacher. My idealism for alternative education did not allow me to behave in a conventional manner and we agreed that it would be better for both the school and me to discontinue this misalignment. I stopped teaching there at the end of my first term, experiencing enormous relief and in no way feeling that I had failed. Where I had failed was in not realising that *basically I did not want to teach in a conventional school* and that all my passion for alternative education was being challenged and frustrated daily. The inner tension rendered me ineffective. All I needed was to realise it and be honest with myself. In his reference, the principal wrote that I was '*a remarkably fine person of unquestionable honesty and integrity...*' and he was honest enough not to say that I was a good teacher well-suited for the conventional system.

Having read many books I got a job as a 'teacher of English'. (Me?)
At least on my first day I look happy enough.

After one semester at high school I teach English to migrants in industry instead.

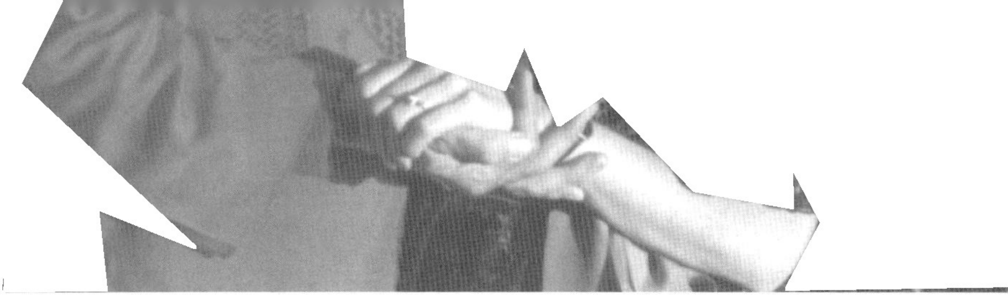

25.

The marriage game

Melbourne 1980s

IN one of our early conversations about sharing our life together, Joy expressed the clear and unequivocal intent to have children. It came across to me as an absolutely non-negotiable item. I had not considered it at that time and my paternal needs, if I had any, had been adequately met by my passion for education and playing with other people's children. However, being presented with the fact that the person I loved and wanted to be with also wanted to have children made me realise that if I was intellectually so keen on sound education, it would not be a bad thing to actually put it into practice where it really matters, that is, with my own children.

After a couple of years of settling in professionally, Joy felt ready. I was nearly forty and thought that we should not wait much longer lest the children feel they are growing up with their grandpa. Joy was teaching in a kindergarten and the question of how they would respond to their well-liked teacher having children out of wedlock immediately arose. So one night in the bath, a place where we seemed to often have our most important conversations, soothed by the relaxed cocoon of warm water topped with scented bubbles, we considered whether it would be better to get married before having children. My anti-marriage stance is well documented in previous pages and in her younger days Joy had also expressed sentiments in that direction. Already in May 1970, ten years earlier I wrote:

'For me, marriage is out of the question – from any point of view – it holds absolutely no water.'

So here we were, two adults clearly not overwhelmingly enamoured with the romanticism of weddings and marriage, yet seriously contemplating whether to indulge in it or not. We would discuss the philosophical, psychological and sociological pros and cons of getting married at great length. My stance was one of complete indifference. Being completely committed to the relationship, it didn't matter one iota to me since I did not believe in the importance of marriage from any point of view at all, and I was strongly convinced that it would not make any difference to our relationship. I simply said, *'If you'd like to get married we will, if you don't want to, we'll have children without it,'* believing that in the end it wouldn't have any derogatory consequences for them. To me marriage was not a matter of moral principle. I see it as just an old-fashioned convention invented to regulate the rampant desire to procreate and to ensure the male's domination over women's fertility. It is still popular for romantic and commercial reasons and mainly adhered to by religious folk who think marriage is '*made in heaven*'.

I also knew of the Hindu concept of 'social duty' and their view that attending to domestic life is a stage in spiritual development. I was equally familiar with the Jungian concept of archetypal influences, different ones exerting their power at different times. I had a couple of years earlier reviewed, for Cosmos, Robert de Ropp's (author of the famous book, *The Master Game*) autobiography. He had called this 'social duty' father-archetype, somewhat derogatorily the 'Domestic Oaf', who wants little more than physical comfort and sexual gratification and, as he put it to '*Eat, drink and copulate, have your mate and children around you, grow your own food and be independent.*' If that's what we were about to do, in my terms, play the 'Marriage Game', then we might as well play the 'Wedding Game' as well.

So on 27 November 1982, we did play the 'Wedding Game'. We never considered that it should be a church wedding. I simply could not have brought myself to make promises in the name of 'God' in the conventional meaning of that word while at the same time rejecting that concept in its formal religious sense. Our relationship was much more meaningful than to make a public mockery of it. We also agreed that we not dress up in the stereotypical uniform of bride and groom, but rather each find a suitable outfit acceptable to the other. Joy wore harem pants and a matching camisole top of deep turquoise with a contrasting navy transparent lace-like patterned three-quarter tunic draped over it. There was a matching sash tied around her waist and she wore soft flat shoes. I wore second-hand Chinese green silk pants with traditional floral patterns, reminding me of my empathy with Taoism, a red Indian shirt, putting me in touch with the wisdom of Advaita Vedanta I had learned about from Nataraja Guru, and sandals, reminding me that humility is important. Everybody thought we looked great together.

We created our own ceremony where we mixed water (belonging to Joy's zodiacal sign) and earth (my sign) to make mud pies, referring to a joking comment we made when we first discovered our birth signs. We exchanged gifts – a ring from me to Joy which she wanted, and a jade statue of a Chinese sage from Joy to me since I never wore any jewellery and could not see myself wearing a wedding ring which, in essence, symbolises the link of a chain tying you to the other person. We crafted our own vows and wrote our own ceremony, we affirmed aspirations to each other rather than 'until death us do part' commitments. A friend of Joy's improvised on the cello and someone read a few poems from Kahlil Gibran. At one stage I had thought we might use Fritz Perls' Gestalt prayer, but it might have sounded a little too indifferent for a wedding so we decided against it. Our plain round wedding cake had the Chinese Tai Chi symbol on top representing the intertwining of opposites, like the partners in a meaningful relationship. Alf Foote, who had invited me to the Transpersonal Conference where we had met, was the celebrant. Joy's brother was the best man, and since I had no family here Joy's closest friend Arija was bridesmaid. Joy has often reminded me that on that day I looked the happiest she had ever seen me. Of course, it was a celebration of our togetherness and of the promise of our future together, whatever that would turn out to be. To me it felt much more like a great party with lots of friends than a wedding with all its formality and seriousness.

The fact that we did not see marriage as the sacrament and the compulsory binding that religious people see it to be does not mean we didn't take it seriously and that we were not committed to doing the best we could for as long as possible, considering all the people involved in the situation. As long as relationships are mutually enhancing, no matter how much the struggle to maintain harmony, something is gained. But, inevitably, people change and not always parallel to one another. They may, in fact, change away from each other and become less and less mutually enhancing to the point where it may become counter-productive to remain together.

In my case, there is no doubt that I had changed over the

years of marriage. It seemed to me that one day I was thirty-five and the next I was fifty with a 'wife and two children', and more dramatically, there was now a disconnect! Respect, care and admiration remained but, intended or not, harm was done for which I need to take an unquantifiable amount of responsibility. When one or both of the partners in a relationship no longer benefit from being in the relationship, then it is better for both that the relationship discontinues. It is to both our credit that we recognised when our marriage had reached the point of diminishing return, and agreed to dissolve it in 2000, after nearly twenty years, without ugly acrimony. We continue to cooperate constructively for the benefit of our children and not to undermine each other's credibility as parents. The children, of course, were old enough to take a mature view of the situation and they were not in the minority amongst their friends for having to deal with a two-location family.

Yes, of course, the process of letting go of something that was so intensely glorious to begin with and the taking asunder of elements that were so tightly bound together is painful and difficult, not withstanding my practice in 'letting go'. But pain, difficulty and letting go were not new to me. For years I used to go to sleep thinking I may not wake up in the morning, convincing myself I had better let go of everything as I closed my eyes. You don't get to be good at anything without daily practice, especially the difficult things.

When reflecting earlier on my leaving the conventional school I taught at, I wrote that the main reason for leaving was probably because I did not want to adapt to that environment out of principle, and that all I needed was to realise such and be honest with myself to see clearly what to do next. Given my view of marriage before actually getting married, even though I completely agreed to do it at the time, it was again not surprising to discover the fact that fundamentally I did not want to be married. As long as things were fine it didn't matter, but once they were no longer mutually enhancing, I began to wonder whether at least one of the causes of this was that I did not want to be married.

Of course, if one partner of a marriage feels that way, it is not possible to say that to the other partner without doing serious damage to their self-esteem. It will inevitably be seen as a personal rejection. If you loved them you would want to be married to them, wouldn't you? I tried to convince myself that when I rejected Roman Catholicism, I did not reject certain people I knew who were Catholics and that when I rejected teaching at a conventional school, I did not reject those particular children. Therefore, in the same way, by rejecting marriage as an institution, I was not rejecting Joy. But it didn't fly for me any more than it did for her. Logically my argument was sound, but emotionally it didn't make sense. There were still compatibilities between us when things started to go poorly, but the basic romantic 'face' of love had faded and without it the conventional expectations of marriage are not met.

The expectations married people have of each other and the expectations others around the couple have of them have a serious impact on the comfort of the people who are expected to behave in certain ways, subtle as these may be. This, I am sure, is not the whole story but in my observation (and psychological and sociological studies bear it out) people's expectations have an influence on their behaviour and performance, both intellectually and physically. Just ask Eliza Doolitle. I was completely wrong in being convinced that being married would not make any difference to our relationship.

Around that time I had become familiar with the work of Dr Julian Hafner, a psychiatrist specialising in marital and family problems. In *The End Of Marriage: Why Monogamy Isn't Working* he wrote: '*Marriage is almost universally accepted as normal and desirable in Western societies. The existence of such a fundamen-*

tal institution as marriage is simply not questioned by most people. Instead, it is for many their main goal in life. The institution of marriage is rarely questioned because social pressures to achieve it are so powerful and persuasive. The major aim of this book is to trace the origins of these social pressures and to describe their negative effects... Let me emphasise that I am not against the idea of people living as couples. I firmly believe that being in a special, harmonious mutually supportive and equal relationship can add much to wellbeing and happiness. But I believe also that comparatively few of us actually live in such partnerships.' He goes on to explain that one of the main reasons marriage fails is due to its compulsory nature – compulsory to enter it, and compulsory to stay in it. Drawing on his experience of helping married couples for over twenty years, he writes, '*During therapy, one or both partners usually talked of feelings of being trapped in the marriage, unable to change it or escape from it.*' Referring to sex roles within marriage he observes that, '*the rigid and stereotypical attitudes to these have destructive effects on the health of both men and women.*' This made sense to me then.

The question, '*When did you realise that love had gone?*' is impossible to answer. There is no date or time when it happens. Love does not switch on or off like a light globe. Fondness, care, appreciation and basic respect may well outlast separation and may never disappear because there is no reason to. The absence of mutually enhancing benefits from the emotional giving in a relationship does not mean that deliberate destructiveness must take over. Priorities may change and egos may be bruised, but the individual's maturation process must go on.

And then, there are also expectations of people who have separated, one of them being that they find a new partner. That expectation rests on the assumption that one has to have a partner (back to 'compulsory coupledom') and that to live by yourself is either unhealthy or terribly lonesome or both, neither of which need be the case. I recently read in a well-known author's autobiography that if his wife died he 'would get another one' because he couldn't bear living alone. I am sure he speaks for many people of both genders. I am not implying here that seeking company from other people is a form of abuse, only that locking another person, deliberately and until death, into a marriage for the purpose of company is a form of compulsive behaviour and an affront to human dignity.

If we see marriage and having children as the only worthwhile or meaningful pursuit in life, then after having accumulated possessions, after having chased sex partners, after having played the marriage game and when the duties of parenthood have come to an end, it is not surprising that for people with this viewpoint their world becomes empty and lonely to the extent of causing both physical and psychological pathology.

However, as de Ropp reminds us, all those games are 'subsidiary to the Master Game.' The aim of the Master Game is to 'attain full consciousnesses' instead of being asleep living in romantic dreams and delusions created by the 'narrow shell of personal ego'. Even though all the world's religious masters had as their original aim the emergence from that narrow shell of ego and the liberation into the light of full consciousness these aims seem forgotten and the process has been turned into yet another game, the 'Religious Game', with its aim now being 'salvation'. This game has lost its original purpose and therefore, like all the other games, fizzles out or becomes an end in itself, needing compulsion, like the marriage game, to remain alive at all.

But the Master Game, as clearly distinguished from the religious 'please save me game', is not a popular game. That game, de Ropp tells us, '*can only be played by people whose observations of themselves and others have led them to the conclusion that man's ordinary state of consciousness, his so-called waking state, is a form of somnambulism, and is not the highest level of consciousness of which he is capable.*'

Even though I have made a good attempt at understanding the Master Game, intellectual comprehension, while a useful start, is not enough, and much work remains to be done, with or without a 'partner'. If living life itself is not a sufficiently meaningful activity to be engaged in, filling one's life with other people simply to fill the void becomes a rather utilitarian use of the human being. Is that why marriage is so attractive – the promise of companionship for the rest of your life, so you will never have to be lonely?

27 November 1982. Joy and I marry in 'hippy' style.
Alf Foote, who organised the Transpersonal Conference
where we met, is the celebrant.

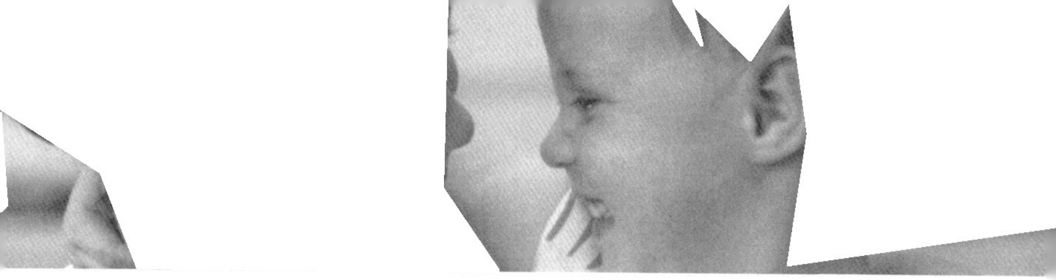

26.

Our children are our teachers

Melbourne 1984

HAVING gotten the wedding and the short honeymoon (a few days by the beach somewhere near Somers) out of the way, we spent a few years enjoying being the two of us. We moved to another house and established a household. Then it was time to think about children.

In his book *Warrior's Way*, De Ropp had reminded me that: '*They are poor indeed who have never had children. Our children are our teachers. In them we see repeated the fall of man, the lapse from innocence, the growth of the false ego clouding the essence, the corrosive effect of what passes for education, and the poisonous influence of our collective bad karma.*' It was time to let some other teachers in and do their thing on us.

We were both healthy and young enough so we didn't expect any complications and Joy became pregnant immediately. We went to birth classes, did the exercises and opted for a home-birth under the careful guidance of a doctor and midwife. It all went well, as expected, right up until the due date. The labour, however, was very long and very painful for Joy and frustrating for me even though I was there and helped in whatever way I could. Joy got into the bath and I was there supporting her, but you can't do much as a bystander. Eventually a normal and healthy boy emerged. We called him Johann, although his school friends often called him Jo or Yogi.

The first weeks of parenting, especially with the first child, are a mixture of euphoria and struggle. They are tiring and demanding and you don't always know what to do. At the same time there is such intense pleasure at seeing those tiny features develop into more proportioned parts of the body and every day new capacities appear, new expressions reveal themselves, new sounds emerge and more relationship develops. We had him sleep between us and we could hardly stop staring and admiring him.

While the result was fantastic, I felt the cost to Joy had been too high to want to do it again, and I wanted to stop at one child. Joy argued, successfully in the end, that to have two is much better than one, for the children's sake. Ultimately, it was she who would have to go through it and if she was prepared, then so was I. Two and a half years later, as easily as the first had been difficult, Joy gave birth to Natasha. We now had one of each. She was a more peaceful child and looked literally like an angel. At her twenty-first birthday party in my little speech I reminded her of the fact that she still looks like an angel, even though her wings have not yet sprouted.

We had two children now and the deeply warming pleasure of seeing them interact together, seeing them being companions to each other, observing them playing and learning together, far outweighed the extra work of having two. Joy was right, it was better, for all of us.

More importantly, we were and still are learning from them. I agree with de Ropp that they *are our teachers*. I remember clearly that, when I started seeing the children as having come to teach me how to be a better parent and how to be a better person and how to gain insights into what is permissible and what is not and why, how much easier it all went. There was much less of a struggle for conformity and obedience and much more of an adventure into discovering what we could learn together, me from them and them from me.

One of the biggest lessons I discovered, with a shock, was the impact that the upbringing we have received has on the parenting we deliver, regardless of the intellectual intention to prevent such. It happened when Johann was only about three and did not do what I asked, or defied me in some way. To my horror, I slapped him on the face. I was immediately ashamed and saddened, but when I saw where it came from and that it was not what I had wanted to do, it never occurred again. In my case, however, the origin of that physically punitive response did not come from my parents as I do not recall either my mother or father ever physically hurting me. But when I looked into my memory bank, I saw that it had occurred numerous times at boarding school, dished out by both the supervising brothers, the teachers at school and the bigger boys if I didn't do what they wanted.

Parenthood is by no means the only way to find meaning in life, even though biologically it makes a lot of sense. Moreover philosophy of education makes little sense without the practice of education. Yet, surely the most powerful form of education is to model to our own children whatever little wisdom we have so that it may rub off a little, should they be predisposed to take it on. Being a parent, like being married, is a phase in the journey we take. While they are always our offspring, '*our children are not our children*' to begin with, as Kahlil Gibran so eloquently put it, so they are not our children once they are independent and self-sufficient either. That we need to let go of them is another of the main lessons they teach us. As we wanted to be independent and free from control and restrictions when we were teenagers, so do they need to gain that independence. Any form of subtle influence or attachment for our own sake, because we are not ready to let go, makes it more difficult for them to gain that necessary independence, and is no less bad parenting than to impose unreasonable restrictions during early childhood. The letting go of course is a gradual process, and needs to be graded in accordance with their capacity to handle the responsibility that comes with freedom and less by our capacity to let go. If children could be free only when parents are ready to let go, some children would never be free – for some even after the death of their parents.

After the separation from Joy the children both came to me every other weekend. They also came often before or after school as I lived close to the high school where they attended. Gradually I invited them to be flexible and change the arrangement if other opportunities arose they would prefer to take part in. Eventually I left it entirely up to them when to come and they continue to visit regularly, clearly because they want to.

They are both in their twenties now and we are reaping the fruits of our parenting efforts. Looking back at these efforts, both ours and theirs, we see a nice basket of fruits. Of course it is easy to become a doting parent and we often forget the struggles and only see the good parts, but I will try to remain objective.

In Joy's immediate family it seems to have been standard to teach all the children music, so it is not surprising that two of them, her brother Phil and Joy, turned out to be specialist music teachers. All the children of these two, almost naturally (either genetically or via 'memes') now also play musical instruments. Johann started off with the violin before he moved to electric guitar, after a short spell on acoustic guitar and the saxophone. He just enjoys playing. Natasha started with the piano (which she did to AMEB level 7) and added the flute later (which she took to level 6) and did both to VCE level. They both played in bands at Blackburn High School, reputedly the best music school in Australia, with a music staff of over a dozen teachers.

They both juggle, largely due to the influence of Joy's brother Phil, and Natasha is currently the vice president of the Monash University Juggling Club. She is also the treasurer of the student chocolate club (maybe influenced by her Belgian father's love thereof), a club designed to increase social interaction; presumably on the assumption that most people like chocolate and therefore that they will get lots of members.

Physically they have both played basketball for years and Johann still does. He was also a volunteer court sweeper for the Melbourne Tigers, a job he obtained at age fourteen without any help from us. He often ascribes his physical balance to a few years of gymnastics at the young age of seven or so, and maybe also from the friendly wrestling we used to do, until he became too strong for me. Natasha has been doing creative dancing for years and regularly participates in the annual performances of her dancing school.

In the last few years they have both travelled solo overseas and may well have been bitten by the same bug I was at their age.

At the early stage of primary school Johann had some reading problems but he blossomed as soon as he entered high school and did consistently well. However, when he reached university he exceeded all our hopes and ended with a First Class Honours degree in Commerce and Finance, and with extremely little help from me, as I am practically financially illiterate. He now has a full-time job as a corporate analyst in the city. Natasha is at Monash doing a double major in Psychology and Sociology planning to also go for Honours. I take it she is not planning to be the only member of the family without a First Class Honours degree. Her current passion is 'Positive Psychology' and I admit that here there may well have been some unashamedly open influence from me.

As far as I know neither have ever gone to a hairdressing salon; I have always cut their hair and will continue to do so until my skill falls below their standard.

Ever since we separated, Joy and I join with the children at their birthday and usually go out to dinner together, during which we have often reminded ourselves that we did a good job together for and with them.

I shall always be grateful to Joy and the children for having given me the opportunity to learn so many lessons. They have been, and continue to be, among my most important teachers.

15 May, 1985.
Johann André comes to live with us.

My children: Natasha and Johann.
Above: Natasha's first day of school, 1994.
Below: dressing up for a party, 1996.

27.

Education and the humanisation of the corporation

Melbourne since 1984

AFTER leaving high-school teaching, I taught English to migrants in the workplace. The Australian Migrant Education Services had an industrial arm; we went to the factories to try to improve the English of migrant workers. Having been a migrant myself and having had to struggle without knowing the language, I knew well what they were up against. Sometimes these sessions where held at four in the afternoon after a long day of heavy work and many would doze off even though I tried to make it engaging and fun. Of course some of them who may have been in Australia for many years did not really want to learn English as they lived in language ghettoes and felt no need.

It was while doing a series of sessions at ACI in Spotswood, where they made beer bottles among other things, that the training manager who was showing me around told me about all the other things they did to educate workers and management in industry. This gave me the idea that I could undertake those kind of tasks (I was a qualified educator wasn't I?) and I thought that it would be more rewarding, both financially and professionally, than trying to teach English to dozing migrant.

So I did some research into this field to prepare myself and I looked for ads in the paper. After a fairly rigorous selection process, I obtained the position of Senior Training Officer at a car manufacturing company in Clayton, south-east of Melbourne. It was a bit of a culture shock both for me and them. After finding out about my background at least one manager was heard to comment, '*Not another bloody academic!*'.

This post was my apprenticeship to my current career and while I had much to learn, the principles of good education and general psychology, which I already knew, came in very handy. I was familiar with Maslow from my work on Transpersonal Psychology and was delighted to find that he had much to say about management and the value of work in the process of becoming more whole as a person. I took my cue from him and many others in always taking the approach that the value of workplace training should serve the employees personally as much as the company they work for. Work is not divorced from private life, and if life is about growing and learning, that does not stop at the office or on the shop floor.

Moving from an academic environment to a factory was a personal challenge for me and stretched my interpersonal flexibility – I learnt a lot about politics in the workplace.

One of the early lessons I learnt was coping with the 'us versus them' attitude between management and the workers. When some of the union representatives went to a negotiating course one day, our training department was asked to provide negotiating training for managers so they could keep their own in bargaining with the workers. While it is true that much unashamed exploitation has occurred, and continues in some cases today, this open antagonism is very much misplaced in a workplace where staff are well looked after. In the end, they should both work cooperatively to achieve the objectives of the organisation and both benefit from it proportionally. Fortunately, younger people are not taking bad management as much as we used to, and are more prepared to stand up to it or leave.

After three years I was ready to step up to consulting and I moved to an employer organisation providing advice on training and development services to its members. During my time there a trade delegation from Belgium came to visit led by the then Prince (now King) Albert of Belgium. I was invited to the reception and introduced to him. We spoke for about a minute in three languages – where do you come from, how long have you been here, that sort of thing – and that was my sixty seconds of life with the Royals.

I learned much about presenting public seminars and writing training material during my time there and how to consult with prospective buyers of my services. I never considered myself a sales person but I became good at teaching negotiating skills and I see it as a more useful skill than selling in the traditional sense of that word.

A few years later I was invited to become part of the Melbourne office start-up team of a global American training company which had Mickey Mouse as its mascot, which is not to say that it was a Mickey Mouse outfit, far from it. The story goes that in its early days the company did some work for Walt Disney and he paid for a particular project with the permission to use the Mickey image as its mascot. Employees were given a Mickey watch on joining to remind them to be punctual but also to have fun while working. My title there was 'Performance Consultant' and many of our clients were Australian divisions of American corporations who had a global contract with our company. I travelled extensively throughout Australia in those days and always made sure I brought something back for the children which they appreciated a lot.

During one of my assignments with a large Australian utility, a letter of complaint against me personally was sent to our head office in Sydney. Several issues were raised, ranging from incompetence to rudeness. I was stunned. Fortunately our managing director knew me well enough to realise that none of this was likely to have happened. It did not take a lot of investigating on his part to discover that internal politics was behind the allegation. Processing the attack on my professional behaviour was not the only challenge – a few months later I was to return to the same company with the person who had made the complaint as a member of the group I was to train. I managed to treat her with the same courtesy as I did everyone else and actually enjoyed my sense of personal control.

One of the many benefits of working for that company was that en route to the United States for a two-week product training session I was able to stop over in Belgium to visit my brothers and their children. Mother had passed away about ten years before, at age eighty-one. Freddy told me she had more or less faded away, becoming undernourished, and was found dead in her little flat one day.

It was an eerie experience walking around the centre of Gent where very little had changed in the thirty years since I had first left. It was like walking on to the set of an historical film where the actors had not yet dressed in their period costumes. It was fascinating also to see my brothers as older people and their children as adults and parents. The fluency of my rusty Flemish improved dramatically after a couple of days, but it was often difficult to express myself clearly and precisely without reverting to English. It also struck me what a funny-sounding language Flemish really is.

The conference I attended in the United States had company representatives from all over the world and felt like a mini United Nations. It reinforced my experience of the value of meeting people from other cultures and other nations and brought me once again in touch with our basic human commonality and unity. During the conference I had some discussions with the marketing manager responsible for developing the company in Europe, and we agreed that there might be a job for me there given my wide knowledge of the company's products and my ability to speak two European languages as well as English. I thought it would be a wonderful opportunity to travel with the children and let them experience other parts of the world. Upon my return, sharing the prospect (which seemed likely at the time) with Joy caused initial excitement but this rapidly faded to anxiety. Leaving her mother behind loomed as the main obstacle. The job offer never eventuated so the decision did not need to be made.

I increasingly enjoyed my work as a Performance Consultant, facilitating training sessions, strategic-planning meetings, and providing consulting services to a wide range and many levels of organisations, with an international infrastructure supporting me. The money was good, which helped with my obligation as main breadwinner while Joy looked after the children. We had decided that, in the early years, being there for the children was far more important than the extra income. Personally I still saw myself as fulfilling my purpose as educator. I felt that as long as I was contributing to the growth and development of people I could honestly and conscientiously do this task. I could even rationalise to myself that improving the technical skills of a person would provide more job satisfaction for them and make them more employable, increasing their personal market value. So to me it was clear that as long as the balance of the benefits of training and development was as much for the person as for the organisation, we had a fair deal here and that both would gain in the process.

When eventually the Melbourne office was closed and clients

were serviced from Sydney, I was retrenched after seven years. They had treated me well and I had seen it coming. The new manager who had to come from Sydney to tell me about it was more nervous than I was. Letting go of well-respected and competent employees is one of the most painful actions managers have to undertake.

For a while I ran my own training design company, but a one-person business where you have to promote and sell as well as deliver the goods is a challenge. I was lucky that a friend who was a successful training package seller was looking for product at the same time that I was starting to write courses so we did a good deal of business together.

Theoreticians in the field of Organisational Development readily bandy about the concepts of 'life-long learning' and 'the learning organisation', but in the workplace these ideas do not often receive the serious application they deserve. Lots of lip service but often little genuine action. While most of my work, when I actually deal with my session participants, is focused on the development of the individual, all too often the overriding objective and underlying motivation of the organisations which sends them is their relentless drive to increase profit. Yes, I know that profit is a necessary element of doing business. But when it becomes an end in itself and a blinding obsession, we have yet again a 'game', (the game of accumulating wealth for its own sake) distracting us from the essence of what really matters. Satisfying work that enables creative activity and personal growth will lead to excellent performance, there is no doubt about it (ask any hobbyist) and excellent work will lead to profit. But that profit belongs as much to those who do the work as those who own the means to do it, doesn't it, Karl?

The philosophical, political, sociological and psychological arguments against the exploitation of human beings for the sake of mere financial profit are overwhelming. In my experience, that exploitation occurs more frequently than not and is usually carefully disguised, but is occasionally very blatant, and unapologetically executed. Such wilful destructiveness against human dignity could be understood, if not accepted, if the results of these actions made the perpetrators happy and fulfilled human beings, but it doesn't. Wealth and power have never correlated with happiness, compassion and maturity. On the contrary, work-related stress and sickness is on the increase. No wonder some people opt out or feel they are better off on the dole.

There are excellent workplaces of course and there are very decent people who happen to own businesses. In his small but extremely impactful book *Good Business: Leadership, Flow and the Making of Meaning*, Mihaly Csikszentmihaly (yes, that's how it is spelled, I checked it twice) gives many examples where personal values and meaning can flow to benefit the people they employ. He recommends that '*the first and most obvious decision a manager should make when hiring is to ask: Does the candidate fit the goals and values of our organisation?*'.

It may be the most obvious to him (as he is one of the foremost proponents of Positive Psychology), but it is not to many organisations. Values, emotions and constructive dialogues are relatively new to some managers. The 'old' school of management is still well-represented in many industries. Many people rarely consider what really matters, at work or in their private life, and find that deep questioning values and motives is way too difficult. If they think about it at all (or when I ask for it in personal development sessions) top priorities are often as varied as: money, sport, sex, entertainment, excitement, fame, security, their mother, their God and often their children. Some people have told me that it's all about numbers; others think it's all about what you believe, or being saved. When I think about it, as I often do, I see that it is all about adding to increased awareness, not only my personal awareness but our collective species consciousness, human reflective self-consciousness, which we mainly do through learning. Learning from reflecting on our experiences and interactions with other people and the world around us. Of course learning is also at the core of most religions as well as evolution, so what are they arguing about? OK. I know what it is; I studied both sides and settled on learning since it applies to both, even though this may sound like a cop-out.

I frequently express gratitude that I am in a position to earn a livelihood by doing what is probably the most important activity a human being can do. I feel sad for all those people who hate Monday morning and can barely wait till it is Friday afternoon. Yet how satisfying is it do something you like, do it well and learn from it at the same time, and get paid for as well?

Some years ago I heard of a view that capitalism is on a self-destructive path and that the overwhelming preponderance of 'taking' over 'contributing' to global wellbeing inevitably leads to fatal deficit. (And by the way, calling it 'creative capitalism' as some excessively wealthy people do will not make any difference.) Even though I know little about commercial finance, the above view made sense to me. It was therefore no surprise to me when I read recently in *Fortune* that the current Treasury Secretary of the United States Government, Henry Paulson, stated that: '*Raw capitalism is a dead end. I've seen it. When I'm travelling around the world and I look at some of the behaviour when there is just profit motive, that convinces me that you need regulation.*' In *Time Magazine* the lead article headed *The Price of Greed* called some of those same behaviours 'financial madness', 'naked greed' and responsible for creating a 'financial Frankenstein' and asking '*didn't the folks on Wall Street know that someday the music must end?*'. Will we learn from this that profit in itself as a motive for action does not lead to a meaningful life? Not only does it not lead to meaning or even enduring happiness, it is hugely destructive, both psychologically and physically. As the late, two-time Pulitzer Prize winning historian Barbara Tuchman wrote in *The March of Folly* as far back as 1984, '*Why does American business insist on 'growth' when it is demonstrably using up the three basics of life on our planet: land, water and unpolluted air?*'

As a Learning and Development practitioner it is easy to neglect one's own professional development. In my case, from around the time of becoming a Theosophist, learning and growing as a person have become a way of life, my central purpose, as well as a profession.

At an Australian Institute of Training and Development meeting I met Joane Goulding, who with her husband Jim ran the Australian Academy of Hypnotic Sciences. When she discovered that I had just completed my Diploma in Workplace Training, which includes competency-based assessment design, she asked if I could help her with the work involved in becoming a Registered Training Organisation (RTO) as they wanted to be able to issue nationally recognised Training Certificates at the Academy. I certainly could help her but now I was more interested in what they were teaching there. After some further discussions with them we came upon the creative solution that in exchange for the work I would do for them, they would allow me to do their course on Hypnotherapy and Counselling. It turned out not only to be fascinating personal development journey, but a worthwhile contribution to my professional work. I also contributed to their work by giving the lecture on Transpersonal

Psychology, which I thought Hypnotherapists should know about, and later to Joane's book *Sleep Talk – A Gift of Love Through Positive Parenting*. It is also of course where I met Graham who later took me to my birth.

A few years later I attended a promotional talk by a coaching college. Again my interest was fired and during further discussions it turned out that they too needed help with becoming an RTO and writing their assessments. If you think that they also offered me to do their course in exchange for my work for them, you are right. The principles of give and take, reciprocity and mutual gain could hardly be better illustrated (all without any money involved) and are so much more constructive than industrial warfare.

Contemporary couching draws a lot from our understanding of how the brain works and tells us that habits can be changed and that our brain is much more flexible and has 'plasticity' as it is now called. So, yes we can change and age is no impediment. Yes, the resistance to change and the tenacity of early conditioning are formidable obstacles to personal growth, even for those who want to change. But it can be done, and change we must.

I got to know Poppy Pavlidis, the principal of the college, very well and she invited me to her book launch recently, and the rest as they say is history.

Books, as you will have noticed, have always been important teachers to me. They are learning aids and I write all over them and make sidebar notes relating them to other books and ideas. A relatively recent book and one I scribbled in on most pages is *Rebalancing the World: Why Women Belong and Men Compete and How To Restore the Ancient Equilibrium* by Carol Lee Flinders (2003) (no relation to Matthew of the station, I think). You will also have noticed that I have an interest in finding out about what makes women different from men and how to better cope with this, and therefore this title immediately and strongly grabbed my attention. It's a great book, beautifully written (the author has a PhD in literature) and extremely informative. She talks about the values of belonging and those of competing and how they have come to relate respectively to the female and male functions in our society, even though these allocations were not there in the 'ancient equilibrium' of the title. In her recommendations on how to restore that equilibrium she recommends we return to where both men and women blend the best of both those values in themselves and live harmoniously together, instead of 'disharmoniously' as Nataraja Guru called my relationship with Jenny. The reason I mention this is because not only is this a great insight in itself but it instantly revealed to me why I have always been attracted to intelligent women. Intelligent women, it seems, combine the left hemisphere function of the brain in larger proportion with their softer feminine belonging values and are therefore more in equilibrium as a whole person and therefore, given my personal make-up, easier to deal with. If you suspect that this is a sexist statement you will have to read Flinders' book to find out why it isn't.

Things we learn without even trying!

My most recent professional development journey has been to become an Accredited Practitioner of Human Synergistics products, an international provider of incredibly well-researched and profoundly Humanistic processes, courseware and diagnostics for use by Learning and Development consultants and internal change agents and managers. Much of their theoretical underpinnings come from psychology, Maslow in particular, so I felt immediately 'in sync'. My understanding of Hypnotherapy and Transpersonal Psychology, and my coaching skills combined with the Human Synergistic tools, have given me a solid foundation for my work in helping people to be happier and more fulfilled human beings both at work and at home. I enjoy my work enormously and find the opportunity to contribute to other people's growth both rewarding and creative.

There is a widespread trend in workplaces to work longer hours, suffer more stress and upset the so-called work-life balance. Yet if we have a clear purpose in life, and find a way to earn a living contributing to that purpose, work no longer feels like work but simply doing what one wants to do. Yes, there still must be time to do other things as well, if for no other reasons than that we need variety, but the more satisfying and productive our work lives are the longer we can continue to work without getting stressed about it. To find a state of peace in the core of meaningful activity, at work as well as at home, is a goal I still find myself aspiring to.

Leading a trade mission, the then Prince and now King of Belgium visits the Chamber and I am introduced to him. We shake hands and talk in Flemish, French and English for one minute. I guess I've got fourteen minutes of fame left to go.

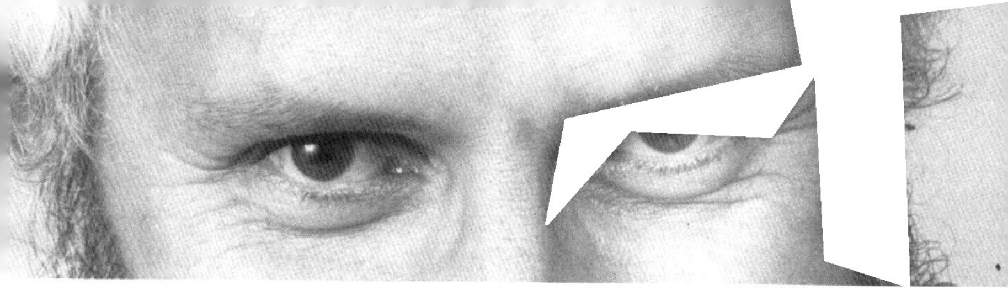

28.

Quantum metaphysics and creative rudder craft

DEEP reflective creative thinking, that unique capacity we humans have, is so frequently under-utilised, not only in the workplace but at home and in families, that I see it as the grossest natural resources squander we are perpetrating, even in our increasingly eco-conscious world. In our sports-mad and possession-dominated so-called Western (war-mongering) civilisation, reflective and creative thinking is often regarded as 'academic', merely useless speculation and boring as hell. Talking of hell, there is a story that goes like this:

'One day a man dies and regains consciousness in an extremely beautiful and luxurious palace. There are servants, all sorts of entertainments laid on, absolutely everything you could want. For a few (celestial) months he enjoys the sheer hedonism available to him, when one day he asks his personal butler for a few suggestions on what is available in terms of meaningful activity. "I am terribly sorry, sir" explains the butler, "but there is nothing here to do that is meaning-

ful." Somewhat annoyed the man replies, "Do you seriously expect me to be here forever and ever without any meaning? I may as well be in hell!" Whereupon the butler asks "Where do you think you are sir?"'

Indeed meaninglessness, lack of purpose and alienation into nihilism has been known to lead to madness, a form of 'hell' really. No wonder teenage suicide in on the increase. Logo therapy tells us, '*This striving for meaning in one's life is the primary motivational force in man.*' But, adds Frankl in *Man's Search for Meaning*, '*… do not ask what is the meaning of life, but ask what is the meaning of your life, what are you making of your life that is meaningful.*'

While looking for a book on an entirely different topic at the local library a few years ago, whether through serendipity or synchronicity, I came upon a volume titled *The Quantum Self.* But it was the subtitle that really sparked my interest: *A Revolutionary View of Human Nature and Consciousness Rooted in the New Physics* by Danah Zohar. At the time of writing my Honours thesis, more than twenty-five years earlier, I had looked into this subject because it relates clearly to Transpersonal Psychology, so I was curious to see what had happened since. Here is not the place to go into the theory of sub-atomic physics in great detail, even if I could, but there are a number of aspects of it that underpin my personal belief, in relation to the meaning of at least *my* life, which I do want to share. Of course if you already know what the meaning of *your* life is, or if you are already convinced that it is meaningless, you could skip this chapter. You are free to choose.

Towards the end of the book Zohar writes:

'In summary, the quantum world-view stresses ***dynamic relationship as the basis of all that is.*** *It tells us that our world comes about through a* ***mutually creative dialogue*** *between mind and body, between the individual and his personal and material context and between human culture and the natural world. It gives a view of the* ***human self which is free and responsible****, responsive to others and to its environment, essentially related and naturally committed, and* ***at every moment creative.****'* (My emphasis added.)

Or as she more simply puts it on the next page, *'It is my conviction that in quantum physics we now have the foundation of a physics upon which we can base both our science and our psychology, and that through a wedding of physics and psychology we, too, can live in a reconciled universe, a universe in which we and our culture are* ***fully, and meaningfully, part of the scheme of things.****'*

From what I understand of this, not being a physicist, I would say that these are big claims and statements with enormous repercussions. Yet, intuitively, and I have a great deal of respect for intuition, I feel she is right. What is more, some of my own experiences support my intuition and those statements, though it is always possible that I am completely deluded, which as we all know, is so easy to do.

Philosophy, science, psychology – all aim to finding answers to the ultimate questions about how things work, how we should live and why there are creatures at all. Traditionally these disciplines have been sealed off from each other into silo-like divisions. More recently, interdisciplinary approaches have become more acceptable and successful in informing each other and therefore they have been able to see further than any one of them independently. One of the most spectacular examples of such collaboration is the coming together of the psychology of consciousness and the new physics or quantum physics. Danah Zohar, a physicist trained at MIT as well as a philosopher trained at Harvard (no amateur this woman), assisted by her psychiatrist husband, makes a valiant attempt to show how both clinical psychology and quantum physics combine to answer all the important philosophical questions. Whether she succeeds is of course a matter of opinion but the effort in itself is laudable and admirable.

She is neither the first nor alone in challenging orthodoxy in these fields but I think she stands out in her conviction, compared to other often overly-tentative theorists.

In the past, philosophers have looked at the nature of matter as much as physicists have. As far back as 1965, Popper already called the bedrock of physical science 'as solid as a swamp', and before him, Quine contested that '*physical objects and the gods of Homer differ only in degree not in kind.*' More recently, Stuart Hameroff has collaborated with Roger Penrose, the distinguished physicist, to write about the '*relevance of quantum physics theory to the understanding of consciousnesses.*'

So, does a theory of physics (the study of matter) which leads to consciousness as its basis have anything to contribute to the question of the meaning of my life, and yours too of course?

Allan Hobson, director of the Neurophysiology Laboratory at Harvard Medical School, says '*The monistic view of consciousness [the materiality of consciousness] is obviously incompatible with this fondest of all of humankind's hopes, [immortality]... so* ***we baulk at realising that when our brain dies, our consciousness dies with it.***' (My emphasis added.)

Yet, if consciousness as explained by quantum theory is all pervasive (and on the basis of all manifestation throughout the universe it must be infinite), and we are part of it, we too are infinite, or at least our influence on it is, '*a universe in which we and our culture are fully, and meaningfully, part of the scheme of things.*'

At least so claims Zohar. So, it may be true that we are dependent upon our brains for personal reflective self-consciousness, but universal consciousness as such is part of a bigger picture nevertheless.

The next big question is: being part of such a big universe guided by the rules of quantum physics, do I have any choice or freedom left? While most of us experience some degree of freedom, there are still some determinists, in psychology, science and even theology, who claim that this is an illusion. Here again Zohar points out that quantum physics provides 'proof' that we are free, albeit in a limited degree. '*The "Uncertainty Principle" of Quantum theory teaches that... fundamentally reality itself is essentially* ***indeterminate****, that there is no clear, fixed, underlying "something" to our daily existence that can ever be known. Everything about reality is and remains a matter of probabilities. In quantum terms, this fuzzy, indeterminate margin of thought is the necessary precondition of all thought [and] is the* ***physical basis of our creativity and our freedom****.*' (My emphasis added.)

So we do have choice and we do have freedom. But what about genetics and conditioning? Some people have likened life to a card game. You are dealt a hand (of genetic propensities) and there is nothing you can do to alter what you get. But what you do with the hand you have been given and how well you play the game with what you have is still up to you, and what's more you CAN learn to play better. The most important choice of all, that you always have, is your attitude to what you have and the circumstances you find yourself in.

Another analogy is that your free will is like the rudder of a boat. The conditions of the sea are a given by the natural world around you and the structure of your boat is inherited through your genes and your conditioning. But how you steer that boat by the skilful use of the rudder can be learned and taken hold of. We can also make more effective rudders and steer them in a more knowledgeable manner, with some focus and learning from experience.

In short, we can learn the '*art of creative rudder making*' and learn to use rudders more ingeniously to survive the stormy seas. But that does not mean that we need to start worshipping the rudders we make or turn rudder making into a religion any more than we should worship Buddha's finger that pointed towards the wisdom he saw. We also need to let go of the old rudders when we invent more effective ones.

This brings us to the question of relationship as explained by quantum physics, at least according to Zohar: '*The whole notion of "separate" has no foundation in reality.*' And, we could ask, as in the Zen principle that '*everything is one*'?

'*One of the most fundamental tenets of quantum theory, the Principle of Complementarity, which states that each way of describing being, as a wave or as a particle, complements the other and that the whole picture emerges only from the "package deal"*',' writes Zohar. Again we could ask, like the complementarity of 'Yin and Yang' in ancient Chinese philosophy?

'*The physics by which the wave function of our various past sub-selves can overlap with, and hence get taken up into, our present self is the physics by which psychotherapists get their patients to relive past experiences in the "now", thus robbing them of their isolation and their sting and wedding them to the present.*' Again Zohar. Is this what I did when I took care of my baby self to overcome what had happened at birth being rejected by my mother?

This does indeed sound like the Buddhist Diamond Sutra as Zohar herself suggests: '*There is said to be a network... so arranged that if you look at one [part] you see all the others reflected in it. In the same way, each object in the world is not merely itself but involves every other object, and in fact is every other object.*' Like a hologram?

In 1980 when I was writing my thesis for my Honours year in Philosophy of Education I researched some aspects of physics as they related to Transpersonal Psychology. I was particularly struck then and now for his congruence with the above, when I came across Kenneth Pelletier's book '*Towards a Science of Consciousness*', published in 1978, twenty-two years before Zohar. In it he wrote that '*Today, the newest theories of quantum physic, an influx of Eastern meditative and religious systems, the rise of human potential growth centres, and a renewed interest in the functions of the mind – all are conveying and necessitating the consideration of a new science, a science of consciousness*' and '*The contemporary trend to the unification of mind and body in a holistic science of consciousness promises to revitalise psychology's ties to the natural and life sciences.*' After dealing with most of the issues noted above he concludes that, '*What is required now is a balance between the scientific inquiry concerning neurophysiology and the mapping of the phenomenology of consciousness through disciplined introspection.*' The Master Game no less? Zen at its scientific best?

I want to make one last comment about '*The Quantum Self*'. Zohar quotes psychiatrist Jerome Frank as saying that, '*All psychotherapies, despite their diversity, share a value system which accord primacy to individual self-fulfilment or self-actualisation. The individual is seen as the centre of his moral universe...*' to which she then adds that '*All [psychotherapies] regardless of their aims, stoke the fires of narcissistic over-attention to self*' citing Jung as a 'glaring exception'.

What I also researched when I was writing my thesis were various approaches to psychotherapy because of my interest in Transpersonal Psychotherapy. In my humble opinion, it is a gross distortion to lump all psychotherapies in the same basket for a start, but, more importantly, they certainly do not all stoke the fires of narcissism, if indeed any of them do. Certainly Jungian psychotherapy does not and neither do Rogerian, nor Gestalt nor Logo therapy, and least of all Transpersonal Psychotherapy, which by its very name is aiming at *going beyond the self.*

Maslow himself, the father of both Humanistic Psychology and of Transpersonal Psychology added 'self-transcendence' to his hierarchy of needs and very clearly stressed that the ultimate 'need' of the human being is to transcend the self. Rogers clearly wanted to make the self 'whole' for it to be healthy and sane, not narcissistic and self-indulgent. What sane psychotherapist would have narcissism as the aim of psychotherapy? The gap between healthy self-love as a prerequisite to the love of others and narcissism is very wide indeed. I agree we should not promote egocentricity, but what we do need is the preservation of a healthy and socially well-functioning self. Yes, we should also promote 'life-centricity' and focus on the preservation and development of life as a whole, including ourselves, until we are ready for transcendence. As Maslow and many others pointed out, building a well functioning self-esteem is a need on the way towards self-transcendence. To expect people to self-transcend when they are still in need of grounding in the social world is somewhat like telling babies not to develop their crawling skills and asking them to get on with walking upright immediately.

Life-centricity means to be pro-life, not just my life, not just my family or my compatriots but of all life, as one unity, as quantum theory clearly suggests. More importantly, none of this requires me to postulate a personal god upon whose grace I am dependent to survive after death. What quantum physics seems to require of me, by virtue of our unity and diversity, is to respect others who are still in need of a God, in the same way that I must respect those who are still in the process of building a well-grounded social self, or learning to crawl, because that's where they are at in their learning. Learning and personal growth, I am told, is perfectly acceptable to most religions as it is to those who prefer evolution as an explanation of what is. Either way, learn, grow and be happy.

To transcend the boundaries of personal selfhood and consciousness as in the Master Game, and help others to see its wisdom if they so wish, is a worthwhile activity in life and has for me been and continues to be a meaningful journey.

What happens when my journey ends, what happens to the '*certain kinds of connectedness and continuity*' I now call myself, hardly matters, and should certainly not dictate how I live life in the here and now. I should live it in accordance with the best information I have and the best insights my intuition can deliver me. Moral developmental theory tells us that doing things for rewards, like a seat in heaven or to avoid punishment such as burning in hell, is not the highest morally developed way of life.

Indeed, as Elisabeth Kubler-Ross has said in her autobiography '*Dying is nothing to fear. It can be the most wonderful experience of your life. It all depends on how you have lived.*'

Throughout my life I have been given many opportunities to practise letting go and in many cases I have chosen to consciously. I have also consciously tried to learn many lessons, many of which I have learned by trying to teach others. I have had the opportunity to learn much and gain some knowledge, but, as Jung pointed out, knowledge 'must be converted into ethical obligation' and he warned of the phenomenon he called 'inflation', being bloated with self-importance. We often hear it said that it is not important what you know but who you know. We could paraphrase it and say: '*It is not important <u>what</u> you know but <u>how you use</u> the knowledge you have*'.

It seems that the concept of death and the idea of not existing any more is an almost impossible notion to accept for many people. Is this the last taboo in our culture?

In his both amusing and profound book *The Book of Dead Philosophers* (2008), Simon Critchley reviews what philosophers have said about death and how they have died. He explains how many humans suffer the 'terror of annihilation' and points out that '*the fear of death enslaves us towards either temporary oblivion or the longing for immortality*'. The desperate search for entertainment and excitement, or the wild inventions of survival beyond death do not seem to permit any alternatives, and we forget that **the value and meaning of life is in the living of it,** neither the escape from it or the waiting till afterwards. At any rate why are we so afraid of dying? If you do not believe in an after-life and you die, you won't be there to feel a thing, so why worry? If you do believe in an after-life and the required actions to make it come true then all you have to do is live by the required actions and presto, there you are, no need to worry. Either way it's not a problem. Should we conclude from this that people who are afraid of dying even though they know what they should do to earn a good after-life are not doing it and fear negative consequences?

If living meaningfully makes for a good death, then I am ready for it, whenever it comes, or whenever I chose it to come. But there is much work to be done in this world and as long as I can, I want to make my death, and thereby my life, even better.

Once I was asked what I would want written on a tombstone, if I were to have one, as an epitaph. I wrote: '***Here lies Noël, magnificently insignificant***'. Equally magnificent and splendid as all the other wonderful creatures on earth and, at the same time in the larger scheme of things, individually as a tiny temporary particle of the totality of things, utterly insignificant.

Even though I shared my story and some of the insights I have gained on the way, on the off-chance that it may be useful to you the reader, I recommend that you disregard what *I* have learned and ask yourself what *you* have learned from reading this story.

And remember Krishnamurti's words: '*So you have to find out for yourself what you are and to learn how to observe yourself. Nobody can give guidance; can give light, to another. Only you yourself can do that, you have to stand completely alone. If you belong to anything, follow anybody, you are already entering into corruption.*' Challenging stuff!

Postscript

OFTEN people have asked me about the origin of the surname Odou. I knew we had family in France and I assumed naturally that we were simply a Belgian branch of the family. During my travels through Russia, however, some people told me that Odou could be an accidentally modified version of Odov, apparently a common name in that part of the world. Since then, I used to reply that it could be either French or Russian, but that I was unsure which. I had sympathy with both cultures so I personally had no preference and would be happy if it was both.

Since starting to write my story, two sources of information have finally confirmed that it is definitely French. The first one came from a genealogical research company which stated that the family name Odou was found in Languedoc, an ancient province in the south of France probably as early as the sixteenth century. They were well established in the region of Toulouse and Nimes, and had lands and titles. In the mid-seventeenth century, the family name Odou appeared on the list of French migrants to

North America and Canada and there are reference to Odous in California, Massachusetts, Ohio and Tennessee. One Odou, who turned up in the US a little later, was the daughter of a French diplomat. She was originally a nurse but turned to embalming and was the founder of the first embalming school for women, the Lina D Odou Embalming Institute established in 1901 in New York.

The second confirmation came from that overwhelmingly vast source of information: the World Wide Web or the Internet. Many municipalities around the world have now listed their birth and death registers on the web. A casual browsing around led me to a whole swag of Odous all born in the small town of Halluin situated practically right on the border of France and Belgium. The earliest entry I found was one Joannes Odou, born some time before 1630 (which could have been the date they started keeping records) and who died there in 1669. In 1651 he married Joanna Dupont who was also born some time before 1630 and died in Halluin in 1689. One of their sons, Antoine Odou (29/3/1654 – 2/6/1721), was listed as the mayor of Halluin.

While all this was interesting information, there was something much more fascinating to come. After some more scrolling and digging I came upon the entry for a certain Emile Odou who was also born in Halluin in 1854 and had died on 24 December (my own birthday!) 1899 in, *of all places*, Melbourne Australia! I could hardly believe my eyes. Surely there must be some mistake here? A little over a hundred years ago a man from Halluin with my surname dies on my birthday in the city I have now lived in for the last twenty-five years; what are the statistical probabilities of that happening?

I immediately resolved to check the accuracy of this information with the Melbourne Deaths Registry Office. After duly filling in an elaborate request form asking me for the purpose of my inquiry and my relationship to the deceased I received, about three weeks later, a certified copy of page 15209 of the '*Register of deaths in the district of Melbourne in the Colony of Victoria*'. In stylish nineteenth century handwriting it told me that Emile's profession was 'woolbuyer' which explains why he had come to Australia in the first place. The spinning and weaving looms of France and Flanders must have been sufficiently hungry for Australian wool to send a buyer to check out the goods.

Emile, unfortunately for his family and his employer, according to the record, died of pneumonia three months after his return arrival in 1899 aged forty-five. In the column under the heading '*Signature, Description and Residence of Internant*' there is the clearly legible signature of a *S. W. Bland, Customs Agent, 183 Collins Street City*, today still the main business street in Melbourne. (It is incidentally also the street where both my son Johann and I work, although at different companies.) The certificate also recorded that Emile had married Jane Leroux at the age of thirty-three in Tourcoing, (a town next to Halluin) France.

The last column of this old document brought the saddest news of all. Their children '*In order of Birth*' were: '*Marie Alix (Dead); Marie Alix (Dead); Elor [?] age 3; Emile age 2; Marie Agnes age 1.*' Had the registry officer made a mistake to enter Marie Alix twice? Unlikely. Had Marie Alix reincarnated and died again? Even less likely. It was not until I finally traced the actual tombstone to the Brighton cemetery (a beachside suburb of Melbourne) that the mystery of the double entry was cleared up. On the cross of the stone the inscription reads '*Ici repose Marie Alix Odou, nee a Melbourne 24 Octobre 1890 et decede 25 Novembre 1891*'. (Here rests Marie Alix Odou born in Melbourne on the 24th of October 1890 and died on 25 of November 1891.) On the marble plate below the inscription reads '*Ici repose le corps de Marie Alix Odou nee a Tourcoing 11 Aout 1893 et decede a Brighton Beach le 29 Novembre 1895 a l'age de deux ans et 3 mois.*' (Here rests the body of Marie Alix Odou born in Tourcoing on 11 August 1893 and died at Brighton Beach on 29th November 1895 at the age of two years and 3 months.)

What exactly happened here is unclear, but some of the dates would suggest that Emile and Jane came to Australia for a stint during which Marie Alix 'one' was born and died. Since Marie Alix 'two' was born in Tourcoing, but died in Australia, they must have come back for a second stint, during which she died here. If he had been in Melbourne only for three months before he died, as the death certificate states, Emile must have left and come back again. Unfortunately Emile's death certificate does not tell us where his other children where born so they could have been born in either Australia or France.

If the following chronology is correct, Emile and Jane must have travelled at least two or three times between France and Australia. It also shows that Jane gave birth to five children between 1890 and 1898 and lost her husband the following year, and that if Marie Agnes were alive today, she would only be 106 years old. Where are her children?

They may well be alive today. An attempt to contact them has had no success so far.

1854	Emile Odou is born in Halluin France
1887	Emile, aged thirty-three, marries Jane Leroux
?	Emile and Jane come to Australia
1890	Marie Alix 'one' is born in Melbourne
1891	Marie Alix 'one' dies in Melbourne
?	Emile and Jane return to France
1893	Marie Alix 'two' is born in Tourcoing
1895	Marie Alix 'two' dies in Melbourne
1896	Elor is born (Since he was three when Emile died.)
1897	Emile junior is born (Since he was two when Emile died.)
1898	Marie Agnes is born (Since she was one when Emile died.)
1899	Emile returns to Australia in October and dies in December.

Natasha visits the grave of Marie Alix Odou
in Brighton Cemetery, 2003.

Some of the books that have had an influence on my life and my thinking

Arguelles, Jose. *The Transformative Vision: Reflections on the Nature and History of Human Expression*. Shambala, 1975.

Arguelles, Miriam & Jose. *The Feminine: Spacious as the Sky*. Shambala, 1977.

Assagioli, Roberto. *Psychosynthesis*. Penguin, 1965.

Bennett-Goleman, Tara. *Emotional Alchemy: How Your Mind Can Heal Your Heart*, Rider, 2001.

Benoit, Hubert. *The Supreme Doctrine: Psychological Studies in Zen Thought*. The Viking Press, 1955.

Benoit, Hubert. *Let Go: Theory and Practice of Detachment According to Zen*. Samuel Weiser, 1973.

Benoit, Hubert. *The Many Faces of Love*. Routlege & Kegan Paul, 1955.

Biddulph, Steve. *Manhood: A Book About Setting Men Free.* Finch Publishing, 1994.

Biddulph, Steve. *Stories of Manhood: Journeys into the Hidden Hearts of Men.* Finch Publishing, 2000.

Blavatsky, Helena Petrovna. *The Secret Doctrine: A Synthesis of Science, Religion and Philosophy.* Theosophical University Press. First published in 1888.

Blofeld, John. *The Zen Teaching of Huang Po.* Grove Press, 1958.

Bois, Samuel. *Explorations in Awareness.* Philosphere Publishers, 1957.

Capra, Fritjof. *The Tao of Physics: An Exploration of the Parallels Between Modern Physics and Eastern Mysticism.* Fontana, 1975.

Chang, Jolan. *The Tao of Love and Sex: The Ancient Chinese Way to Ecstasy.* Panther, 1977.

Cooper, John. *Yin & Yang: The Taoist Harmony of Opposites.* Aquarian Press, 1981.

Critchley, Simon. *The Book of Dead Philosophers.* Melbourne University Press, 2008.

Csikszentmihalyi, Mihalyi. *Good Business; Leadership, Flow and the Making of Meaning.* Penguin Books, 2004.

Csikszentmihalyi, Mihalyi. *Flow: The Psychology of Optimal Experience.* Harper Perennial, 1990.

Dawkins, Richard. *The Blind Watchmaker.* Folio Society, 2007.

De Bono, Edward. *The Mechanism of Mind.* Simon & Schuster, 1969.

De Ropp, Robert. *Warrior's Way*. George Allen & Unwin. 1980.

De Ropp, Robert. *The Master Game: Beyond the Drug Experience*. Delta, 1968.

Doublet, Serge. *The Stress Myth*. Ipsilon. 2000.

Ferguson, Marilyn. *The Aquarian Conspiracy: Personal and Social Transformation in the 1980s*. J.P. Tarcher, 1980.

Feyerabend, Paul. *Against Method: Outline of an Anarchistic Theory of Knowledge*. Verso, 1975.

Feyerabend, Paul. *Science in a Free Society*. NBL. 1978.

Fowles, John. *The Aristos*. Pan Books, 1965.

Frankl, Viktor. *Man's Search for Meaning: An Introduction to Logotherapy*. Touchstone, 1962.

Freire, Paulo. *Education: The Practice of Freedom*. Writers and Readers Publishing Cooperative, 1973.

Goleman, Daniel. *Emotional Intelligence*. Bantam. 1995.

Goleman, Daniel. *Destructive Emotions and How to Overcome Them*. Bloomsbury. 2003.

Grof, Stanislav. *The Holotropic Mind: The Three Levels of Human Consciousness and How They Shape Our Lives*. Harper, 1990.

Grof, Stanislav. *The Cosmic Game: Explorations in the Frontiers of Human Consciousness*. Hill of Content, 1998.

Grof, Stanislav. *Spiritual Emergence: When Personal Transformation Becomes a Crisis*. Penguin Putnam, 1989.

Hafner, Julian. *The End of Marriage: Why Monogamy Isn't Working*. Century, 1993.

Harding, Esther. *The Way of All Women: A Psychological Interpretation*, Rider. 1971.

Huxley, Aldous. *Island*. Penguin, 1962.

Huxley, Aldous. *The Perennial Philosophy*. Fontana, 1946.

Koestler, Arthur. *The Roots of Coincidence*. Picador, 1972.

Koestler, Arthur. *The Act of Creation*. Pan, 1969.

Krishnamurti, Jiddu. *Beginnings of Learning*. Victor Gollancz, 1975.

Krishnamurti, Jiddu. *Tradition and Revolution*. Orient Longman, 1972.

Krishnamurti, Jiddu. *Krishnamurti on Education*. Orient Longman, 1974.

Kubler-Ross, Elisabeth. *Death: The final stage of Growth*. Prentice Hall, 1975.

Ladas, Alice, et. al. *The G Spot: and Other Recent Discoveries About Human Sexuality*. Corgi Books, 1982.

Ladner, Lorne. *The Lost Art of Compassion; Discovering the Practice of Happiness in the Meeting of Buddhism and Psychology*. Harper, 2004.

Lao Tzu. *Tao Te Ching*. Unwin Books, 1972.

Leduc, Violette. *La Batarde*. Panther, 1964.

Linssen, Robert. *Zen: The Wisdom of the East*. Bay Books, 1972.

Linssen, Robert. *Living Zen*, Grove Press, 1960.

Lloyd, William. *The Karezza Method or Magnetation: The Art of Connubial Love.* Self Published, 1931.

Maslow, Abraham. *Toward a Psychology of Being.* Van Nostrand, 1968.

Maslow, Abraham. *The Farther Reaches of Human Nature.* Penguin, 1973.

McKinney, J. P. *The Structure of Modern Thought.* Chatto & Windus. 1971.

Merrell-Wolf, Franklin. *The Philosophy of Consciousness Without an Object: Reflections on the Nature of Transcendental Consciousness.* Julian Press, 1973.

Merrell-Wolf, Franklin. *Pathways Through to Space: A Personal Record of Transformation in Consciousness.* Julian Press, 1973.

Merton, Thomas. *The Way of Chuang Tzu.* Unwin Books, 1965.

Moore, John. *Sexuality Spirituality: A Study of Feminine/ Masculine Relationship.* Elements Books, 1980.

Mott, Francis. *The Universal Design of Creation.* Mark Beech Pub. 1964.

Murchie, Guy. *The Seven Mysteries of Life: An Exploration in Science and Philosophy.* Rider, 1978.

Myss, Caroline. *Sacred Contracts: Awakening Your Divine Potential.* Bantam Books, 2001.

Myss, Caroline. *Why People Don't Heal and How They Can.* Bantam, 1997.

Nataraja Guru. *An integrated Science of the Absolute.* East West University of Brahmavidya, 1977.

Ornstein, Robert. *The Psychology of Consciousness.* W.H. Freeman, 1972.

Pearce, Joseph, Chilton. *Magical Child: Rediscovering Nature's Plan for Our Children.* E. P. Dutton. 1977.

Peck, M. Scott. *The Road Less Travelled.* Simon and Shuster, 1978.

Pelletier, Kenneth. *Toward a Science of Consciousness.* Delta, 1978.

Perls, Frederick. *Gestalt Therapy.* Delta Books, 1951.

Pirsig, Robert. *Zen and the Art of Motor Cycle Maintenance: An Inquiry into Value*s. Corgi Books, 1974.

Porter, Muriel. *Sex, Power and the Clergy.* Hardie Grant, 2003.

Reich, Wilhelm. *The Function of the Orgasm.* Panther, 1968.

Actual Freedom: A new non-Spiritual down to earth Freedom. The Actual Freedom Trust, 1997.

Rogers, Carl. *Freedom to Learn.* Charles Merrill, 1969.

Rogers, Carl. & Stevens Barry. *Person to Person: The Problem of Being Human – A New Trend in Psychology.* Real People Press, 1967.

Rowan, John. *The Transpersonal Psychotherapy and Counselling.* Routledge, 1993.

Saul, John Ralston. *On Equilibrium.* Penguin, 2001.

Seligman, Martin. *Learned Optimism.* Random House. 1990.

Senzaki, Nyogen & Reps, Paul. *Zen: A Pathway to Enlightenment*. Ohara, 1977.

Smith, Ingram. *The Transparent Mind: A Journey With Krishnamurti*. Edwin House Publ. 1999.

Stevens Barry. *Don't Push the River.* Real People Press, 1970.

Stone, Justin. *Abandon Hope! A Way to Fulfilment*. Sun Books, 1974.

Suzuki, D.T. *An Introduction to Zen Buddhism*. Rider, 1969.

Talbot, Michael. *Mysticism and the New Physics*. Routledge,1980.

Tomio, Hirai. *Zen Meditation Therapy*. Japan Publications, 1975

Vaughan, Frances. *Awakening Intuition*. Anchor Books, 1979.

Watts, Alan. *The Wisdom of Insecurity*. Rider, 1976.

Watts, Alan. *Psychotherapy East and West*. Ballantine, 1961.

Watts, Alan. *The Way of Zen*. Penguin, 1957.

Watts, Alan. *Tao: The Watercourse Way*. Penguin, 1979.

Welwood, John. *Towards a Psychology of Awakening: Buddhism, Psychotherapy, and the Path of Personal and Spiritual Transformation*. Shambhala, 2002.

Wilber, Ken. *The Spectrum Of Consciousness*. The Theosophical Publishing House, 1977.

Wilber, Ken. *No Boundary: Eastern and Western Approaches to Personal Growth*. Whole Mind Series, 1979.

Wilber, Ken. *The Atman Project: A Transpersonal View of Human Development*. The Theosophical Publishing House, 1980.

Wilson, Colin. *Origins of the Sexual Impulse*. Panther, 1963.

Zohar, Danah. *S.Q. Spiritual Intelligence: The Ultimate Intelligence*. Bloomsbury, 2000.

Zohar, Danah. *The Quantum Self*. Bloomsbury, 1994.

Magnificently Insignificant

by Noël Odou

ISBN 9781921221866

		Qty
RRP	AU $24.99	....
Postage	AU $ 5.00	....
	TOTAL* $________	

* All prices include GST

Name: ....

Address: ....

Phone: ....

Email Address: ....

Payment:

❑ Money Order ❑ Cheque ❑ Amex ❑ MasterCard ❑ Visa

Cardholder's Name:..

Credit Card Number: ....

Signature:...

Expiry Date: ....

Allow 21 days for delivery.

Payment to: Better Bookshop (ABN 14 067 257 390)
PO Box 12544
A'Beckett Street, Melbourne, 8006
Victoria, Australia
Fax: +61 3 9671 4730
betterbookshop@brolgapublishing.com.au